Adjusting to Globalization

Adjusting to Globalization

Edited by
David Greenaway
University of Nottingham

 **Blackwell** Publishing

© 2005 by Blackwell Publishing Ltd

BLACKWELL PUBLISHING
350 Main Street, Malden, MA 02148-5020, USA
108 Cowley Road, Oxford OX4 1JF, UK
550 Swanston Street, Carlton, Victoria 3053, Australia

The right of David Greenaway to be identified as the Editor of the Editorial Material in this Work has been asserted in accordance with the UK Copyright, Designs, and Patents Act 1988.

First published 2005 by Blackwell Publishing Ltd

Library of Congress Cataloging-in-Publication Data has been applied for

ISBN 1-4051-3169-1

A catalogue record for this title is available from the British Library.

Set in 10/12pt Times Ten
by SNP Best-set Typesetter Ltd, Hong Kong

For further information on
Blackwell Publishing, visit our website:
www.blackwellpublishing.com

Contents

List of Contributors

Carl Davidson   - Professor of Economics, Michigan State University

Peter Egger   - Professor of Economics, University of Munich

Noel Gaston   - Professor of Economics, Bond University

Sourafel Girma   - Senior Lecturer in Economics, University of Leicester

Amy Jocelyn Glass   - Associate Professor, A&M University

Holger Görg   - Lecturer in Economics, University of Nottingham

David Greenaway   - Professor of Economics, University of Nottingham

Saqib Jafarey   - Reader in International Economics, City University, London

Lori G. Kletzer   - Professor of Economics, University of California, Santa Cruz

Richard Kneller   - Senior Research Fellow, University of Nottingham

Wilhelm Kohler   - Professor of Economics, Tübingen University

Sajal Lahiri   - Professor of Economics, Southern Illinois University

Steven J. Matusz   - Professor of Economics, Michigan State University

Douglas Nelson   - Professor of Economics, Tulane University and Professorial Research Fellow, University of Nottingham

Michael Pfaffermayr   - Professor of Economics, Innsbruck University

Editorial Note

The papers in this volume were presented at a conference on "Adjusting to Globalisation" held at the University of Nottingham in June 2002 and hosted by the Leverhulme Centre for Research on Globalisation and Economic Policy. After the normal refereeing process, the papers were first published as a Special Issue of the *Review of International Economics* in 2004. Given the topicality of the subject matter and high quality of the contributions, Blackwell decided to also publish the papers in this stand-alone volume, for which I am grateful. I am also grateful to Susan Berry for assistance in preparing the final manuscripts. Finally, I would like to acknowledge support from the Leverhulme Trust under Programme Grant F114/BF for their support for the conference.

David Greenaway
University of Nottingham

Chapter 1

Trade-related Job Loss and Wage Insurance: a Synthetic Review

Lori G. Kletzer

1. Introduction

Most, if not all, papers in the area of "Globalization and Labor Markets" contain at least several sentences noting the large and positive net benefits of free trade, and the corresponding ability of free trade's winners to compensate the losers. The presumption that the losers can be compensated (at least partially if not fully) is strong, and often seems to serve as adequate justification for promoting policies that advance free trade. These presumptions have long been problematic in policy and political contexts, and are steadily being challenged in the academic literature.

One key problem for the argument that the gains from trade are always large enough to (fully) compensate the losers (without exhausting the benefits) is that presumptions of an ability to compensate have only weakly translated into a record of compensation policies and programs. The record of trade liberalizations undertaken by the US is not matched by a record of policies to compensate workers for their trade-related job loss. The creation of, and reforms to, trade adjustment assistance (TAA) has some parallels to rounds of trade liberalization, but the important dimension is in results, and on this score there is little sense that TAA brings to workers any sense of adequate compensation.[1]

The highly visible nature of job loss, along with the failure of current federal adjustment programs to compensate workers for their losses, clearly weakens popular support for the view that economic integration brings widespread benefits. Yet opinions about trade liberalization do become more favorable when it is linked to worker adjustment programs (Scheve and Slaughter, 2001). The public sense remains strong that fairness dictates compensation for workers affected by trade.

Over the past 15 years, at first quietly and then with more momentum since 2000, wage insurance has emerged as a potential additional adjustment policy tool, particularly in the context of free trade.[2] The relevant papers here are Lawrence and Litan (1986), Baily et al. (1993), Jacobson et al. (1993), Jacobson (1998), Burtless et al. (1998), and Kletzer and Litan (2001).[3] In the US policy arena, the idea of wage insurance has reached a level of prominence perhaps surprising for a largely "academic" idea.[4] Due in part to the success of the globalization backlash in highlighting American job losses, the leadership of the US Senate tied legislation that granted presidential trade-promotion authority to an amendment expanding and reauthorizing TAA. One of the TAA program expansions contained in the Trade Act of 2002 is a targeted program of wage insurance.[5]

Over the recent past, the distance between adjustment discussions of the "policy" literature and those of mainstream academic international trade has narrowed.

The academic literature on adjustment costs and compensation schemes is distinguished by a number of theoretical articles.[6] Within the traditional full-employment model of trade, Dixit and Norman (1980, 1986) proposed a scheme of commodity taxation to compensate the losers. With this compensation scheme in place, trade liberalization leads to a Pareto improvement. One clear shortcoming of the traditional full-employment trade model is its inability to address the central issue of how to compensate unemployed workers for their job loss. In this spirit, Brecher and Choudhri (1994) showed that a Dixit–Norman commodity tax scheme may not work in the presence of unemployment because fully compensating the losers may require using all the gains from trade. Feenstra and Lewis (1994) showed that imperfectly mobile factors create similar problems for a commodity tax scheme. Importantly from a labor-market policy perspective, Feenstra and Lewis went on to show that commodity taxes paired with trade adjustment assistance (predicated on subsidizing workers moving across industries) can lead to Pareto gains from trade. Brander and Spencer (1994) considered several designs for trade adjustment assistance from the perspective of efficiency costs and distributional objectives. One of the designs considered is a version of wage insurance, as described by Lawrence and Litan (1986), that Brander and Spencer labeled "tapered assistance," where assistance is an increasing function of the wage loss. In their most basic case (nonmarket opportunities known and uniform across individuals), Brander and Spencer found that unconditional tapered assistance, offered to workers taking new jobs as well as workers who do not (using the value of leisure as a wage-equivalent), achieves full efficiency and dominates other programs from a distributional point of view. They went on to note that this result cannot be generalized beyond the basic model. Moving fully to a model of trade where workers seeking employment must first complete costly training and job search, two papers by Davidson and Matusz (2001, 2002) analyze worker adjustment costs and policy alternatives in a general-equilibrium framework with trade liberalization. In the 2002 paper, the main point is to consider various compensation policies, most prominently a wage subsidy/wage insurance scheme. Given the current policy prominence of this idea, these developments are welcome. As the TAA expansions introduced in the Trade Act of 2002 are implemented, the academic literature can help raise questions for evaluation and assessment.[7]

This paper seeks to promote further integration of empirical and theoretical discussions of trade and worker adjustment. From my recent studies of the costs of job loss, I develop a set of stylized facts of trade-related job loss, with a focus on worker characteristics and labor market consequences. These stylized facts are relevant to any (credible) model of trade liberalization and adjustment costs. I then discuss the basic ideas of wage insurance and summarize the little that is known about how a program might work if implemented in the US. A final section provides a list of issues for a model of trade that will be consistent with the empirical stylized facts, and sets out questions for future research.

2. What We Know about Imports and Job Loss[8]

"Trade-related job loss" is a familiar, if ambiguously defined, phrase. As commonly understood and implemented in policy, trade-related job loss means job loss due to increasing imports, and a trade-displaced worker is a worker for whom increased imports have contributed to job loss. This definition may appear precise, but many operational ambiguities arise. In addition, within academic circles there are further complications that arise from the complexity of empirically capturing the causal nature of the "trade and employment change" question; see Kletzer (2002b) for details. At a minimum, it is important to state the obvious: we have no way of knowing for certain whether a given worker is trade-displaced, nor do we have any widely agreed-upon ways of identifying the share of workers in a given industry who are trade-displaced. Those caveats in place, it is important to acknowledge that a notion of trade-displacement exists in public discourse. A sensible approach for policy-relevant analysis is to try to define the term in a way that is grounded in economic analysis. In what follows, I seek to identify workers whose job loss is associated with rising imports. I am not claiming to prove that trade or imports are the cause of the job loss.[9]

In Kletzer (2001), I classified manufacturing industries by their degree of import competition in the following way: "high" import-competing industries, those in the top quartile of a ranking of import share changes during the period 1979–94; "medium" import-competing for industries in the middle two quartiles; and "low" for the bottom quartile. The top quartile contains industries with an increase in import share exceeding 13 percentage points. By applying this import-competition definition to the Displaced Worker Surveys, I obtained samples of workers who, by the industry of the lost job, are "trade-displaced" workers in the sense of being displaced from industries facing increased import competition.[10]

Table 1 lists the high import-competing (or import-sensitive) industries. These industries are the most likely to produce import-competing job loss, and we can usefully consider workers displaced from these industries to be import-competing displaced workers. At this point, these are the workers who face adjusting to new labor market circumstances. Industries are listed in Table 1 in order of estimated total number of workers displaced during the period 1979–99, from largest to smallest.[11]

My judgments moved several industries into the high-import category: motor vehicles, tires and inner tubes, blast furnaces, other primary metals, and cycles and miscellaneous transport all have a history of import competition, are large and visible employers, but experienced increases in import share just below the top quartile cutoff.[12] The high-import group contains the handful of industries commonly considered to be import-competing: apparel, footwear, knitting mills, leather products, textiles, blast furnaces, radio and television, and toys and sporting goods. As I report in more detail in the book, my criterion for import-competition is robust. The top-ten industries accounting for NAFTA–TAA certifications over the period 1994–2000 are all in the high import-competing group.[13]

Using a somewhat conservative count of displaced workers, I estimate that 16.8 million workers lost jobs in all of manufacturing during the period 1979–99, about 37% of the total nonagricultural job loss of 44.9 million.[14] During this period, manufacturing represented, typically, about 18% of total nonagricultural employment. The high import-competing group accounted for 38.4% of manufacturing displacement, at 6.45 million workers. During the 1979–99 period, these industries accounted for just under 30% of manufacturing employment. In a larger context, averaged over the period 1979–99, the high import-competing manufacturing industries accounted for 5.2% of total nonagricultural employment. By my measures, job losses from these industries accounted for 14.2% of nonagricultural displacement.

More recently and more narrowly, I examined the extent of job loss related to NAFTA and imports, and concluded that NAFTA-import-related job loss accounted for 24–27% of manufacturing job loss over the 1993–99 period. For the economy

Table 1. High Import-competing Industries and Job Displacement, 1979–99

	Total displaced 1979–99	Share of total mfg. displaced	Mean job loss rate	Change in import share			1979 import share
				1979–94	1979–85	1985–94	
Electrical machinery, I	1,576,095						
Electrical machinery	1,180,706	0.070	0.040	0.206	0.071	0.135	0.107
Radio, TV	395,389	0.024	0.105	0.147	0.046	0.101	0.151
Apparel, I	1,135,668						
Apparel	1,135,668	0.068	0.056	0.250	0.103	0.146	0.132
Transportation equipment, I	985,760						
Motor vehicles	918,066	0.055	0.043	0.101	0.086	0.016	0.173
Cycles & misc. transport	67,694	0.004	0.084	-0.063	-0.022	-0.041	0.291
Machinery, except electrical, I	905,514						
Electronic computing eqpt.	513,988	0.031	0.045	0.384	0.086	0.298	0.103
Construction & material moving machines	350,900	0.021	0.053	0.177	0.091	0.087	0.060
Office & acct machines	40,626	0.002	0.030	0.372	0.083	0.289	0.080
Metal industries, I	494,660						
Blast furnaces	361,428	0.022	0.053	0.071	0.074	-0.003	0.119
Other primary metal	133,232	0.008	0.072	0.002	0.022	-0.020	0.189
Misc. manuf industries	335,091	0.020	0.051	0.190	0.110	0.080	0.186
Leather & leather products	246,451						
Footwear	184,417	0.011	0.087	0.359	0.219	0.140	0.348
Leather products	57,337	0.003	0.122	0.391	0.195	0.196	0.269
Leather tanning & finish	4,697	0.000	0.074	0.117	0.073	0.045	0.160

Table 1. Continued

	Total displaced 1979–99	Share of total mfg. displaced	Mean job loss rate	Change in import share			1979 import share
				1979–94	1979–85	1985–94	
Professional & photographic equipment	240,200						
Scientific & controlling	163,503	0.010	0.028	0.154	0.042	0.112	0.074
Photographic eqpt.	67,754	0.004	0.032	0.140	0.052	0.088	0.121
Watches, clocks	8,943	0.001	0.091	0.413	0.226	0.187	0.387
Rubber & misc. plastics	192,960						
Other rubber products	113,144	0.007	0.044	0.157	−0.013	0.169	0.086
Tires & inner tubes	79,816	0.005	0.045	0.096	0.038	0.058	0.130
Textiles, I	159,177						
Knitting mills	137,725	0.008	0.034	0.159	0.097	0.061	0.061
Misc. textile	21,452	0.001	0.045	0.015	0.014	0.001	0.119
Other							
Toys & sporting goods	155,970	0.009	0.060	0.278	0.148	0.130	0.229
Pottery & related	26,471	0.002	0.073	0.133	0.105	0.027	0.313
Totals/means	6,454,017	0.384	0.059	0.185	0.085	0.100	0.169

Source: Taken from Kletzer (2001, Table 2.1). Author's calculations from the NBER Trade Database and the Displaced Workers Surveys, 1984–2000.

overall, NAFTA-import-related job losses are more modest, accounting for 10.7% of total job loss.[15]

These job loss numbers will strike some as compelling, and others as less so. There has been much debate over the number of workers or jobs affected by trade (Scott, 2001). To understand adjustment costs, it is important to understand workers—who they are and how they are affected by import-related job loss. Briefly, I will summarize what is known about the characteristics of displaced workers and basic post-displacement outcomes.

Table 2 reports a set of worker characteristics. Compared to workers displaced from other sectors of the economy, such as wholesale and retail trade, utilities, or services, manufacturing workers are slightly older, notably less educated, with longer job tenures, somewhat more likely to be minority, and far more likely to be production-oriented (just less than one-half of manufacturing displaced are lower-skilled blue-collar workers—fabricators, laborers, etc.). Twenty-one percent of manufacturing-displaced are high-school dropouts, compared to 11.9% of the nonmanufacturing-displaced. This difference widened in the 1990s as compared to the 1980s: the high-school dropout share fell throughout the economy, but more so outside of manufacturing. Manufacturing workers are less likely to be college graduates: over 1979–99, workers with a college degree or higher comprised about 14% of manufacturing-displaced and 22% of nonmanufacturing-displaced.

Import-competing workers are similar to other displaced manufacturing workers, with respect to age, educational attainment, and job tenure (see Table 3). Import-competing workers are very slightly older (a larger share are 45–54 years of age). The most striking difference between import-competing displaced workers and other displaced manufacturing workers is the degree to which import-competing industries employ and displace women. Women account for 45% of import-sensitive displaced workers, compared to 37% of overall manufacturing-displaced. Some industries stand out: women account for 80% of those displaced from apparel, 66% of those displaced from footwear, and 76% of those displaced from knitting mills (part of the textiles industry). Women dominate the group of displaced workers from these import-competing industries as a result of their high representation in employment.

Turning to outcomes, about 65% of manufacturing displaced workers were re-employed at their survey date, as compared to 69% of nonmanufacturing displaced workers. This difference, 4.3 percentage points, is not large, but it is statistically significant. The likelihood of re-employment was markedly higher in the 1990s than in the 1980s. Import-competing displaced workers are a little less likely to be re-employed (63.4% were re-employed at their survey date) than other displaced manufacturing workers (65.8% re-employed). Particularly for the high import-competing group, re-employment was more difficult in the 1980s with a lower rate of 62.3%, than it was in the 1990s when 65.4% of workers were re-employed on average (see Table 4).

Among the re-employed, high import-competing displaced workers have large average earnings losses, about 13% at the mean. This average earnings loss is significantly different from workers displaced from industries with the least exposure to imports, but not the medium import group. These large average losses mask considerable heterogeneity: 36% of import-competing displaced workers report earning the same or more after displacement as they earned before the job loss, and 25% reported earnings losses of 30% or more. This spread is very similar to manufacturing as a whole.

Drawing these elements together, there are few striking differences between import-competing displaced workers and other manufacturing workers, based on average

Table 2. Characteristics of Displaced Workers, 1979–99

	Manufacturing	Transportation, communications, utilities, wholesale & retail trade, services
Age at displacement:		
20–24 years	0.144	0.164
25–34	0.333	0.344
35–44	0.254	0.256
45–54	0.168	0.153
55–64	0.101	0.082
Average age, years (SD)	38.6	37.3
	(11.5)	(11.2)
Education:		
Less than high school	0.210	0.119
High-school graduate	0.437	0.365
Some college	0.215	0.294
College degree +	0.137	0.222
Average years of education (SD)	12.3	13.2
	(2.6)	(2.4)
Job tenure at time of displacement:		
Less than 3 years	0.402	0.510
3–5 years	0.227	0.229
6–10 years	0.156	0.133
11–20 years	0.131	0.082
>20 years	0.084	0.045
Average job tenure, years (SD)	6.5	4.6
	(7.8)	(6.2)
Share female	0.369	0.504
Share minority	0.176	0.170
Share displaced from full-time jobs	0.956	0.837
Predisplacement occupation:		
White collar	0.307	0.645
Skilled blue collar	0.188	0.075
Unskilled blue collar	0.480	0.138
Services	0.023	0.140
Weekly earnings on the old job:		
Mean (SD)	$396.88	$368.65
	($250.89)	($269.19)
Share earned less than $200/wk	0.18	0.28
Share earned more than $800/wk	0.06	0.07
Share re-employed at survey date	0.648	0.691
For re-employed:		
Mean change in log earnings (SD)	−0.121	−0.038
	(0.473)	(0.575)
Median change	−0.047	0
Share with no earnings loss or earning more	0.35	0.41
Share with earnings losses greater than 15%	0.35	0.29
Share with earnings losses greater than 30%	0.25	0.21

Source: Taken from Kletzer (2001, Table 3.1).
Workers displaced from agriculture, mining, construction, forestry and fishing excluded.

Table 3. Characteristics of Displaced Manufacturing Workers by Industry Level of Import Competition, 1979–99

	High import competition	Medium import competition	Low import competition
Age at displacement:			
20–24 years	0.131	0.149	0.157
25–34	0.323	0.338	0.340
35–44	0.267	0.240	0.262
45–54	0.174	0.169	0.155
55–64	0.104	0.103	0.087
Average age, years (SD)	39.1	38.4	37.8
	(11.4)	(11.6)	(11.3)
Education:			
Less than high school	0.213	0.219	0.182
High-school graduate	0.427	0.444	0.446
Some college	0.212	0.210	0.229
College degree +	0.148	0.126	0.142
Average years of education (SD)	12.3	12.3	12.5
	(2.7)	(2.6)	(2.5)
Job tenure at time of displacement:			
Less than 3 years	0.388	0.398	0.442
3–5 years	0.221	0.231	0.230
6–10 years	0.168	0.154	0.134
11–20 years	0.130	0.133	0.125
>20 years	0.091	0.083	0.069
Average job tenure, years (SD)	6.8	6.5	5.9
	(7.9)	(7.8)	(7.7)
Share female	0.449	0.304	0.351
Share minority	0.190	0.165	0.167
Share displaced from full-time jobs	0.966	0.960	0.924
Predisplacement occupation:			
White collar	0.313	0.286	0.345
Skilled blue collar	0.180	0.209	0.155
Unskilled blue collar	0.488	0.478	0.466
Services	0.018	0.025	0.029
Weekly earnings on the old job:			
Mean (SD) (1995 dollars)	$402.97	$400.41	$375.11
	($273.39)	($236.55)	($230.52)
Share earned less than $200/wk	0.24	0.16	0.18
Share earned more than $800/wk	0.07	0.06	0.05

Source: Taken from Kletzer (2001, Table 3.2).

characteristics. It is useful to look beyond the averages and at the distribution of these characteristics. Table 5 reports on a set of characteristics, expanded from Tables 3 and 4, just for the high import group of industries and workers.

High import competition industries vary from the low-wage (apparel, footwear, knitting mills, leather products) to the high-wage (computers, blast furnaces, tires and inner tubes, construction and material moving machines, motor vehicles). Across the board, the lower-wage industries employ and displace large shares (and often large numbers) of women. A few industries stand out: women account for 79% of displaced workers

Table 4. Post-displacement Outcomes in Manufacturing, by Industry Level of Import Competition, 1979–99

	High import competition	Medium import competition	Low import competition
Share re-employed at survey date	0.634	0.654	0.668
For re-employed:			
Mean change in log earnings (SD)	−0.132	−0.126	−0.086
	(0.475)	(0.469)	(0.475)
Median change	−0.047	−0.062	−0.027
Share with no earnings loss or earning more	0.36	0.34	0.38
Share with earnings losses greater than 15%	0.35	0.36	0.34
Share with earnings losses greater than 30%	0.25	0.25	0.26

Source: Taken from Kletzer (2001, Table 3.3).

from apparel (compared with their 82% employment share in 1978). In footwear, women represent 66% of displaced workers, from a 70% 1978 employment share. In leather products, women were 73% of the displaced, and 69% of 1978 employment. From knitting mills, women account for 80% of displaced workers. Understanding gender differences in the incidence and consequences of import-competing job losses is a subject for another study. What is clear here is that the burden of import-competing job losses falls on women, in large part because traditionally women have been employed in these high import-competing industries.[16]

Lower educational attainment also describes these lower-wage industries. High-school dropouts comprise 25–50% of those displaced from these industries. A few industries stand out: textiles, apparel, leather products, footwear. The fraction of high-school dropouts is notably lower in the higher-wage industries, in the range of 7–10%. We expect our traditional import-competing industries to be relatively low-skilled, and their displaced workers face readjustment starting from modest levels of formal schooling. Their on-the-job skills are more difficult to observe, but formal schooling and on-the-job training are known to be positively correlated. We should expect these workers to face difficult readjustments.

Many high import-competing displaced workers were well-established in their jobs. Long tenures clearly characterize the higher-wage industries. Half of the displaced from tires and inner tubes reported being in the job ten years or more before the job loss. Even in the lower-wage industries, sizeable shares (around 20%) of displaced workers had been in the job at least ten years. Just being in a job for 10 years can mean rusty job search skills and a general lack of information about current labor market conditions.

For workers with little formal schooling and long tenures, job loss can be a costly experience. For the high import-competing group as a whole, the likelihood of re-employment is less than two-thirds (at 63.5%), and it varies from a low of 38% for leather products to a high of 83% for photographic equipment. Almost all, 97%, of these workers were employed full-time before displacement, making weak labor force attachment, from the worker side, an unlikely cause for the low re-employment rates.

For most high import-competing workers, the time needed to find a new job is within the usual 26-week period of eligibility for unemployment compensation. Half of these

Table 5. Characteristics of "High" Import-competing Workers, Rank-ordered by Number of Workers Displaced, 1979–99

| | Mean old-job earnings | Share female | Share high-school | | Share w/ tenure >10yrs | Share re-employed | Change in weekly earnings | | Share w/ earnings loss >30% | Share w/ jobless >26 wks |
			Dropouts	Grads			Median	Mean		
Electrical machinery	$412.16	0.484	0.139	0.414	0.184	0.673	-0.033	-0.143	0.22	0.222
Apparel	$236.37	0.791	0.378	0.447	0.181	0.556	-0.041	-0.083	0.199	0.203
Motor vehicles	$448.32	0.248	0.196	0.503	0.287	0.622	-0.117	-0.228	0.35	0.296
Electronic computing eqpt.	$588.10	0.377	0.068	0.256	0.224	0.737	-0.068	-0.239	0.254	0.134
Radio, TV	$431.61	0.479	0.138	0.431	0.214	0.657	-0.003	-0.071	0.192	0.252
Blast furnaces	$509.54	0.111	0.203	0.465	0.39	0.617	-0.36	-0.493	0.446	0.367
Construction & material	$489.36	0.178	0.152	0.415	0.219	0.678	-0.17	-0.296	0.307	0.3
Misc. manuf. industries	$327.01	0.46	0.236	0.416	0.14	0.638	-0.023	-0.173	0.229	0.201
Footwear	$240.26	0.662	0.427	0.439	0.194	0.543	-0.071	-0.072	0.239	0.329
Scientific & controlling	$464.28	0.403	0.087	0.311	0.128	0.717	0.021	-0.088	0.17	0.198
Toys & sporting goods	$333.96	0.506	0.212	0.312	0.117	0.619	-0.03	-0.153	0.245	0.23
Knitting mills	$223.05	0.759	0.368	0.487	0.167	0.609	-0.024	-0.107	0.225	0.263
Other primary metal	$444.22	0.252	0.189	0.563	0.257	0.581	-0.061	-0.157	0.306	0.207
Other rubber products	$311.23	0.533	0.261	0.522	0.297	0.683	0	-0.166	0.231	0.101
Tires & inner tubes	$605.57	0.247	0.085	0.309	0.485	0.689	-0.42	-0.464	0.487	0.315
Photographic eqpt.	$526.49	0.223	0.137	0.414	0.385	0.777	-0.077	-0.15	0.254	0.236
Cycles & misc. transport	$352.04	0.219	0.221	0.647	0.136	0.681	0	-0.203	0.255	0.251
Leather products	$226.64	0.734	0.525	0.321	0.17	0.378	-0.089	-0.106	0.254	0.335
Office & acct machines	$464.81	0.432	0.095	0.462	0.167	0.612	0.206	0.175	0.117	0.237
Pottery & related	$267.02	0.454	0.376	0.386	0.229	0.396	-0.223	-0.464	0.338	0.214
Misc. textile	$282.40	0.666	0.379	0.559	0.222	0.511	-0.077	-0.328	0.398	0.242
Watches, clocks	$403.63	0.268	0.098	0.434	0.241	0.777	0.01	-0.066	0.128	0.169
Leather tanning & finish	$322.83	0.368	0.098	0.471	0.202	0.635	0.158	0.101	0.092	0.109
High import-competing average	$402.97	0.449	0.213	0.427	0.221	0.635	-0.047	-0.132	0.253	0.24
Manufacturing average	$396.88	0.369	0.211	0.437	0.215	0.648	-0.047	-0.121	0.252	0.221
Nonmanufacturing average	$368.65	0.511	0.119	0.365	0.127	0.691	0	-0.038	0.212	0.127

Source: Taken from Kletzer (2001, Table 3.4).
Changes in weekly earnings are changes in log(earnings).

workers had unemployment spells of 8 weeks or less. Interestingly, 27% of workers were unemployed for less than one week (this group is included in the half with spells of less than one week). Yet a full quarter of workers were unemployed for more than 26 weeks (six months), where standard unemployment compensation is exhausted. There is a wide variation in the incidence of long spells of unemployment (jobless for six months or longer) across the high import-competing industries. In some industries, relatively few workers were jobless six months or more (10% in other rubber products, and leather tanning and finishing) and in others long periods of joblessness was a more likely experience (36.7% in blast furnaces, 32.9% in footwear, 31.5% in tires and inner tubes).

The mean earnings loss was 13.2%. The range of earnings losses is striking across the high import-competing industries. Mean earnings losses from two of the high-wage industries were greater than 45% (blast furnaces, and tires and inner tubes). Mean earnings losses from other high-wage industries were notably smaller; e.g., motor vehicles at 23% and photographic equipment at 15%. Lower-wage industries have lower mean and median earnings losses, and we expect some of that effect statistically (i.e., high-earning workers have more earnings to "lose" as they drop down in the earnings distribution than do lower-earning workers). High-wage industries have a greater share of their workers reporting large (greater than 30%) earnings losses. With their predominance in lower-wage industries, women have slightly smaller mean earnings losses than men (12% compared to 15%), a difference that is not statistically significant.

Simple statistical models of re-employment and earnings losses can be used to understand the variation in outcomes across workers. Tables 6 and 7 report estimates from a logit analysis of survey-date employment, first for the full sample (Table 6) and then for the manufacturing subsample (Table 7).[17] Certain characteristics stand out:

1. Younger workers are more likely to be re-employed. Workers who are 25–34 years of age or 35–44 years of age are about 11 percentage points more likely to be re-employed than workers who were 45 years of age or older at the time of displacement.
2. Education matters too. Compared to high-school dropouts, workers with a college degree (or higher) are 25 percentage points more likely to be re-employed, high-school graduates 9.4 percentage points more likely, and workers with some college experience 11 percentage points more likely to be re-employed.
3. The overall health of the economy and the labor market matters a great deal. A worker displaced from nondurable goods manufacturing in the strong economy of the mid-to-late 1990s (1993–99), 45 years of age or older, a high-school dropout, more than 10 years' tenure on the old job, full-time at the time of displacement, nonminority and married had a predicted chance of re-employment of 53.7%. The same worker, displaced during the deep 1980s recession (1981–83), had a 34.5% chance of re-employment, more than one-third (35.7%) lower. While it may not be enough (particularly for older, less educated, and more tenured workers), a strong labor market clearly provides the necessary setting for displaced workers to find the next job.

As an illustrative example, take a representative import-competing displaced worker (displaced from nondurable goods manufacturing in the mid-to-late 1990s, 45 years of age or older, a high-school dropout, more than 10 years' tenure on the old job, full-time at the time of displacement, nonminority, and married). This worker has a predicted likelihood of re-employment of 54%. If that worker was younger, say 25 to 44

Table 6. Change in the Probability of Re-employment (marginal effects)

	(1) Full sample	(2) Full sample	(3) Full sample
Nondurable goods mfg.	−0.0598**	−0.0274*	−0.0269**
	(0.0193)	(0.0128)	(0.0104)
Durable goods mfg.	−0.0289*	−0.0226*	−0.0423**
	(0.0129)	(0.0099)	(0.0094)
Transport, Comm., Utility	−0.0098	−0.0027	−0.0259
	(0.0177)	(0.0146)	(0.0142)
Age at displacement:			
20–24 years		0.0940**	0.0851**
		(0.0107)	(0.0110)
25–34 years		0.1097**	0.1052**
		(0.0079)	(0.0079)
35–44 years		0.1106**	0.1101**
		(0.0096)	(0.0098)
Education:			
High-school graduate		0.1058**	0.1116**
		(0.0079)	(0.0081)
Some college		0.1599**	0.1622**
		(0.0083)**	(0.0084)**
College		0.2494**	0.2434**
		(0.0093)**	(0.0093)**
Job tenure:			
Less than 3 years		0.0106	0.0191
		(0.0103)	(0.0106)
3–5 years		0.0376**	0.0463**
		(0.0101)	(0.0104)
6–10 years		0.0294**	0.0366**
		(0.0104)	(0.0106)
Displaced from full-time job		0.1019**	0.0780**
		(0.0094)	(0.0090)
Minority		−0.1063**	−0.1029**
		(0.0084)	(0.0084)
Married		0.0193**	0.0116
		(0.0070)	(0.0067)
Female			−0.0973**
			(0.0062)
Year displaced:			
1979–80	−0.0764**	−0.0747**	−0.0736**
	(0.0150)	(0.0157)	(0.0152)
1984–89	0.0569**	0.0538**	0.0567**
	(0.0086)	(0.0083)	(0.0083)
1990–92	0.0510**	0.0366**	0.0383**
	(0.0088)	(0.0091)	(0.0090)
1993–99	0.1774**	0.1717**	0.1773**
	(0.0098)	(0.0098)	(0.0099)
Years since displacement	0.0828**	0.0794**	0.0805**
	(0.0034)	(0.0037)	(0.0037)
Constant	−0.0911**	−0.3918**	−0.3251**
	(0.0133)	(0.0206)	(0.0212)
Observations	35,435	35,222	35,222

Source: Taken from Kletzer (2001, Table 4.1).
Standard errors are in parentheses. *significant at 5%; **significant at 1%.

Table 7. Change in the Probability of Re-employment, Manufacturing Sample (marginal effects)

	(1)	(2)	(3)	(4)
High import-competing	−0.0408*	−0.0345**	−0.0206	−0.0206
	(0.0198)	(0.0124)	(0.0130)	(0.0134)
Medium import-competing	−0.0068	0.0002	−0.0030	−0.0040
	(0.0160)	(0.0141)	(0.0126)	(0.0126)
Age at displacement:				
20–24 years		0.1074**	0.0944**	0.1065**
		(0.0209)	(0.0206)	(0.0208)
25–34 years		0.1196**	0.1122**	0.1185**
		(0.0137)	(0.0138)	(0.0136)
35–44 years		0.1115**	0.1090**	0.1126**
		(0.0180)	(0.0186)	(0.0186)
Education:				
High-school graduate		0.1050**	0.1063**	0.1090**
		(0.0118)	(0.0119)	(0.0121)
Some college		0.1456**	0.1392**	0.1387**
		(0.0126)	(0.0128)	(0.0132)
College		0.2716**	0.2554**	0.2540**
		(0.0167)	(0.0177)	(0.0178)
Job tenure:				
Less than 3 years		0.0422**	0.0576**	0.0619**
		(0.0135)	(0.0141)	(0.0143)
3–5 years		0.0644**	0.0788**	0.0836**
		(0.0150)	(0.0156)	(0.0159)
6–10 years		0.0652**	0.0758**	0.0798**
		(0.0141)	(0.0140)	(0.0142)
Displaced from full-time job		0.1117**	0.0818**	0.0722*
		(0.0297)	(0.0305)	(0.0301)
Minority		−0.1111**	−0.1024**	−0.1056**
		(0.0138)	(0.0141)	(0.0142)
Married		0.0388**	0.0284**	0.1068
		(0.0098)	(0.0097)	(0.0140)
Female			−0.1049**	0.0023
			(0.0111)	(0.0136)
Female*married				−0.1768**
				(0.0260)
Year displaced:				
1979–80	−0.0968**	−0.0979**	−0.0949**	
	(0.0212)	(0.0236)	(0.0228)	
1984–89	0.0684**	0.0726**	0.0744**	
	(0.0123)	(0.0118)	(0.0120)	
1990–92	0.0551**	0.0487**	0.0491**	
	(0.0136)	(0.0140)	(0.0134)	
1993–99	0.1803**	0.1854**	0.1901**	
	(0.0152)	(0.0170)	(0.0174)	
Years since displacement	0.0944**	0.0935**	0.0941**	
	(0.0048)	(0.0055)	(0.0058)	
Constant	−0.1392**	−0.4903**	−0.4263**	−0.4770**
	(0.0191)	(0.0375)	(0.0355)	(0.0357)
Observations	13,846	13,795	13,795	13,795

Source: Taken from Kletzer (2001, Table 4.2).
Standard errors are in parentheses. *significant at 5%; **significant at 1%.

years old instead of 45 years or older, the chance of re-employment rises to nearly 66%. As a high-school dropout, the chance of re-employment is about 65%. For a college graduate, re-employment jumps to 78.5%. These differences are a striking illustration of the importance of education (which can be changed) and age (which cannot) in getting the next job. And the effect of more formal schooling is stronger for younger workers than for older workers.

My analysis finds that losing a job and having to find another can be difficult for many workers. The difficulties may not end with re-employment. If the new job pays less than the old one, the costs of job loss can continue for years. For a sample of Pennsylvania workers, Jacobson et al. (1993) found earnings losses equal to approximately 25% of predisplacement earnings, five or six years after job loss.

An analysis of re-employment earnings is more limited using the Displaced Worker Surveys, where earnings are measured as weekly earnings, and the available comparison is between weekly earnings at the time of displacement and, if re-employed, weekly earnings at the time of the survey. Earnings losses can be measured by comparing earnings on the old job to those on the new job. This measure will "miss" earnings growth that would have occurred on the old job, in the absence of displacement. Manufacturing displaced workers experience large earnings losses on average, 12% at the mean, compared to a loss of just under 4% for nonmanufacturing displaced workers.

Among the re-employed, import-competing displaced workers experience sizeable average weekly earnings losses of about 13%. This large average loss masks considerable variation: one-third of import-competing displaced workers report earning the same or more on their new job as they earned on the old job, and one-quarter reported earnings losses of 30% or more. This average and distribution is very similar to what I find for manufacturing workers as a group. Older, less educated, lower-skilled production workers, with established tenures on the old job, are more likely to experience earnings losses in excess of 30%.

Straightforward OLS estimates of earnings loss specifications help clarify an emerging profile of workers who experience costly job losses (Kletzer, 2001). Earnings losses rise with previous job tenure and age and are smaller for more educated workers. Among manufacturing workers, high import-competing workers do not have significantly larger earnings losses than the less import-competing group.

Re-employment Sector

The pattern of re-employment by industrial sector can help us understand the range of outcomes available to displaced workers. Some basic knowledge of the re-employment sector is also applicable to a larger question of the impact of free trade on employment and wages. With shifts in comparative advantage, how is labor reallocated across industries?

Table 8 presents detailed information on re-employment outcomes by industrial sector.[18] A few general observations stand out. First, contrary to common perceptions, not all displaced manufacturing workers are re-employed at McDonald's. Overall, just 10% of re-employed manufacturing workers are in retail trade (McDonald's, as an eating and drinking establishment, is in the retail trade sector). High import-competing displaced workers are no more likely than any other manufacturing worker to be re-employed in retail trade. In contrast, 21% of nonmanufacturing displaced workers are re-employed in retail trade.

Second, there is considerable re-employment within manufacturing. High import-competing displaced workers, 100% of whom were displaced from nondurable goods and durable goods manufacturing, are being re-employed in manufacturing, at a level of about one-half. In other words, considering just those workers re-employed when surveyed (about two-thirds of those displaced), fully one-half of import-competing displaced workers are re-employed back in manufacturing. Incorporating the 0.634 re-employment rate, we can note that about one-third (0.329) of all high import-competing displaced workers return to manufacturing after their job loss. Another one-third are re-employed in the nonmanufacturing sectors and the remaining one-third are not re-employed.

Workers who return to their old sector may retain the value of some specific skills, keep earning union rents, and maintain their position in internal job ladders. All these factors are expected to mitigate earnings losses, and they do, as can be seen in Table 8. For manufacturing workers, regaining employment in manufacturing greatly reduces earnings losses. Mean earnings losses are smallest for workers re-employed in durable goods (at 4.5%), and next smallest in nondurable goods (5.8%). Median earnings losses are even smaller, at no loss for durable goods and 3.7% for nondurable goods.

While earnings losses are small for the "average" high import-competing worker re-employed in manufacturing, there is still considerable variation in earnings changes. About one-fifth of these workers suffer earnings losses in excess of 30% (see Table 8). Even within manufacturing, skilled (but older) workers may find themselves unfamiliar with standards, processes, and procedures instituted by manufacturing firms since the mid-1980s. That 20% of workers with very large earnings losses is, however, considerably smaller than the corresponding shares for workers re-employed in other sectors.

Displaced manufacturing workers who gain re-employment in manufacturing also experience the shortest median weeks of joblessness (6–8 weeks), as compared to workers re-employed elsewhere. This may be a result of searching first in familiar labor markets in manufacturing, and turning to less familiar markets and networks only after some period of unsuccessful search. These spells of joblessness are well within the standard period of eligibility for unemployment compensation (at 26 weeks).

Wholesale and retail trade, finance, and services provide about 3% of import-competing displaced worker re-employment. Mean earnings changes are highly variable, ranging from a 6% loss in finance, insurance and real estate, to 34% loss in retail trade. A large share of such workers (25–40%) report earnings losses exceeding 30%. Retail trade and business and personal services together account for nearly 20% of import-competing displaced re-employment, and mean earnings losses are large, on the order of 22–33%. Given the prevalence of part-time work in wholesale and retail trade and services, a switch from full-time to part-time may help explain the large re-employment earnings losses.

These patterns of re-employment are both expected and perhaps unexpected. The patterns show both considerable reallocation along with some maintenance of employment in "old" industries. They suggest a partial reallocation of labor, one that may be consistent with a short (1–3 year) horizon. It is not at all clear that a complete reallocation should be expected, given the presence of specific factors. The "old" manufacturing sectors may be engaged in a form of long-term employment decline, but that process is not uniform across firms or industries. Production continues, normal turnover continues, some employment opportunities remain open. For workers with specific skills, re-establishing a spot in manufacturing makes sense; it minimizes earnings losses. It also suggest avenues for re-employment efforts that do not involve formal (re)training. At the same time, the pattern of re-employment, particularly for manufacturing workers, shows that when workers are reallocated, it can be at considerable cost.

Table 8. Re-employment Sector, Earnings Changes and Jobless Durations, by Industry Level of Import Competition

Level of import competition	Agriculture	Mining	Construction	Manufacturing		Transport, utilities	Trade		Finance, insurance real estate	Services		Govt	Total
				Nondurables	Durables		Wholesale	Retail		Personal, business	Professional		
High													
Number	19,379	23,672	190,065	853,687	1,887,237	259,336	221,516	556,987	214,245	524,750	462,936	93,906	5,307,716
Share	0.0036	0.0044	0.0358	0.1608	0.3555	0.0488	0.0417	0.1049	0.0403	0.0988	0.0883	0.0176	1.000
Median earnings chg.	-0.181	-0.078	-0.086	-0.037	0	-0.01	-0.07	-0.262	0	-0.113	-0.149	-0.128	-0.048
Mean earnings chg.	-0.294	-0.064	-0.13	-0.058	-0.045	-0.118	-0.133	-0.334	-0.058	-0.223	-0.255	-0.062	-0.125
Median wks.	38	9	12	8	6	6	8	8	6	6	13	10	8
Medium													
Number	67,091	27,302	394,009	949,850	2,089,635	302,265	257,804	538,684	217,211	551,787	470,198	131,914	5,997,750
Share	0.0112	0.0045	0.0656	0.1583	0.3484	0.0503	0.0429	0.0898	0.0362	0.0919	0.0783	0.0219	1.000
Median earnings chg.	-0.261	-0.041	-0.053	-0.023	-0.029	0	-0.131	-0.251	-0.136	-0.228	-0.197	-0.055	-0.063
Mean earnings chg.	-0.29	0.144	-0.062	-0.034	-0.041	-0.075	-0.149	-0.29	-0.218	-0.298	-0.225	-0.114	-0.118
Median wks.	6	10	6	4	6	9	6	8	9	6	8	8	6
Low													
Number	31,944	3,943	125,304	559,789	535,946	156,584	125,062	261,557	93,893	281,170	299,028	61,134	2,535,354
Share	0.0125	0.0015	0.0494	0.2207	0.2113	0.0617	0.0493	0.1032	0.037	0.1109	0.1179	0.0241	1.000
Median earnings chg.	-0.048	0.182	0	-0.006	0.018	0	-0.043	-0.19	0.018	-0.052	-0.163	-0.331	-0.028
Mean earnings chg.	-0.157	0.008	-0.155	-0.012	0.026	0.048	-0.052	-0.217	-0.074	-0.15	-0.166	-0.393	-0.077
Median wks.	8	0	8	4	5	6	4	6	4	6	10	7	6
Nonmanufacturing													
Number	164,442	62,076	896,199	951,046	1,491,502	2,172,656	1,324,330	4,488,224	2,276,067	3,368,766	4,659,912	579,645	22,400,000
Share	0.0073	0.0027	0.04	0.0424	0.0665	0.0969	0.0591	0.2003	0.1016	0.1504	0.208	0.0258	1.000
Median earnings chg.	-0.062	0.084	0	0.003	0.051	0	0	-0.028	0.001	0	0	0.039	0.000
Mean earnings chg.	-0.113	0.086	0.016	0.039	0.073	0.009	0.009	-0.037	-0.019	-0.034	0.007	0.101	-0.003
Median wks.	3	4	4	5	4	3	4	3	4	4	3	6	4

Source: Taken from Kletzer (2001, Table 6.1).
Changes in earnings are changes in log(earnings).

These results also suggest that a uniform manufacturing-to-services view of labor reallocation is simplistic. Rather than thinking that entire industries are in decline, it is more realistic to think that some firms/activities in an industry decline while other firms/activities start up or expand.

3. Stylized Facts of Import-competing Job Loss

From the summary discussion above, we can draw out a set of stylized facts about import-competing job loss. These stylized facts can provide some useful benchmarks for models of trade and trade liberalization with adjustment costs. Proposed policies for addressing adjustment costs should have some consistency with these stylized facts.

1. Import-related job loss is a sizeable share of US manufacturing job loss, and a much smaller share of economy-wide job loss.
2. Similar to manufacturing workers displaced for other reasons, import-competing displaced workers are older, less formally educated, and more tenured than displaced nonmanufacturing workers. Generally, these are not the characteristics of workers who succeed in training programs.
3. The probability of re-employment is low for import-competing displaced workers (relative to nonmanufacturing workers), with sizeable earnings losses on average.
4. Import competition is associated with low re-employment rates because the workers vulnerable to rising import job loss experience difficulty gaining re-employment, based on their individual characteristics. The characteristics that limit the re-employment of import-competing displaced workers are the same characteristics that limit the re-employment of all displaced workers: low educational attainment; advancing age, high tenure, minority status, marital status. Workers with high tenure and/or low skill may confront serious skill-related adjustment problems, along with having rusty job search skills. Facing the loss of a wage premium, UI benefits will be relatively generous, allowing slower job search.
5. For most workers, the costs of job loss occur as re-employment earnings losses. Less formally educated workers experience the greatest difficulty maintaining earnings. More generally, re-employment earnings losses rise with age, fall with education, rise with (old) job tenure. Workers with these characteristics appear to need the most help. Wage insurance could be considered (partial) compensation for lost specific skills.
6. Re-employment in manufacturing minimizes earnings losses (on average). An advantageous outcome for production workers with manufacturing-specific skills is to stay employed in manufacturing. Earnings losses are reduced by re-employment within the narrow set of "old" industries, and even more so by re-employment in the old detailed industry. Re-employment in services is associated with the largest earnings losses. There may be little retraining associated with these moves. Wage insurance has potential for reducing these losses.

4. Wage Insurance: Compensation or a Fix for the Unemployment Insurance System?

In recent discussions about addressing some of the costs of trade-related job loss, wage insurance has resurfaced as a mechanism for (partially) compensating workers for their re-employment earnings losses. With the range of earnings changes found in the Displaced Worker Surveys, the costs of such a program are reasonable in dollar terms and a very small fraction of the estimated benefits for the US from freer trade (Kletzer and Litan, 2001).

How Would a Wage Insurance Program Work?

Wage insurance is a supplemental benefit program designed to cover some of the earnings losses following displacement, in a way that stimulates re-employment. As proposed in Kletzer and Litan (2001), eligible workers would receive some fraction, perhaps half, of their weekly earnings loss. The fraction could vary by age and tenure of the worker. Payments begin only when a worker has a new (full-time) job and could continue for up to two years following the initial job loss, as long as the new job paid less than the old job. Annual payments could be capped at $10,000/year. By "topping up" earnings if the new job pays less than the old, and only for a specified period, the program offers re-employment incentives, in contrast to the incentives introduced by UI and training subsidies. With the re-employment incentive, the program can also be seen from an active labor market policy perspective, in the spirit of re-employment bonuses.[19]

For example, if an eligible high import-competing worker made $600 per week on the old full-time job and found a new full-time job paying $520 (13% less), the supplemental payment would be $40/week, for a total weekly earnings of $560.[20] At a 30% earnings loss, the new job would pay $420/week, the payment would be $90, for a weekly earnings of $510. Here, the supplement could encourage a worker to take a job paying significantly less than the old job, yet with the supplement, the earnings loss is reduced by half.

The re-employment incentive in wage insurance is seen clearly when contrasted with UI benefits. Generally, payments under UI are limited, replacing a little less than 50% of the average worker's previous earnings. In 1999, average weekly earnings for a production worker in wage and salary employment was $457, and the average weekly unemployment benefit was $212.[21] Table 9 summarizes the numbers above, and adds the UI comparison.

Wage insurance raises the return to search, and more so for workers with greater re-employment losses. A higher wage insurance replacement rate further increases the return to job search, while it reduces the worker's incentive to search for a (different) higher-paying job (but only during the eligibility period). If the supplement interval is fixed and limited, say to two years, the present value of the supplement declines with the duration of unemployment and poses an incentive for a quicker return to work. There is a "winners" theme here, as workers who have difficulty finding a job (particularly if required to be full-time) will receive a smaller supplement than workers with short unemployment spells.

High-tenure, lower-skill manufacturing workers will find wage insurance to have greatest value. These workers are visible and have clout. They are not high-wage

Table 9. Comparison of Hypothetical Pre- and Post-displacement Earnings, Wage Insurance Benefits, and Unemployment Insurance Benefits

Old job	New job	New job + supplement	UI benefit
$600	$520	$560	$300
$600	$420	$510	$300
$600	$300	$450	$300

workers; they are earning a wage premium over their alternative. Wage insurance is more valuable to these workers than it is to lower-wage workers. Lower-wage displaced workers will find it relatively easier to find an equivalent job and therefore will be less likely to experience large earnings losses. This introduces a potentially important distributional issue.

Restricting eligibility to full-time employment raises some questions. Earnings losses are a product of both changes in wages and changes in hours. Either wages or hours, or both, could be lower on the new job. Particularly for lower-skill workers, most readily available jobs will be part-time, as well as at low wage rates. Limiting benefits to those who find one of a limited supply of full-time jobs will end up awarding the "winners." On the other hand, if the earnings supplement is applied to earnings losses arising from changes in hours worked, effective pay on new part-time jobs could be quite high. For example, as discussed by Parsons (2000), if a particular worker's earnings loss arises solely from working part-time on the new job, that worker will have an opportunity to work half the hours (as compared to the old job) at three-quarters pay. This level of subsidy could induce a sizeable shift to part-time work.

In this sense, wage insurance has some clear roots in the literature of optimal UI policy design. Moral hazard questions are well-recognized in the UI literature, in particular a UI-recipient worker's reduced incentive to leave unemployment due to a reduction in the net return to securing a job. This moral hazard issue broadly explains why UI benefits are only partial compensation for lost earnings and why the duration of benefit eligibility is limited (usually to 26 weeks). Baily (1978) proposed a front-loaded redundancy payment (equal to expected earnings loss), to be followed by a lower payout for incremental weeks of unemployment. This scheme separates compensation for job loss from unemployment insurance and avoids creating incentives for extending a spell of unemployment. See Parsons (2000) for a more complete discussion.

The re-employment incentive aspect of wage insurance gives rise to (some of) the standard set of questions. Will an earnings supplement encourage workers to look sooner or more intensely? Will it broaden the range of job offers considered? Will the supplement lower reservation wages, easing consideration of entry-level jobs in expanding industries, jobs that provide training in new skills and prospects for advancement? In short, will wage insurance lead to shorter unemployment durations, increased earnings, and changes in UI benefit receipt?

The focus on re-employment incentives stands out as a contrast to the longer-term compensatory wage subsidies discussed in Davidson and Matusz (2002). Structuring a program with a relatively short eligibility period, starting with the date of job loss, creates the incentive and addresses UI concerns, yet limits the compensatory nature of the program. Not enough is known about the long-term nature of displaced worker earnings losses. What is known, however, is that these earnings losses exist five to six years after job loss, not just at two years (Jacobson et al., 1993). This co-mingling of goals within wage insurance (compensation versus unemployment insurance fix) has not been carefully considered to date.

Evidence From a Wage Insurance Trial

The Earnings Supplement Project (ESP) was a Canadian multisite demonstration program to test wage insurance for a group of displaced workers (and also for a different group of repeat users of unemployment insurance). Human Resources Development Canada (HRDC) funded the project, and the demonstration was conducted by the Social Research and Demonstration Corporation (SRDC).[22] Shortening the re-employment process was the goal of the supplement trial and the program evaluation reflected this intent. The supplement was seen as a possible additional tool in an active labor market policy. From Bloom (1999, p. ES-1):

> "The primary goal of the supplement for displaced workers was to shorten their often long and painful re-employment process and to provide them with a source of income in a form that promoted employment. It was hoped that doing so would help to compensate displaced workers for the losses they incurred due to economic change. In addition, it was hoped that, by encouraging re-employment, the supplement would reduce the cost of unemployment benefits."

The ESP used a randomized experiment research design to measure the effect of the supplement on employment, earnings, and UI benefit receipt. Eligible applicants were assigned to one of two groups: a supplement group, which was offered the supplement, along with all standard UI benefits and services, and a control (standard) group, not offered the supplement, but eligible for all standard UI benefits and services. The process was started with the filing of a regular UI claim, when workers were screened for displaced worker eligibility. The assignment to one of the two groups (by the SRDC research team) did not occur until the worker received a first UI benefit check. This process focused the study on UI benefit recipients, not on all displaced workers. In addition, the average time between ESP application and random assignment was eight weeks. The full reports (Bloom, 1997, 1999) contain all the details.

The basic structure of the program was as follows. For eligible displaced workers who became re-employed within a 26-week period, in a full-time job (minimum 30 hours/week), in a new job that paid less than the old job, the supplement covered 75% of the earnings loss for each week worked, for up to two years after random assignment. The supplement was capped at a maximum of $250/week, and was based only on UI-insured earnings (earnings beyond the maximum UI insured amount did not count toward calculating the payment). Workers returning to their old job with their previous employer were not eligible.

For this discussion, some relevant findings (all taken from Bloom, 1999) were as follows.

1. During the one-year intake period, 8,144 displaced workers were enrolled in the study sample, with 5,912 not expecting to return to their employer. The Canadian displaced worker sample was fairly similar, in basic characteristics (age, education, job tenure), to a sample of manufacturing displaced workers from the US Displaced Worker Survey.
2. Most supplement group members were well-informed about the basic provisions of the program. Also, there was broad interest in the supplement program. The HRDC report interprets this survey evidence as an indication from workers that there was little to lose from the program.
3. About 20% of displaced workers in the supplement group received supplement payments. Take-up rates were higher for older workers, and those who had previously held a high-wage job. On average, recipients were paid $8,705 for 64 weeks of full-time employment during the two-year period. The minimum payment was $1, and the maximum $25,750. Thus total payments were quite large, and likely an important component of income during the two-year receipt period. In-depth interviews of supplement recipients revealed that the ESP was an important source of temporary income (over 90% of interviewees responded that the supplement made at least a fair or big bit of difference to total income).

4. There was a modest increase in full-time employment at the end of the six-month eligibility period. ESP increased the percentage of displaced workers who became re-employed full-time by 4.4 percentage points. About half of the increase was due to a shift from part-time to full-time employment and half to an increase in overall employment. Higher re-employment rates for the supplement group occurred in the fourth to sixth months following random assignment.
5. ESP may have caused some workers to take jobs that paid less than the ones they would have taken otherwise. Hourly wages were 2.5% less than they would have been otherwise ($0.33). This could reflect a broadening of the range of job opportunities considered.
6. Virtually no effect was seen on the amount or duration of unemployment benefits received by supplement group members. This result follows from the time delay in the difference in re-employment rates discussed above in point 4. The employment boost occurred late in the ESP eligibility period and this period started two months after job loss, leaving little time left for unemployment benefit receipt to be reduced.
7. Among supplement group nonrecipients, when asked "why," 42% responded that "they couldn't find a job in time," and 8% replied "couldn't find a job working 30 hours/full-time."

One conclusion is that the earnings supplement produced very modest effects on job search, in terms of promoting rapid re-employment and reduced UI receipt. For this group of workers, an earnings supplement as compensation may be a more useful framework. The supplement can deliver compensation (and improve worker welfare), in a way that promotes employment, yet be judged on its compensatory merits rather than on how it addresses standing problems in the unemployment insurance system.

5. Conclusions

Given these stylized facts about trade-related job loss, what does a model of trade liberalization and compensation need to do? Clearly it should generate involuntary job loss. As noted in Kletzer (2002b), workers face a high risk of job loss from industries with a rising share of imports in domestic supply. There is a subset of industries—those with both high and increasing import shares, where the rate of job loss is high—that confront sustained import competition. Beyond this subset, the relationship between rising import share and high rate of job loss is considerably weaker. This means that growing imports play a small role in job loss in the economy as a whole, but a large role in traditional import-competing industries. These findings are consistent with Bernard and Jensen (2002), who find the probability of shutdown higher in industries that face increased import competition from low-income countries using establishment-level data. These findings are also consistent with Trefler (2001), who, for the most impacted industries from the US–Canada FTA, finds tariff cuts reduced employment by 15% and the number of plants by 8%. To date, a key weakness of theoretical models of trade and liberalization is the absence of involuntary separations. With flexible wages (and prices), the mechanism separating workers from firms is a voluntary one, following a decline in the wage.

Second, worker skills (and perhaps capital too) must have a degree of sector specificity. A worker's current skill level can have implications for sectoral mobility. Between some sectors, mobility is possible only after training. Mobility between other sectors is not constrained by a need to retrain, but without training, a new job in a new sector will pay less than the old job.

Third, consider three (or maybe four) broad sectors. Two are within manufacturing, one being high-skill manufacturing industries (perhaps export-oriented), and the other a set of lower-skill manufacturing industries (import-competing). In the service sector, there is a set of lower-skill services industries, where workers can enter without training, and then a medium-skill services sector (entry with training). For empirical completeness, we might consider a high-skill services sector, where there is entry by formal education only. This sector is not likely to be very relevant to the current set of displaced workers.

Let trade liberalization displace workers from the lower-skill manufacturing sector. Displaced workers can enter the high-skill manufacturing sector only with retraining (similarly with medium-skilled services). Re-employment in the old, lower-skill manufacturing sector is possible, as vacancies occur. This outcome requires waiting for a vacancy (wait unemployment), and is associated with relatively small earnings losses. Without training, a trade-displaced worker can seek re-employment in lower-skill services, with large earnings losses.[23]

Broadening the policy discussion beyond training may be one of the most useful results of the recent emergence of wage insurance in policy discussions. Very little has been said here about training and its value. Training does help some displaced workers, but overall the evidence suggests an appraisal similar to Jacobson (1998, p. 505), "that training should be used sparingly," and that "policymakers appear to underrate the ability of most workers to acquire substantially more human-capital-enhancing knowledge on the job rather than in the classroom." It is worth noting that wage insurance may have a training incentive, because by narrowing earnings losses, it can encourage workers to consider entry-level jobs that offer on-the-job training.

There are several questions for future research. The new US wage insurance program within TAA will hopefully provide information on how the re-employment incentive works and the nature of program cost savings. It seems important to continue to consider how the compensatory aspects of wage insurance interact with the aspects that speed returning to work. In regard to the longer-run, labor market outcomes under wage insurance should be compared to TAA/training, for different groups of workers.

References

Baily, Martin Neil, "Some Aspects of Optimal Unemployment Insurance," *Journal of Public Economics* 10 (1978):379–402.

Baily, Martin Neil, Gary Burtless, and Robert E. Litan, *Growth with Equity: Economic Policy-making for the Next Century*, Washington, DC: Brookings Institution (1993).

Bernard, Andrew B. and J. Bradford Jensen, "The Deaths of Manufacturing Plants," NBER working paper 9026 (2002).

Bhagwati, Jagdish N. (ed.), *Import Competition and Response*, Chicago: University of Chicago Press (1982).

Bloom, Howard, Barbara Fink, Susanna Lui-Gurr, Wendy Bancroft, and Doug Tattrie, *Implementing the Earnings Supplement Project: a Test of a Re-employment Incentive*, Social Research and Demonstration Corporation (1997).

Bloom, Howard, Saul Schwartz, Susanna Lui-Gurr, with Jason Peng and Wendy Bancroft, *Testing a Re-employment Incentive for Displaced Workers: the Earnings Supplement Project*, Social Research and Demonstration Corporation (1999).

Brander, James A. and Barbara J. Spencer, "Trade Adjustment Assistance: Welfare and Incentive Effects of Payments to Displaced Workers," *Journal of International Economics* 36 (1994):239–61.

Brecher, Richard A. and Ehsan U. Choudhri, "Pareto Gains from Trade, Reconsidered: Compensating for Jobs Lost," *Journal of International Economics* 36 (1994):223–38.

Burtless, Gary, Robert Z. Lawrence, Robert E. Litan, and Robert Shapiro, *Globaphobia: Confronting Fears about Open Trade*, Washington, DC: Brookings Institution (1998).

Davidson, Carl and Steven J. Matusz, "On Adjustment Costs," manuscript, Michigan State University (2001).

———, "Trade Liberalization and Compensation," Leverhulme Centre for Research on Globalization and Economic Policy, research paper series 2002/10 (2002).

Decker, Paul T. and Walter Corson, "International Trade and Worker Displacement: Evaluation of the Trade Adjustment Assistance Program," *Industrial and Labor Relations Review* 48 (1995):758–74.

Decker, Paul T. and Christopher J. O'Leary, "Evaluating Pooled Evidence from the Reemployment Bonus Experiments," Upjohn Institute staff working paper 94-28 (1994).

Dixit, Avinash and Victor Norman, *Theory of International Trade*. Cambridge: Cambridge University Press (1980).

———, "Gains from Trade without Lump-sum Compensation," *Journal of International Economics* 21 (1986):111–22.

Feenstra, Robert C. and Tracy R. Lewis, "Trade Adjustment Assistance and Pareto Gains from Trade," *Journal of International Economics* 36 (1994):201–22.

Jacobson, Louis, "Compensation Programs," in S. M. Collins (ed.), *Imports, Exports, and the American Worker*, Washington, DC: Brookings Institution (1998):473–537.

Jacobson, Louis, Robert LaLonde, and Daniel Sullivan, *The Costs of Worker Dislocation*, Kalamazoo, MI: W. E. Upjohn Institute for Employment Research (1993).

Kletzer, Lori G., "Job Displacement," *Journal of Economic Perspectives* 12 (1998):115–36.

———, *Job Loss from Imports: Measuring the Costs*, Washington, DC: Institute for International Economics (2001).

———, "Globalization and American Job Loss: Public Policy to Help Workers," Industrial Relations Research Association, *Perspectives on Work* 6 (2002a):28–30.

———, *Imports, Exports and Jobs: What Does Trade Mean for Employment and Job Loss?* Kalamazoo, MI: W. E. Upjohn Institute for Employment Research (2002b).

Kletzer, Lori G. and Robert E. Litan, "A Prescription to Relieve Worker Anxiety," Institute for International Economics Policy Brief PB01-2 (2001).

Lawrence, Robert Z. and Robert E. Litan, *Saving Free Trade: a Pragmatic Approach*, Washington, DC: Brookings Institution (1986).

Leigh, Duane, *Does Training Work for Displaced Workers? A Survey of Existing Evidence*, Kalamazoo, MI: W. E. Upjohn Institute for Employment Research (1990).

Parsons, Donald O., "Wage Insurance: a Policy Review," *Research in Employment Policy* 2 (2000):119–40.

Scheve, Kenneth F. and Matthew J. Slaughter, *Globalization and the Perceptions of American Workers*, Washington, DC: Institute for International Economics (2001).

Scott, Robert E., "NAFTA's Hidden Costs: Trade Agreement Results in Job Losses, Growing Inequality, and Wage Suppression for the United States," *NAFTA At Seven: Its Impact on Workers in All Three Nations*, Economic Policy Institute Briefing Paper (2001).

Trefler, Daniel, "The Long and Short of the Canada–US Free Trade Agreement," NBER working paper 8293 (2001).

United States Trade Deficit Review Commission, *The US Trade Deficit: Causes, Consequences, and Recommendations for Action*, Washington, DC: US Trade Deficit Review Commission (2001).

Notes

1. TAA has held center stage in the limited mix of worker adjustment policies since the mid-1970s. Overlapping with the evaluation literature, a number of papers consider the evidence on

TAA and training for displaced workers. For examples, see Decker and Corson (1995) and Leigh (1990).

2. As noted below, Davidson and Matusz (2002) refer to wage insurance as a wage subsidy. Brander and Spencer (1994) use the phrase "conditional tapered assistance."

3. Wage insurance gained visibility in November 2000 when recommended by the US Trade Deficit Review Commission (2000).

4. See *Wall St Journal*, 31 August 2001, p. A1, and *Wall St Journal*, 13 May 2002, p. A4.

5. The House and Senate approved the granting of presidential trade-promotion authority, with the TAA expansion, just before their summer recess, and President Bush signed the bill in early August. The targeted wage insurance program was added, along with the establishment of a refundable tax credit, payable in advance, to cover 65% of the cost of health insurance for TAA eligible workers. See the *Washington Post*, 7 August 2002, p. A06.

6. The discussion here of the theoretical literature is brief. Other early contributions are contained in Bhagwati (1982).

7. This discussion of the theoretical literature is hardly exhaustive. See Bhagwati (1982) for early contributions.

8. This section borrows heavily from Kletzer (2001).

9. Chapter 5 of Kletzer (2002b) discusses the descriptive and causal aspects of the question.

10. The Displaced Worker Surveys are biennial supplements to the Current Population Survey.

11. Industries are defined and listed at a three-digit CIC level of detail. For readability, some three-digit industries are grouped together under more aggregated (or two-digit) headings.

12. One industry, aircraft and parts, was moved from the high-import to the medium-import group, despite its increase in import share, because it had little history of import competition (on the basis of a low level of import share in the mid-1970s).

13. The sole exception is Sawmills, a top-ten NAFTA–TAA industry, but a medium import-competing industry under my definition.

14. This number will be different from the often-cited declines in employment in manufacturing. Manufacturing employment decline is a net loss in employment, the difference between employment gains (through new hires, rehires, and recalls) and reductions in employment (through quits, layoffs, displacements, retirements, and deaths). See details in Kletzer (2002b).

15. See Kletzer (2002a).

16. Lower average job tenure for women and inverse seniority-based layoff rules, along with part-time status, may account, in part, for women's high incidence of displacement.

17. Tables 6 and 7 report marginal effects. Coefficient estimates are available on request.

18. The table is a very basic "re-employment matrix," reporting the industrial sector from which workers were displaced (categorized by the level of import-competition of their old industry) and the industrial sector of re-employment. The table contains four main rows, labeled "high," "medium," "low" (for the import-competing nature of the manufacturing industries) and "non-manufacturing" for the remaining private nonmanufacturing sectors of the economy (utilities, wholesale and retail trade, services). This last row serves as a comparison group for manufacturing. Workers are displaced from one of these four big rows. They are re-employed in one of 12 columns, where columns designate new industrial sectors. Within each cell, defined as a main row intersecting with a column, five measures are reported.

19. Re-employment bonuses are lump-sum payments to unemployed workers who find jobs within a specified limited timeframe. Four randomized experiments have tested the idea, in Illinois, New Jersey, Washington state, and Pennsylvania. See Decker and O'Leary (1994).

20. Mean earnings on the old job for high import-competing displaced workers is $600/week (in 1999 $), and the mean earnings change for this group was a loss of 13%.

21. As reported in *Economic Report of the President* (January 2001), Tables B-45 and B-47.

22. My discussion here is taken from Bloom (1997, 1999).

23. A question to consider is whether some workers, based on a characteristic, can be trained, and others not, with the nontrainees eligible for wage insurance.

Chapter 2

An Overlapping-generations Model of Escape Clause Protection

Carl Davidson and Steven J. Matusz

1. Introduction

"A Member shall apply safeguard measures only to the extent necessary to prevent or remedy serious injury and *to facilitate adjustment*."
Article 5, Uruguay Round Agreement on Safeguards (emphasis added)

"If the Commission makes an affirmative determination, it recommends to the President the action that will *facilitate positive adjustment* by the industry to import competition."
USITC (1998) (emphasis added)

Between January 1974 and January 2002, the United States International Trade Commission (USITC) completed investigations of 73 petitions for import relief filed under the aegis of section 201 of the Trade Act of 1974.[1] This act permits interested parties to petition the USITC for relief from injurious but fair foreign competition. Any relief granted is intended as a temporary measure, providing the industry with time to adjust to changing circumstances.

Of the 73 completed investigations, 40 resulted in affirmative findings by the Commission. After forwarding their recommendations to the President of the United States, 24 of these cases resulted in some form of import relief, almost half of which as recommended by the Commission, with the remainder being modified by the President.

As the excerpts from the Uruguay Round Agreement on Safeguards and the USITC indicate, safeguard measures are intended, in part, to facilitate adjustment to changes in the international environment. Adjustment typically entails becoming "leaner and meaner" to more effectively compete in the international marketplace. As such, part of "facilitating adjustment" can be viewed as providing time so that resources can be withdrawn from declining industries in an orderly fashion. It has been suggested that the government may also have equity considerations in mind when providing such relief, as this passage from Baldwin (1989) clearly articulates:

"Other authors stressing the income distribution goals of government, like Cheh (1974) and Lavergne (1983), argue that trade policies of governments are motivated by a desire to minimize (or delay) adjustment costs, especially to workers. In examining the Kennedy Round of multilateral trade negotiations, Cheh found a pattern of low tariff cuts in industries with high proportions of elderly workers, declining employment, and rising import penetration ratios."

By providing temporary protection, the government gives young workers time to retrain and make a smooth transition to the growing export sectors while simultaneously softening the blow to the older workers who face bleak re-employment prospects if they try to change their occupation so late in life.

Our goal in this paper is to explore the efficiency consequences of using temporary protection to smooth out the adjustment process following an unexpected, permanent improvement in a country's terms of trade.[2] We assume that the government's primary motivation in providing such relief is twofold. First, it is intended to either reduce or delay the adjustment costs imposed on the young workers who switch occupations as a result of the terms-of-trade shock. Second, it is intended to lessen the blow to the older workers who find that they regret decisions made earlier in life because they could not anticipate the improvement in the terms of trade. Thus, while the government's primary motives may be equity driven, our goal is to assess the welfare consequences of the government's actions.[3] We do so in the context of a simple overlapping-generations model where all newborn agents must decide whether to seek employment in the export sector or the import-competing sector. In making their choices, agents trade off the potentially higher wage that the export sector has to offer with a lower probability of actually finding a job in that sector. Since young agents have a longer time horizon, more young workers than old choose to search for jobs in the export sector. An unexpected improvement in the terms of trade surprises old workers who cannot undo the decisions they made while young. As a result, some old workers who had not planned to search for work in the export sector end up changing their plans, adding to the pool of searchers. As the pool of searchers in the export sector swells, congestion externalities may arise, making it harder to secure employment. This is particularly harmful to old workers since they have less time left to find new jobs than their younger counterparts. By providing temporary protection, the government can stem the tide of searchers, reduce congestion, and make the transition to the new steady state smoother.

We are not the first to examine the broad issue of trade and adjustment costs, nor even the first to examine the more narrowly defined issue of temporary protection and adjustment costs. Several empirical studies—including those by Magee (1972), Baldwin et al. (1980), and Trefler (2001)—address the size and scope of adjustment costs. Theoretical work by Mayer (1974), Mussa (1974, 1978), Neary (1978), and Davidson and Matusz (2001) emphasizes the importance of taking the adjustment process into account when making welfare judgments. More directly relevant to this paper are the studies by Cassing and Ochs (1978), Lapan (1976, 1978, 1979), Michealy (1986), Mussa (1986), Ray (1979), Karp and Paul (1994, 1998), and Gaisford and Leger (2000) that explore the optimal policy path for liberalization in the presence of adjustment costs.[4] One key insight from this research is that, in the absence of factor market distortions, there is no justification on efficiency grounds for gradual liberalization. However, if there are factor market imperfections then some sort of government intervention, either in the form of temporary protection or some sort of labor market policy, is warranted.[5]

Several of these papers focus on congestion externalities as the source of the factor market distortion. Cassing and Ochs (1978) provide an explicit model of the search process and show that the market-induced rate of adjustment is suboptimal when congestion externalities are present. In contrast, Karp and Paul (1994, 1998) and Gaisford and Leger (2000) do not model the source of the externality—they simply assume that the social cost of adjustment exceeds the private cost of adjustment. Both papers then show that government intervention can raise welfare, although Karp and Paul (1994, 1998) focus on tariff policy while Gaisford and Leger (2000) argue that there are always superior policies available.

Our work is similar to Karp and Paul's in that we show that if a change in the terms of trade leads to a temporary enlargement of the pool of searchers, and if this creates congestion, then a temporary import tariff that slows down the movement of workers into the export sector might actually increase the value of output (measured at world prices). However, our work is unique in at least three respects. First, by using an overlapping-generations model in which the congestion externalities are carefully modeled, we are able to highlight how the unexpected improvement in the terms of trade affects the young and old as well as the current and future generations in fundamentally different ways. We consider this to be important, since, as we noted above, there is empirical evidence that concern about the welfare of older workers plays a role in the government's policy choices. Second, we show that there are conditions under which the congestion externalities in our model lead to multiple steady-state equilibria that can be Pareto-ranked. As a result, it is possible that with free trade the change in the terms of trade may push the economy into a new steady state characterized by low job acquisition rates and low output in the export sector. However, if the government intervenes by providing temporary protection to the import-competing sector, the adjustment process may be slowed down enough to steer the economy towards a different steady state that is characterized by higher job acquisition and production rates in the export sector. This leads to the third unique feature of our analysis. In previous work, when the new long-run free-trade equilibrium is reached, there are no lasting effects from the period of temporary protection. This need not be the case in our model—temporary protection may lead to a permanent change in the allocation of resources and this permanent change may be welfare-enhancing.

We present our model and examine the decision problem faced by workers in the next section. We then solve for the steady-state equilibrium and the transition path between equilibria in section 4, where we also demonstrate how temporary import protection can avert the congestion externality. Since a tariff is distorting, we include a discussion of the costs and benefits associated with a temporary tariff, and argue that it will be welfare-improving if the magnitude of the minimum tariff necessary to reduce congestion is relatively small. In section 5, we turn to the issue of multiple equilibria and show how a temporary tariff can have a permanent effect on the long-run allocation of resources.

2. An Overlapping-generations Model

Assumptions

We consider an overlapping-generations model where labor is the only factor of production. Workers are indexed by ability a, which is distributed uniformly over $[0, 1]$. Each worker lives for two periods and is replaced by an identical worker upon death. We refer to a generation as "young" or "old" if it contains workers in their first or second period of life, respectively. Correspondingly, we use superscripts "y" and "o" to refer to variables that pertain to a given generation at a particular time. We normalize the measure of workers in each generation to 1. Combined with our assumption about the distribution of ability, this means that for any $a^g \in [0, 1]$, the measure of workers in generation g with $a < a^g$ is a^g, while the measure with $a > a^g$ is $1 - a^g$.

There are two goods which we label X (an export good) and M (an import-competing good). Each worker, regardless of ability, can produce one unit of M per period. By contrast, each worker employed in the export sector can produce a units of output per period. With competitive labor markets, constant-returns-to-scale technology, and no other inputs, each employed worker is paid the value of his or her marginal product, which also equals the total value of his or her production.

We assume that the economy is small, choose the export good as *numéraire*, and define P_t as the exogenously given world price of the import-competing good.

We assume that a worker can always obtain a job in the import-competing sector and keep that job for his or her entire life. By contrast, a worker who wishes to be employed in the export sector must search, and there is some positive probability the worker will not find a job in that sector. We use π_t to denote the probability of "success" for a worker searching for a job in the export sector at time t, and it is assumed that workers have rational expectations concerning π_t.

While we do not explicitly model the search process, what we have in mind is an underlying model in the spirit of the classic work by Mortensen (1982) and Pissarides (1990) in which firms in the export sector post vacancies while workers search for employment.[6] Workers know the number of jobs available and the size of the search pool, but they do not know which firms have unfilled vacancies until they visit them. In such settings, a worker who chooses to search for an export sector job makes it harder for the other searchers in that sector to find employment. These congestion externalities distort incentives and lead to suboptimal equilibria. Our focus is on how the government can use temporary protection to improve the efficiency of the adjustment process by controlling the rate at which workers switch sectors. Consistent with previous search theoretic models of unemployment, we are assuming that the government possesses the same information as the workers, and thus cannot eradicate the information problem that generates the equilibrium unemployment.[7]

The main reason that we do not explicitly model the search process is that its exact nature is not important for our purpose—all that matters is that the congestion externalities are present.[8] This can be captured in a simple manner by assuming that the probability of finding a job in the export sector is a decreasing function of the measure of workers searching for export-sector jobs, as we do in section 3 below. Carefully modeling the search process itself would greatly complicate the analysis without providing any additional insight.

The Worker's Decision Problem

At the start of each period, unemployed workers (including all newborns) must decide whether to accept certain employment in the import-competing sector or search for employment in the export sector. Moreover, each worker who enters the period employed must decide whether to keep his/her job or look for a job in the other sector.[9]

The decision for workers in the old generation is simple. Expected one-period income from searching in the export sector at time t is $\pi_t a$, whereas the certain income of taking a job in the import-competing sector is P_t. Assuming risk-neutrality, workers who are not already employed in the export sector with $a \geq P_t/\pi_t$ will choose to search for a job in that sector, while the remaining workers will choose to work in the import-competing sector. We define this critical level of ability as a_t^o and refer to any old worker with this ability as the marginal old worker.[10]

The problem for workers in the young generation is more complicated. Define $V_{St}^y(a)$ as the expected lifetime income of a young worker who searches for a job in the export sector, and use $V_{Mt}^y(a)$ to denote the expected lifetime income for a young worker who accepts a job in the import-competing sector.[11] Then:

$$V_{St}^y(a) = 2\pi_t a + (1 - \pi_t)\max\{P_{t+1}, \pi_{t+1}a\}, \tag{1}$$

$$V_{Mt}^y(a) = P_t + \max\{P_{t+1}, \pi_{t+1}a\}. \tag{2}$$

If a young searcher achieves success, she earns a while young, and a when old.[12] If the searcher does not find a job, she has the option of searching again when old, or taking a job in the import-competing sector. Similarly, a worker who accepts a job in the import-competing sector earns P_t while young, and has the option of searching when old.

We define a_t^y as the value of ability that equates (1) and (2) and refer to any young worker with this ability as the marginal young worker. Figure 1 illustrates two qualitatively different solutions for a_t^y. On the left, some workers who are young at time t will choose to search for a job in the export sector, but if they are not successful, they will return to the import-competing sector when they become old. These workers have ability $a \in [a_t^y, a_{t+1}^o)$. It is in their interest to "test the waters" of the job market. The potential to receive two periods of high wages is worth giving up one period of low wages. But as they near the end of their work life, the potential to receive higher wages no longer offsets the loss of a single period of low wages.

If the marginal young worker depicted on the left in Figure 1 fails in her search for an export sector job, she will not choose to repeat the search when old. Instead she will choose to accept a job in the import-competing sector. This implies that, for this marginal young worker, $\max\{P_{t+1}, \pi_{t+1}a_t^y\} = P_{t+1}$. We can now equate (1) and (2) and solve to obtain

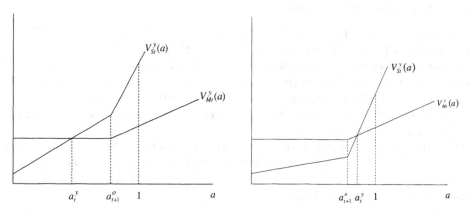

Figure 1. Solving for the Marginal Young Worker. Left: Testing the Waters. Right: Delayed Search

$$a_t^y = a_t^o \left\{ \frac{1 + \pi_t(P_{t+1}/P_t)}{2} \right\}. \tag{3a}$$

The situation depicted on the right in Figure 1 is different. Fewer workers choose to search when young than when those same workers become old. For these delayed searchers, $\max\{P_{t+1}, \pi_{t+1}a_t^y\} = \pi_{t+1}a_t^y$. Equating (1) and (2) and solving yields

$$a_t^y = a_t^o \left\{ \frac{1}{2 - \pi_{t+1}} \right\}. \tag{3b}$$

Alternative assumptions about the parameters underlie the qualitatively different solutions depicted in Figure 1. For example, in "testing the waters" it is the case that $a_t^y < a_{t+1}^o$. Using (3a) and our solution for a_t^o, we find that this inequality holds if

$$\frac{P_t}{\pi_t} \left\{ \frac{1 + \pi_t(P_{t+1}/P_t)}{2} \right\} < \frac{P_{t+1}}{\pi_{t+1}}. \tag{4}$$

For example, reducing π_{t+1} or P_t or increasing P_{t+1} will lead eventually to the satisfaction of the inequality expressed in (4). All of these partial derivatives are sensible. A reduction in π_{t+1} causes a fall in the expected wage of a worker searching in period $t + 1$, while an increase in P_{t+1} boosts the attractiveness of jobs in the import-competing sector.

Similarly, for "delayed search" it is clear that $a_t^y > a_{t+1}^o$. Using (3b) and our solution for a_t^o, this inequality is satisfied if

$$\frac{P_{t+1}}{\pi_{t+1}} < \frac{P_t}{\pi_t} \left\{ \frac{1}{2 - \pi_{t+1}} \right\}. \tag{5}$$

Since $\pi_{t+1} \leq 1$, delayed search can occur only if the price of the import-competing good falls between periods t and $t+1$ (which reduces the wage in the import-competing sector) or if $\pi_{t+1} > \pi_t$ (which increases the probability of a successful search).

3. Steady States and Transition Paths

The Steady-state Allocation of Resources

The measure of searchers at time t, (S_t), equals the sum of young searchers (S_t^y) and old searchers (S_t^o), where the measure of young searchers is $S_t^y = 1 - a_t^y$.

Finding the measure of old searchers is more difficult. Only old workers with $a \geq a_t^o$ *who are not already employed* in the export sector will search for a job in that sector. There are two possibilities. If $a_t^o > a_{t-1}^y$, then all workers with $a \geq a_t^o$ would have searched for a job in the export sector when they were young. With a success rate of π_{t-1}, we can deduce that $S_t^o = (1 - \pi_{t-1})(1 - a_t^o)$.

Alternatively, if $a_t^o < a_{t-1}^y$, then there are some old workers who choose to search in period t who did not search when they were young. In this case, we have $S_t^o = (1 - \pi_{t-1})(1 - a_{t-1}^y) + (a_{t-1}^y - a_t^o) = (1 - \pi_{t-1})(1 - a_t^o) + \pi_{t-1}(a_{t-1}^y - a_t^o)$. We can combine both possibilities into a single equation:

$$S_t^o = (1 - \pi_{t-1})(1 - a_t^o) + \pi_{t-1}\max\{0, a_{t-1}^y - a_t^o\}. \tag{6}$$

The second part of (6) can be interpreted as the measure of old searchers who would have gotten a job when young had they searched, and therefore would not be searching when old. Of course, this term is zero if all old searchers also searched when young.

In a steady state, $P_t = P$ and $\pi_t = \pi$ for all t. From our discussion at the end of the last subsection, we can rule out the possibility of delayed search in a steady state. Therefore, all steady states are characterized by the left of Figure 1. Let $\bar{S}^y$ and $\bar{S}^o$ denote the steady-state measures of young and old searchers, and define $\bar{S} = \bar{S}^y + \bar{S}^o$. We note that the steady-state measure of searchers in each generation is a function of both P and π. We focus on the relationship between P and the measure of searchers in the remainder of this section, turning to the relationship with π in section 4.

An Unexpected Improvement in the Terms of Trade

Suppose now that there is a permanent, unexpected improvement in the terms of trade. To help keep track of events, we normalize time by setting $t = 1$ when the terms of trade improve. We can then model a permanent improvement in the terms of trade by assuming that $P_t = P_H$ for $t \leq 0$ and $P_t = P_L$ for $t \geq 1$, where $P_L < P_H$. We begin by investigating how this change in world prices affects worker behavior and the value of output.

Intuitively, the improvement in the terms of trade will push some workers out of the import-competing sector to search for jobs in the export sector. As we noted earlier, it is standard to assume congestion externalities exist so that as the pool of searchers swells the probability that an individual worker will find a job falls. This notion is captured by assuming that π_t is a decreasing function of S_t. While it is natural to think of this function as continuous, doing so complicates our analysis considerably without providing any additional insight.[13] Thus, for illustrative purposes we postulate the following as a simple form for this function:

$$\pi(S) = \begin{cases} \pi_H & \text{if } S \leq \tilde{S}, \\ \pi_L & \text{if } S > \tilde{S}. \end{cases} \tag{7}$$

We assume that workers have rational expectations about the time path of π_t. As we show in section 5, there are cases in which there are multiple rational-expectations steady-state equilibria. In addition, there may be more than one rational-expectations transition path that leads from the initial steady-state equilibrium to the new one. Since we deal with this issue explicitly later in the paper, in this section we focus on the case in which the new steady-state rational-expectations equilibrium is unique as is the transition path that leads to it.

To solve for this equilibrium as well as the transition path, we first specify the workers' expectations regarding the time path for π_t, and then show that these expectations are consistent with equilibrium behavior. The case that we are interested in is the one in which congestion causes the probability of success to temporarily fall from its steady-state value of π_H to π_L immediately after the improvement in the terms of trade. We then want π_t to rise back up to π_H in the next period and remain there forever afterward. That is, we assume that $\pi_t = \pi_H$ for $t \neq 1$ and $\pi_t = \pi_L$ for $t = 1$. This set of beliefs will be rational if $S_1 > \tilde{S} \geq S_t$ for all $t \neq 1$.

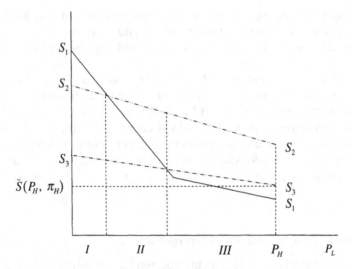

Figure 2. The Measure of Searchers during the Transition to the New Steady State

The measures of searchers in each of the three periods following the terms-of-trade shock are depicted in Figure 2 (the detailed derivations for this figure are provided in the Appendix). Since S_t (for $t = 1$–3) is shown as a function of P_L for $P_L \leq P_H$, this figure reveals how the total measure of searchers varies with the degree of improvement in the terms of trade. There are several features worth noting. First, as expected, the measure of searchers in each period is a decreasing function of P_L since smaller terms-of-trade improvements cause fewer workers to seek export sector jobs. Second, the curve S_1S_1 is kinked because small deviations of P_L from P_H do not produce regret in old workers. That is, all old workers who search when the price is P_L also searched when they were young. In contrast, large deviations of P_L from P_H induce some old workers to search for the first time. It is this surge of old workers entering the export-sector labor market for the first time that can cause the congestion that the government may want to ease. Finally, from Figure 2 it is evident that there are three ranges for P_L that lead to different patterns for the measures of searchers over time. A rational-expectations equilibrium of the type that we are seeking exists for relatively low values of P_L (those in region *I*).[14] That is, this is the region in which $S_1 > \tilde{S} \geq S_2 \geq S_t$ for $t \geq 3$.[15]

In region *I* of Figure 2, the change in the terms of trade is dramatic and congestion reduces the probability of finding a job in the export sector. In this case, there are important implications for the distribution of income between current members of the young and old generations, as well as between current and future generations. To sort out how the different groups of workers are affected, it is useful to consider the following four questions as they pertain to the old workers at $t = 1$: Does the change in the terms of trade alter their labor market behavior? Do they regret any decisions made when young? Are they harmed by the unexpected change in the terms of trade or do they benefit from it? Is their experience any different from the clones that replace them in the future?

The answers to these four questions are provided in Lemmas 1–4 below. However, before these lemmas can be stated, we need to introduce some new notation. Let $\bar{a}^y$ and $\bar{a}^o$ denote the ability levels of marginal young and old workers in the initial steady state, respectively; and let a_1^o represent the ability level of the marginal old worker in period 1. In addition, let $\tilde{a}^y$ denote the ability level of a marginal young worker at time zero *if the change in the terms of trade could be anticipated.*[16] From our earlier analysis, we know that $\bar{a}^y < \bar{a}^o$. It is also the case that (compared with the actual number of young searchers) more young people would search in period zero if they anticipated the improvement in the terms of trade. That is, $\tilde{a}^y < \bar{a}^y$. The only question is whether a_1^o is less than or greater than $\tilde{a}^y$. There are two cases to consider. Either $\tilde{a}^y < a_1^o < \bar{a}^y < \bar{a}^o$ or $a_1^o < \tilde{a}^y < \bar{a}^y < \bar{a}^o$, with the particular ordering depending upon the underlying parameters of the model.[17] For brevity, we consider the first case in the text and relegate treatment of the second case to the notes.

LEMMA 1. *When there is an unexpected terms-of-trade improvement the old workers who change their labor market behavior are the ones with $a \in [a_1^o, \bar{a}^o]$ who are not already employed in the export sector. These workers had planned on taking jobs in the import-competing sector but now search for export sector jobs instead.*

PROOF. *By the definition of $\bar{a}^y$, we know that workers born at $t = 0$ with $a < \bar{a}^y$ take jobs in the import-competing sector when young and plan on doing so again when old. By the definition of $\bar{a}^o$ we know that workers born at $t = 0$ with $a > \bar{a}^o$ search for jobs in the export sector when young and plan on doing so again when old if their initial search proves fruitless. Workers with $a \in [\bar{a}^y, \bar{a}^o]$ search for export sector jobs when young and then, if their search is unsuccessful, plan on taking jobs in the import-competing sector when old. By the definition of a_1^o, when the terms of trade unexpectedly change, all old workers with $a > a_1^o$ who are not already employed in the export sector search for jobs in that sector. Thus, it is the old workers who are not already employed in sector X with $a \in [a_1^o, \bar{a}^o]$ who change their behavior—they had planned on taking jobs in the import-competing sector but now, because P has fallen, they search for export sector jobs instead.* □

LEMMA 2. *The old workers who regret the decisions they made when young are those with $a \in [\tilde{a}^y, \bar{a}^y]$. Instead of taking jobs in the import-competing sector they would have rather searched for jobs in the export sector.*

PROOF. *This follows directly from the definitions of $\tilde{a}^y$ and $\bar{a}^y$. If the workers who are born at $t = 0$ could anticipate the change in the terms of trade, then they would search when young if $a > \tilde{a}^y$ and then, if necessary, search again when old if $a > a_1^o$. However, since they do not anticipate the change in P, workers with $a \in [\tilde{a}^y, \bar{a}^y]$ take jobs in the import-competing sector when young instead. Note that a subset of these workers, those with $a \in [\tilde{a}^y, a_1^o]$, regret not having searched when young, yet do not change their behavior when old.* □

LEMMA 3. *The unexpected terms-of-trade improvement benefits the old workers who are employed in the export sector and harms those who are employed in the import-competing sector. Those who seek X-sector jobs could gain or lose—they are harmed by the reduction in the job acquisition rate in period 1 but benefit from the fall in the consumer price index.*

PROOF. *Those employed in the export sector benefit from the fall in the consumer price index, while those employed in the import-competing sector see their real incomes fall.* □

LEMMA 4. *If we compare the experience of the old workers in the current generation with the experience of the clones that replace them in future periods, there are two differences worth highlighting. First, the clones with $a \in [\tilde{a}^y, \bar{a}^y]$ are not surprised by the low price for good M and therefore search for export sector jobs when young. Second, by the time the clones age, the congestion will have abated and the job acquisition rates will have returned to the relatively high value.*[18]

PROOF. *The first difference follows directly from the definitions of $\tilde{a}^y$ and $\bar{a}^y$. The second difference is due to the fact that we are focusing on the rational-expectations equilibrium in which the job acquisition rate falls for only one period.*

With the aid of Lemmas 1–4, we are now in a position to examine the sort of equity considerations that the government might have in mind when instituting a temporary tariff on the import-competing good. If the decision is based on the welfare of the lowest ability workers, then the government must be primarily concerned with the old workers in this group—the temporary tariff keeps their real incomes from falling as far as they would without protection. Deardorff (1987), making use of Corden's Social Welfare Function, suggests that this may be one reasonable equity-based explanation for temporary protection. He argues that the government's goal may be to prevent a significant fall in the real income of a significant sector of the economy. However, it should be clear that a temporary tariff could achieve this goal only for the old workers with low ability levels. For the young, a temporary tariff may *delay* the fall in real income, but it cannot *prevent* it. If the government truly wanted to use tariffs to prop up the wages of the young workers with low ability levels, it would have to institute a permanent tariff.

It is also unlikely that the government is concerned about the workers with the highest ability levels. While it is true that these workers are harmed by the fall in π when they are old, most of them will already have high-paying jobs in the export sector and will benefit from the lower consumer prices. In addition, these are the workers at the highest end of the income distribution.

This leaves us with the workers with $a \in [\tilde{a}^y, \bar{a}^o]$.[19] Workers with ability levels in the low end of this range regret that they did not search when young (Lemma 2), and those with ability levels at the high end of this range are forced to change their behavior and search for export sector jobs when the prospects for finding such a job are relatively bleak (Lemma 1).[20] These are also the workers who are in a fundamentally different position than the clones that replace them because they were unable to anticipate the improvement in the terms of trade (Lemma 4). Of course, if the government tries to help these workers by instituting a temporary tariff, there are some additional benefits—the old workers with the lowest ability levels have their wages propped up temporarily, and those who are searching for export sector jobs face higher job acquisition rates if the tariff successfully reduces congestion. In addition, the young workers at $t = 1$, who are not surprised by the change in the terms of trade, benefit from the increase in π. These are the young workers we referred to in the introduction—government intervention can reduce or delay the adjustment costs imposed on them by instituting a temporary tariff. It is not clear, however, what the full welfare consequences of such an action would be since tariffs generate distortions as well. In the next subsection we demonstrate that a temporary tariff can alleviate the congestion. We defer the full welfare analysis to the subsequent section.

Temporary Protection

The existence of the congestion externality leaves open the possibility that government intervention could successfully increase economic welfare. The fact that the congestion is temporary suggests that the policy need not be permanent. While the best policies would be those that directly target the externality, they may not be feasible. We therefore explore the effects of a temporary import tariff.

Suppose that the government levies a specific import tariff (τ) during the first period, removing it for all subsequent periods. The purpose of the tariff is to keep enough workers from searching in the first period so that the congestion externality is averted. Since congestion is not a problem in the longer run, the tariff is not needed and is therefore removed.[21]

It will continue to be the case that the economy will be in the new steady state for $t \geq 3$ and therefore the measure of searchers in periods 3 and beyond (both young and old) will remain unchanged.[22] However, the measures of old and young searchers during the first period, and the measures of old searchers during the second period, are impacted by the tariff.[23] In Figure 3, we show how S_1 and S_2 vary with τ, given a price P_L and assuming that $\pi_t = \pi_H$ for all t (the derivation of Figure 3 is provided in the Appendix). The measure of period-1 searchers is monotonically decreasing in the tariff. Higher tariff rates make the import-competing sector more attractive and fewer people search. By contrast, very small tariffs have no impact on the measure of searchers in the second period because all searchers who are old in period 2 also searched when young (in period 1). However, for high enough tariffs, some workers will choose to work in the import-competing sector in period 1 when they are young, but then search in the export sector when they become old and the tariff is removed. Higher tariffs increase the measure of these delayed searchers, implying that S_2 is increasing in the tariff rate.

From Figure 3, there exists a tariff rate ($\hat{\tau}$) such that $S_1 = S_2$. It follows that if $S_1(\hat{\tau}) = S_2(\hat{\tau}) \leq \tilde{S}$, there exists a range of tariffs $\tau \in [\tilde{\tau}, \hat{\tau}]$ that can alleviate the congestion externality. Because any tariff is distortionary, the optimal tariff is either zero or $\tilde{\tau}$.

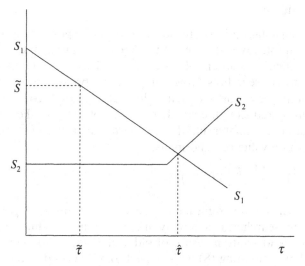

Figure 3. The Measure of Searchers per Period as a Function of the Tariff

4. The Welfare Effects of a Temporary Tariff

A temporary tariff creates both gains and losses. The losses consist of the usual consumption distortion and a production distortion that arises because some workers who would have searched in the absence of the tariff would have found jobs in the export sector, and the value of their output measured at world prices would have been higher than the value of output that they produced in the import-competing sector. The gains occur because all of the workers who continue to search when a temporary tariff is imposed would have also searched in the absence of a tariff. However, because others are drawn to the import-competing sector and excluded from search, the probability of success for the remaining searchers is higher, therefore increasing the value of output obtained from this group of searchers.

Suppose that we measure the gains and losses as a function of the tariff. Suppose further that we have an economy in which $\hat{\tau} > \tilde{\tau}$. This means that in the free trade outcome $S_1 > \tilde{S} > S_t$ for all $t \neq 1$ (i.e., congestion is only a problem in period 1) and that there exists a temporary tariff that the government can use to alleviate the congestion. Then, as τ first begins to rise above zero, there are losses from the consumption and production distortions but there are no gains as long as $S_1(\tau)$ remains above $\tilde{S}$. These losses are a continuous, increasing function of τ. However, as the tariff continues to rise we eventually reach the point where $\tau = \tilde{\tau}$ and $S_1(\tau) = \tilde{S} > S_2(\tau)$.[24] At that point, a marginal increase in the tariff creates discrete gains as the job acquisition rate in period 1 jumps up from π_L to π_H. If these discrete gains dominate the losses accumulated by increasing τ from 0 to $\tilde{\tau}$, then the temporary tariff is welfare-enhancing. It should be clear that this *must* be the case if the free trade value for S_1 is close to (but above) $\tilde{S}$. In that case, it takes only a very small tariff to alleviate congestion and boost job acquisition rates in the export sector. As for the gains and losses, the consumption distortion generated by such a small tariff is of second-order importance, as is the loss due to inducing a very small measure of workers to refrain from search. However, the discrete change from π_L to π_H applies to all of those workers who continue to search, which is nearly all of the workers who would have searched under free trade. Thus, the gains must dominate the losses.

5. Multiple Equilibria

Increasing the steady-state job acquisition rate in the export sector has two contradictory effects on the steady-state size of the search pool. First, for each generation the pool broadens to include workers of lesser ability. This effect tends to increase the steady-state measure of searchers. However, given the breadth of workers who prefer to search for a job in the export sector, a higher success rate leaves fewer old workers unemployed, thereby reducing the steady-state size of the pool. For values of π near one, the second effect dominates and the steady-state measure of searchers is *decreasing* in the steady-state value of π. Formally:

$$\bar{S}(P, \pi) = \left\{1 - \frac{P}{\pi}\frac{1+\pi}{2}\right\} + (1 - \pi)\left\{1 - \frac{P}{\pi}\right\}, \tag{8}$$

where the first term on the right-hand side of (8) (representing the steady-state measure of young searchers) is strictly increasing in π, while the second term (representing the steady-state measure of old searchers) is first increasing and then decreasing in π. Differentiating (8) with respect to π reveals that $\bar{S}$ is decreasing in π if $\pi > (3P/2)^{1/2}$.

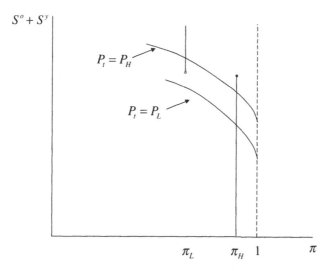

Figure 4. Multiple Steady States

Combining the fact that the steady-state measure of searchers may be decreasing in π with the existence of congestion externalities suggests that there are circumstances under which the economy has multiple steady states, with $\overline{S}(\pi_L) > \tilde{S} > \overline{S}(\pi_H)$. We illustrate this case in Figure 4 where we are assuming that the economy is initially in a steady state with a low level of search ($\pi = \pi_H$). Suppose that the terms of trade unexpectedly improve and that workers correctly anticipate that this will lead to an immediate increase in the size of the search pool. Suppose further that workers expect the job acquisition rate to fall to π_L and remain there permanently. If this is the case the permanent improvement in the terms of trade has pushed the economy into a new steady state with a permanently higher level of search and lower job acquisition rates in the export sector. This provides a new role for the government—it might be possible to use a temporary tariff to keep the economy from moving to the "bad" steady state. If so, the short-run loss associated with the temporary distorting effects of the tariff is likely to be more than offset by a perpetual stream of gains. This would be a situation in which *temporary* protection would lead to a *permanent* change in the allocation of resources.

To analyze this situation, we now assume that the probability of successfully finding a job in the export sector falls permanently to π_L concurrent with the improvement in the terms of trade. As before, young workers adjust immediately to any change. Since there are no changes in the environment beyond the first period, the steady-state measure of young workers is reached immediately. Similarly, it only takes two periods for the measure of old workers to reach its new steady-state value. In Figure 5 we show the total measure of searchers as a function of P_L (note that S_2 represents the size of the search pool in the new steady state since adjustment is complete after only two periods). If the terms of trade improve to a price within range I in Figure 5, then our initial conjecture about the probability of success immediately falling to π_L and remaining there forever is validated. As drawn, this range of prices can be further divided into two subsections. For relatively high prices in range I, the measure of searchers monotonically approaches the new steady state. For lower prices in this range, the measure of searchers overshoots the new steady-state level.

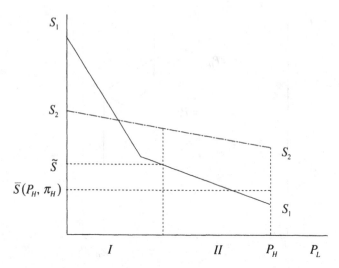

Figure 5. The Measure of Searchers per Period as a Function of Price

If there exists a steady state $\overline{S}(P_L, \pi_H) < \tilde{S}$, then a one-period tariff that holds the measure of searchers at $\tilde{S}$ during the first period of transition has *exactly the same effect* as in the case where the free trade measure of searchers would exceed $\tilde{S}$ in only the first period. In both cases, relieving congestion in the first period has the beneficial impact of reducing the measure of workers who are old searchers in the second period.

Of course, we are not the first to point out that externalities in the search process can lead to multiple steady-state equilibria. Diamond (1982, 1984) and Diamond and Fudenberg (1989) provided models in which positive search externalities may generate this outcome. In their models, workers must search for a trading partner and the fact that more people are trading makes it easier to find a match. If people do not expect many others to search, then it is not in their interest to search and we get an equilibrium with a relatively low level of output. On the other hand, if people expect many others to be searching as well, then their own expected return to search will be high. In this case, we get equilibrium with a high level of search activity and a relatively high level of output. Diamond and Fudenberg argue that there is a role in their model for the government to try to manipulate expectations in order to steer the economy away from the Pareto-inferior steady state. If, by telling workers to expect a bright future with high production, the government can convince workers to search, the government's projections will turn out to be accurate. It is important to note that such a policy will not work in our setting. To see this, suppose we have an economy that, without government intervention, would be pushed into the bad steady state by the terms-of-trade shock. Suppose further that the government tried to avoid this outcome by telling workers that job acquisition rates in the export sector would remain high. If workers believed the government, then more of them would be attracted to the export sector, the size of the search pool would grow even larger, and job acquisition rates would turn out to be low. Thus, propaganda would not work—the government would have to use a temporary tariff instead.

6. Conclusion

It has been argued that if governments are going to liberalize trade that they should do so gradually. One of the rationales offered for this is that by doing so the government can smooth out the transition to the new equilibrium and reduce the adjustment costs imposed on workers. Equity concerns have also been raised about how liberalization will affect workers, particularly older ones, who are employed in the protected sector. Similar concerns arise when economies are hit by terms-of-trade shocks. As a result, governments occasionally provide temporary relief to industries that have been injured by unexpected changes in world prices.

In this paper we have presented an overlapping-generations model that highlights the manner in which current and future generations are affected by unexpected changes in the terms of trade. We have argued that if the government uses *temporary* protection due to equity concerns, then their concerns cannot be about the welfare of those workers who remain trapped in the injured sector. Instead, the government must be concerned about two groups—the older workers who regret the decisions made when they were young or who change their labor market behavior as a result of the terms-of-trade shock, and the young workers who would face low job acquisition rates in the export sector without protection. We have also shown how temporary protection affects the different groups of workers both in the current and future generations.

To capture the notion that adjustment is costly, we have assumed that workers must search for export sector jobs so it takes time for the economy to reach the new steady-state equilibrium. We have shown that if there are congestion externalities present in the search process, temporary protection may be welfare-enhancing, reducing adjustment costs for young and old workers alike. This result is not new—it can be found in Karp and Paul (1994) or Gaisford and Leger (2000). However, a result that is new to this paper is that these congestion externalities can give rise to multiple steady-state equilibria. If this is the case, then a terms-of-trade shock can *permanently* push the economy from a "good" steady state with high job acquisition rates and high output to a "bad" steady state with lower job acquisition and output rates. Government intervention aimed at steering the economy back to the "good" equilibrium is then warranted. However, propaganda aimed at influencing expectations is not enough. The government must also provide some sort of tangible protection to the injured sector. We have shown that there are cases in which a temporary tariff will do the trick.

Appendix

The purpose of this appendix is to provide the detailed derivation of Figures 2, 3, and 5. As for Figure 2, we begin by focusing on the younger generation. The measure of young searchers in the initial and terminal steady states, as well as those in the intervening period, are given in (A1)–(A3):

$$\bar{S}^y(P_H, \pi_H) = \left\{ 1 - \frac{P_H}{\pi_H} \frac{1+\pi_H}{2} \right\}, \tag{A1}$$

$$S_1^y = \left\{ 1 - \frac{P_L}{\pi_L} \frac{1+\pi_L}{2} \right\}, \tag{A2}$$

$$S_2^y = \bar{S}^y(P_L, \pi_H) = \left\{ 1 - \frac{P_L}{\pi_H} \frac{1+\pi_H}{2} \right\}. \tag{A3}$$

Young workers adjust immediately to new circumstances. In particular, they adjust immediately to the simultaneous fall in P and π, and they immediately adjust one more time to the increase in π. This follows since the young workers make all of their decisions after the terms-of-trade improvement occurs.

In contrast, old workers can be surprised, since the change in price occurs in the middle of their life, after they have committed to a course of action based upon their expectations regarding future prices and labor market conditions. The measure of old searchers in the initial and terminal steady states, as well as those in the intervening period, are given in (A4)–(A7):

$$\bar{S}^o(P_H, \pi_H) = (1 - \pi_H)\left\{1 - \frac{P_H}{\pi_H}\right\}, \tag{A4}$$

$$S_1^o = (1 - \pi_H)\left\{1 - \frac{P_L}{\pi_L}\right\} + \pi_H \max\left\{0, \frac{P_H}{\pi_H}\frac{1 + \pi_H}{2} - \frac{P_L}{\pi_L}\right\}, \tag{A5}$$

$$S_2^o = (1 - \pi_L)\left\{1 - \frac{P_L}{\pi_H}\right\} + \pi_L \max\left\{0, \frac{P_L}{\pi_L}\frac{1 + \pi_L}{2} - \frac{P_L}{\pi_H}\right\}, \tag{A6}$$

$$S_3^o = \bar{S}^o(P_L, \pi_H) = (1 - \pi_H)\left\{1 - \frac{P_L}{\pi_H}\right\} + \pi_H \max\left\{0, \frac{P_L}{\pi_H}\frac{1 + \pi_H}{2} - \frac{P_L}{\pi_H}\right\}. \tag{A7}$$

Combining (A1)–(A7), we obtain S_t as a function of P_L for $P_L \leq P_H$. These functions are depicted in Figure 2. As discussed in the text, the curve S_1S_1 is kinked because small deviations of P_L from P_H do not produce regret in old workers while large deviations induce some old workers to search for the first time. This can be seen by examining the second term in (A5)—it is positive and decreasing in P_L for relatively small values of P_L, then turns to zero (and therefore becomes independent of P_L) once P_L surpasses a critical value.

Neither S_2S_2 nor S_3S_3 are kinked. The former is true because the value of P_L plays no role in determining whether the second term in (A6) is zero or positive. The latter is true because the second term in (A7) is always zero since the economy reaches the new steady state at time $t = 3$, and we have already shown that in any steady state there are no old searchers who were not also searchers when young.

As we noted in the text, it is region I of Figure 2 that is of interest to us since this is the range of values for P_L such that $S_1 > \tilde{S} \geq S_2 \geq S_t$ for $t \geq 3$. The existence of range I is guaranteed if $S_1 > S_2$ when both are evaluated at $P_L = 0$. Using (A1)–(A7), this condition reduces to

$$\pi_L > \pi_H\left\{1 - \frac{P_H}{\pi_H}\frac{1 + \pi_H}{2}\right\}. \tag{A8}$$

The incentive to search diminishes as π_L becomes smaller. If this probability is low enough, then the measure of searchers in period 1 is below the measure of searchers in subsequent periods, where the probability of success is higher. Thus, as long as π_L is not too low, a rational-expectations equilibrium of the type we are seeking exists.

Turn next to Figure 3. After the temporary tariff is imposed the measures of young and old searchers during periods 1 and 2 are now given by

$$S_1^y = \left\{1 - \frac{P_L + \tau}{\pi_H}\frac{1 + \pi_H}{2}\right\}, \tag{A9}$$

$$S_1^o = (1 - \pi_H)\left\{1 - \frac{P_L + \tau}{\pi_H}\right\} + \pi_H \max\left\{0, \frac{P_H}{\pi_H}\frac{1 + \pi_H}{2} - \frac{P_L + \tau}{\pi_H}\right\}, \tag{A10}$$

$$S_2^o = (1 - \pi_H)\left\{1 - \frac{P_L}{\pi_H}\right\} + \pi_H \max\left\{0, \frac{P_L + \tau}{\pi_H}\frac{1 + \pi_H}{2} - \frac{P_L}{\pi_H}\right\}. \tag{A11}$$

Combining (A9)–(A11) yields Figure 3. Note that the above three equations differ from their counterparts in two ways. Obviously, the relevant price in the first period is now the tariff-inclusive price. This also shows up in the equation for the measure of old searchers in period 2 because this measure is determined, in part, by the measure of young workers who searched in period 1. The second difference is that all of the probabilities now equal π_H under the assumption that $S_t \leq \tilde{S}$ for all t. Of course, this will not be true for very low values of the tariff. In particular, it will not be true when $\tau = 0$. However, assuming initially that it is true allows us to solve for the minimum tariff that is consistent with this assumption.

Finally, turn to Figure 5. As before, the measures of young and old searchers in the initial steady state are given by (A1) and (A4). If the job acquisition rate falls to π_L and remains there permanently, then the measures of young and old searchers in subsequent periods are now given by (A12) and (A13):

$$S_1^y = \bar{S}^y(P_L, \pi_L) = \left\{ 1 - \frac{P_L}{\pi_L} \frac{1+\pi_L}{2} \right\}, \tag{A12}$$

$$S_1^o = (1-\pi_H)\left\{ 1 - \frac{P_L}{\pi_L} \right\} + \pi_H \max\left\{ 0, \frac{P_H}{\pi_H} \frac{1+\pi_H}{2} - \frac{P_L}{\pi_L} \right\}, \tag{A13a}$$

$$S_2^o = \bar{S}^o(P_L, \pi_L) = (1-\pi_L)\left\{ 1 - \frac{P_L}{\pi_L} \right\} + \pi_L \max\left\{ 0, \frac{P_L}{\pi_L} \frac{1+\pi_L}{2} - \frac{P_L}{\pi_L} \right\}. \tag{A13b}$$

Combining (A1), (A4), (A12), and (A13) yields Figure 5.

References

Bishop, William R., "Investigations Completed Under Section 201 of the Trade Act of 1974," unpublished, USITC, Washington, DC (2002).

Baldwin, Robert E., "The Political Economy of Trade Protection," *Journal of Economic Perspectives* 3 (1989):119–35.

Baldwin, Robert E., John Mutti, and J. David Richardson, "Welfare Effects on the United States of a Significant Multilateral Tariff Reduction," *Journal of International Economics* 10 (1980):405–23.

Cassing, James and Jack Ochs, "International Trade, Factor Market Distortions, and the Optimal Dynamic Subsidy: Comment," *American Economic Review* 68 (1978):950–5.

Cheh, John H., "United States Concessions in the Kennedy Round and Short-run Labor Adjustment Costs," *Journal of International Economics* 4 (1974):323–40.

Davidson, Carl and Steven J. Matusz, "On Adjustment Costs," GEP research paper 2001/24, University of Nottingham (2001).

Deardorff, Alan, "Safeguards Policy and the Conservative Social Welfare Function," in Henryk Kierzkowski (ed.), *Protection and Competition in International Trade: Essays in Honor of W. M. Corden*, Oxford: Blackwell (1987):22–40.

Diamond, Peter, "Mobility Costs, Frictional Unemployment and Efficiency," *Journal of Political Economy* 89 (1981):798–812.

———, "Aggregate Demand Management in Search Equilibrium," *Journal of Political Economy* 90 (1982):881–94.

———, *A Search-Equilibrium Approach to the Micro Foundations of Macroeconomics*, Cambridge, MA: MIT Press (1984).

Diamond, Peter and Drew Fudenberg, "Rational Expectations Business Cycles in Search Equilibrium," *Journal of Political Economy* 97 (1989):606–19.

Falvey, Rod and Cha Dong Kim, "The Timing and Sequencing Issues in Trade Liberalization," *Economic Journal* 102 (1992):908–24.

Gaisford, James D. and Lawrence A. Leger, "Terms-of-trade Shocks, Labor-market Adjustment, and Safeguard Measures," *Review of International Economics* 8 (2000):100–12.

Karp, Larry and Thierry Paul, "Phasing In and Phasing Out Protectionism with Costly Adjustment of Labour," *Economic Journal* 104 (1994):1379–92.

———, "Labor Adjustment and Gradual Reform: When is Commitment Important?" *Journal of International Economics* 46 (1998):333–62.

Lapan, Harvey, "International Trade, Factor Market Distortions, and the Optimal Dynamic Subsidy," *American Economic Review* 66 (1976):335–46.

———, "International Trade, Factor Market Distortions, and the Optimal Dynamic Subsidy: Reply," *American Economic Review* 68 (1978):956–9.

———, "International Trade, Factor Market Distortions, and the Optimal Dynamic Subsidy: Reply," *American Economic Review* 69 (1979):718–20.

Lavergne, Real, *The Political Economy of US Tariffs: an Empirical Analysis*, New York: Academic Press (1983).

Magee, Stephen, "The Welfare Effects of Restrictions on US Trade," *Brookings Papers on Economic Activity* 3 (1972):645–701.

Mayer, Wolfgang, "Short-run and Long-run Equilibrium for a Small Open Economy," *Journal of Political Economy* 82 (1974):820–31.

Michealy, Michael, "The Timing and Sequencing of a Trade Liberalization Policy," in Armeane Choksi and Demetrios Papageorgiou (eds.), *Economic Liberalization in Developing Countries*, Oxford: Blackwell (1986).

Mortensen, Dale, "Property Rights and Efficiency in Mating, Racing and Related Games," *American Economic Review* 72 (1982):968–79.

Mussa, Michael, "Tariffs and the Distribution of Income: the Importance of Factor Specificity, Substitutability and Intensity in the Short and Long Run," *Journal of Political Economy* 82 (1974):1191–203.

———, "Dynamic Adjustment in the Heckscher–Ohlin–Samuelson Model," *Journal of Political Economy* 86 (1978):775–91.

———, "The Adjustment Process and the Timing of Trade Liberalization," in Armeane Choksi and Demetrios Papageorgiou (eds.), *Economic Liberalization in Developing Countries*, Oxford: Blackwell (1986).

Neary, Peter, "Short-run Capital Specificity and the Pure Theory of International Trade," *Economic Journal* 88 (1978):488–510.

Pissarides, Christopher, *Equilibrium Unemployment Theory*, Oxford: Blackwell (1990).

Ray, Edward, "Factor Market Distortions and Dynamic Optimal Intervention: Comment," *American Economic Review* 69 (1979):715–17.

Sykes, Alan, "Protectionism as a 'Safeguard': a Positive Analysis of the GATT 'Escape Clause' with Normative Speculations," *University of Chicago Law Review* 58 (1991):255–307.

Trefler, Daniel, "The Long and the Short of the Canada–US Free Trade Agreement," working paper, University of Toronto (2001).

United States International Trade Commission, "Summary of Statutory Provisions Related to Import Relief," USITC publication 3125, Washington, DC (1998).

Yashiv, Eran, "The Determinants of Equilibrium Unemployment," *American Economic Review* 90 (2000):1297–322.

Notes

1. See Bishop (2002).
2. Thus, our approach differs, in a fundamental way, from the equity-based explanation of temporary protection offered by Deardorff (1987) and the political economy explanation offered by Sykes (1991). Deardorff bases his explanation on Corden's Conservative Social Welfare Function and argues that the government's objective is to prevent a significant fall in real income of a significant sector of the economy. In his setting, safeguard policies "are not intended, as economists more often recommend, to facilitate 'adjustment' in the sense of an

orderly transition to a new equilibrium" (Deardorff, 1987, p. 24). In contrast, the Sykes approach emphasizes that policymakers may experience a change in political support when the terms of trade change and it is therefore in their interest to respond to this change with newly adopted measures of temporary protection. Our analysis is, in no way, meant to dismiss such alternative explanations of temporary safeguard policies. Instead, our goal is to show that if the government is concerned about adjustment, as has been emphasized by a variety of authors in the past, there may be efficiency as well as equity concerns driving their decisions.

3. While we are concerned with the efficiency implications of temporary protection, we make no attempt to derive the *optimal* time path. Indeed, as one referee correctly notes, our two-period overlapping-generations framework precludes any deep analysis of this interesting and important issue.

4. For an excellent survey of the early work in this literature, see Falvey and Kim (1992).

5. Of course, if factor markets are distorted there are generally policy instruments that are preferable to tariffs. Thus, complete liberalization coupled with temporary labor market policies targeted at the source of the distortions is the optimal policy. It has been pointed out that such policies may be politically infeasible, leaving tariffs as the only way to slow down the adjustment process.

6. See also Diamond (1981, 1982, 1984) where the information problems that generate equilibrium unemployment are not explicitly modeled.

7. One way that the government could attack the source of the problem directly is through state-run employment agencies. We follow the standard approach in the search literature by assuming that the government does not do so because it would be prohibitively costly to do so.

8. For recent empirical evidence on the existence and magnitude of congestion externalities in the labor market, see Yashiv (2000).

9. The only people who have the opportunity to switch jobs are those in the middle of their life, who are just turning old.

10. Any old worker for whom $a = a_t^o$ will be indifferent between searching for an export sector job and taking a job in the import-competing sector. Without loss of generality, we break the tie in favor of search.

11. In order to lighten the notation, we assume that the discount rate is zero. This assumption has no substantive bearing on the qualitative features of the model.

12. Of course, this worker always has the option of quitting her job in the export sector when old and taking a job in the import-competing sector. However, since we are interested in the case in which the economy experiences an unexpected improvement in the terms of trade, the worker will never choose to do so.

13. In particular, if the probability of success is a continuous function of S_t, we would have to solve a thorny fixed-point problem in order to find equilibrium.

14. As we show in the Appendix, region I may not exist if π_L is sufficiently low. The condition for existence is given in (A8) in the Appendix.

15. Note that if $S_1 > \tilde{S}$, then it necessarily follows that $S_2 > \tilde{S}$ in range II, and $S_2 > S_3 > \tilde{S}$ in range III. In turn, this would imply that $\pi_2 = \pi_L$ when P_L is in range II, and $\pi_2 = \pi_3 = \pi_L$ if P_L falls within range III. This would contradict our assumption that the workers' expectations concerning π_t are rational.

16. It is straightforward to show that

$$\tilde{a}^y = \max\left[\frac{P_H + \pi_H P_L}{2\pi_H}, \frac{P_H}{\pi_H(2 - \pi_L)}\right].$$

17. There is a third, less interesting case where $\tilde{a}^y < \bar{a}^y < a_1^o < \bar{a}^o$. In this case, the improvement in the terms of trade does not change behavior and does not induce regret.

18. For the sake of brevity, we have glossed over an important issue here—the economy does not reach the new steady state until $t = 3$. Thus, the low job acquisition rates faced by workers at $t = 1$ have effects on those workers born at $t = 2$ as well. While these workers are not surprised by the change in the terms of trade, the search pool that they are a part of may be larger than its steady-state value. As we show in the next subsection, a temporary tariff is effective at

relieving congestion only if it reduces S_1 below $\tilde{S}$ without increasing S_2 above this value. Thus, effective temporary protection cannot harm these workers.

19. For the case in which $a_1^o < \tilde{a}^y < \bar{a}^y < \bar{a}^o$, this interval would be $[a_1^o, \bar{a}^o]$.

20. For the case in which $a_1^o < \tilde{a}^y < \bar{a}^y < \bar{a}^o$, all workers in the interval change their behavior and search for export sector jobs (rather than take jobs in sector M), while only those in the middle of the range (with $a \in [\tilde{a}^y, \bar{a}^y]$) regret their behavior when young.

21. It is possible to create numeric examples where a smaller tariff levied for two periods can also relieve the congestion externality. It is also conceivable that this could be a more efficient policy than the single-period tariff, since deadweight loss is proportional to the square of the tariff. However, our only purpose in this paper is to show that temporary protection can lead to welfare gains. Solving for the *optimal* policy is significantly more complex.

22. This follows because the value of the tariff is zero and the price of the import-competing good is at its new steady-state value from period 2 onwards. It follows that all people born during period 2 make their steady-state choices, as do all people born in subsequent periods. Thus, those who are old in period 3 made their steady-state choices when they were young in period 2.

23. As before, young searchers adjust instantly to any changes in the environment. Therefore the measure of young searchers attains its steady-state value starting in the second period.

24. Since the increase in τ does not push S_2 above the threshold level (by the definition of $\hat{\tau}$), there are no spillover effects on period 2 searchers—although the search pool increases, it does not increase enough to lower job acquisition rates.

Chapter 3

Structural Change and the Labor-market Effects of Globalization

Noel Gaston and Douglas Nelson

1. Introduction

Why is the average citizen so worried about globalization and the average economist so unworried? It is surely true, but unuseful, to say that the citizen and the economist simply do not understand the benefits and costs of globalization in the same way. There are good reasons why the economist feels comfortable arguing that, at least at an aggregate level, globalization is either no big deal or a substantial boon. It would be comforting to conclude that the citizen is simply wrong, with the obvious implication being that a little bit more effort at public education would help reduce globalphobia. There may be a significant element of truth here, but the consequences of introducing irrationality, ignorance, and learning into our models are substantial.[1] It seems to us to be useful to consider the possibility that the widespread concern with globalization emerges as a result of changes that are, to some extent, obscured when we apply standard trade-theoretic methods to understand globalization. In this paper we are interested in effects of globalization that operate on the labor market indirectly by transforming the structures that support one set of equilibria and induce change in those equilibria. We will develop our analysis in terms of the interdependence between economic and political structures in a given national economy. Because the economic and political structures are related, changes in the relationship of a national economy to the global economy can produce profound changes in the political–economic arrangements of a country. In addition to affecting equilibrium wages and employment, such changes could well be unsettling in themselves.

In section 2 we begin by briefly rehearsing the main framework within which most economists (at least trade economists) have considered the effects of globalization, and found them to be essentially unproblematic. We refer to these as *direct effects* of globalization. In section 3 we review some of the research suggesting that globalization has effects on the returns to labor market participation that work through its effects on labor market and political institutions. We refer to these as *indirect effects* of globalization. We believe that this research supports a claim that indirect effects of globalization are sufficiently plausible to consider them in more detail.

Thus, in section 4, we develop a simple model of political economic equilibrium with firm–union bargaining and a welfare state. Using this model, we consider the impact of increased openness. Specifically, we show the effect of globalization on the bargain between the firm and the union (Proposition 1); as a baseline we derive the equilibrium unemployment benefit with a utilitarian policymaker in the closed economy (Proposition 2) and in the open economy (Corollary 1). Since the politics of labor figure prominently in existing work on indirect effects of globalization, we also formally characterize equilibrium with lobbying by labor (Proposition 3). In section 5, we present some empirical work based on a fixed-effects panel model for OECD countries. With respect to the effects of globalization, we find strong evidence of a positive relationship between openness and the unemployment benefit, but a negative relationship between openness interacted with the budget deficit and the unemployment benefit. This suggests that an increase in the government debt to GDP ratio lowers the response of the benefit replacement rate to openness. That is, there is some evidence that, as suggested by some of the work reviewed in section 3 and the model developed in section 4, globalization acts as a constraint on the political economy of labor market outcomes. Section 6 concludes.

2. The Direct Labor Market Effects of Globalization

The professional literature (to say nothing of the popular literature) on the direct labor market effects of globalization is enormous. The essential empirical issue is macroeconomic: accounting for the *economy-wide* rise of the skill-premium at a time when the share of skilled to unskilled workers is rising. Thinking systematically about the role of globalization in this context requires a model of the economy as a whole with sufficient structure that the link to the world economy can be treated explicitly, but simple enough that it generates guidance for both empirical work and policy. Standard low-dimensional trade-theoretic models provide just such a framework and, not surprisingly, they lie at the heart of a sizable majority of the theoretical work and an even larger share of the empirical work on trade (migration, foreign direct investment) and wages.[2]

As the story has now been told many times, in response to early work in the one-sector framework, trade economists successfully argued that the natural framework for thinking about the effect of trade on labor markets, at least from a maintained assumption of competitive markets, was the Stolper–Samuelson theorem and its various generalizations.[3] The theoretical account of trade shocks as running from commodity-price changes to factor-price changes provided a compelling equilibrium mechanism, and some useful rough empirical checks, but the real success came with the development and refinement of the mandated wage regression methodology (Baldwin and Cain, 2000). The solid theoretical foundations of the mandated wage regression approach led to the almost complete displacement of the factor-content study as a framework for empirical study. The interpretation of the empirical results, as well as the appropriate implementation of the framework, is not without controversy, but the aggregate professional prior would seem to have settled on the conclusion that trade has a small effect on the skill-premium (maybe 10–20%), but that other factors (especially technological change) are more important.

The analysis of immigration would appear to be very different, but in fact contains strong similarities to the above story. The obvious problem with the trade-theoretic framework from the perspective of evaluating immigration shocks is that, as long as we assume the commodity and factor markets are competitive and, as seems quite the most plausible assumption, that the number of goods exceeds the number of factors, then we are stuck with what Leamer (1995) calls the *factor-price insensitivity theorem*. This result, which is the single-country analogue of the factor-price equalization theorem, asserts that, under the dimensionality and competitiveness assumptions already mentioned, as long as the economy produces the same types of goods before and after an immigration shock (the endowment remains inside the same cone of diversification), the change in endowment will leave relative factor-prices unchanged. Since the goal is to find globalization effects that might help account for the changing skill-premium, this feature of the trade-theoretic model would seem to be a problem. However, it turned out that most studies found only extremely small effects of immigration on the skill-premium.

To the extent that foreign direct investment (FDI) could be seen as capital arbitrage, factor-price insensitivity would apply there as well. The problem in this case is that economists had long become convinced that FDI was fundamentally not about capital arbitrage. This was the fundamental realization in Hymer's (1960) classic dissertation that is generally credited with beginning the modern theory of foreign direct investment. Starting with Caves (1971), a large body of research has incorporated the insights of the firm-theoretic approach by interpreting FDI as an arbitrage of firm-specific capital. Similarly, monopolistic competition models could be enlisted to analyze FDI by interpreting one input as managerial or headquarters services (Helpman, 1984). But this has always been only uneasily related to the firm-theoretic foundations of the modern theory of FDI. The problems become more obvious when outsourcing becomes part of the picture. We pick up that part of the story in the next section.

3. Indirect Labor Market Effects of Globalization: Some Preliminary Remarks

Implicit in all the comparative static analyses discussed in the previous section is the assumption that the underlying structure of the economy is unchanged by whatever is taken to be the relevant globalizing force—trade, immigration, FDI. However, one of the essential claims in much of the popular writing on globalization, and surely a major source of the general social concern about globalization, is its transformative nature. That is, globalization is taken to transform the economic and political structures in ways that might be obscured when we apply the standard toolkit of trade theory.

Consider the case of global outsourcing, one of the characteristic aspects of contemporary globalization (Feenstra, 1998). From a microeconomic or firm-theoretic point of view, outsourcing is just the reverse process of internalization, which has long been central to the theory of foreign direct investment. However, from the macroeconomic (e.g., trade-theoretic) perspective, internalization and externalization are radical innovations relative to the models used to understand trade and migration. That is, when we come to focus explicitly on outsourcing, it becomes clear that we are dealing with nonmarginal change in production structure that does not really permit simple extension of standard techniques. Where allocation of production among existing facilities is trade-theoretically straightforward, the decision to outsource creates new technologies and transforms the dimensionality of the underlying model.[4] This recognition is increasingly being made in the theoretical literature on outsourcing (Jones and Kierzkowski, 2001; Deardorff, 2001; Kohler, 2001), but empirical work on the link between outsourcing and wages continues to use a mandated wage approach that manifestly does not permit such nonmarginal change (e.g., Feenstra and Hanson, 1999).

In the case of outsourcing, because it directly transforms dimensionality in our standard models, we can see how structural change interferes with inference based on those tools in a straightforward way. The role played by broader social institutions in supporting economic and political–economic outcomes is less well understood, although elements of such an analysis are beginning to be developed in economics, drawing to a considerable degree on existing research in political science and sociology.[5] In this paper we are interested in the relationship between globalization, unions, and welfare states. Loosely speaking, the idea is that part of the support for an equilibrium in which relatively unskilled workers receive high wages comes from the mutually supporting institutions of unions and welfare states. That is, as a result of labor market institutions, in this case a union, some workers receive a higher wage than other otherwise identical workers. There are insiders and outsiders. In addition, because there is unemployment in equilibrium, we will assume that there is some governmental transfer to the unemployed. It should be clear that globalization could change each of the components of this relationship, with implications for equilibrium relative wages. With respect to the first, there is now a sizable body of research examining the relationship between the institutional structure of the unionized sector of an economy (i.e., the extent and centralization of organization) and various measures of macroeconomic performance. Countries with encompassing labor market institutions (i.e., large unionized sectors with centralized bargaining) are characterized by: lower wage inequality (Rowthorn, 1992; Zweimüller and Barth, 1994; OECD, 1997); lower unemployment (OECD, 1997); and higher growth (Calmfors and Driffill, 1988; Rowthorn, 1992; Calmfors, 1993; Danthine and Hunt, 1994). The usual explanation involves the ability of centralized bargaining institutions to internalize negative wage externalities (Calmfors, 1993; Garrett, 1998). That is, where strong sectoral unions pursue wage gains relative to some perceived market wage, resulting in cost-push inflation, reduced employment, lower growth, and intersectoral inequality, the centralized union recognizes these negative externalities and takes them into account in its bargaining. Thus, as unionization has declined, there is some evidence that wage inequality has increased (Freeman, 1998).

Globalization is widely thought to have affected unions. On the one hand, globalization is generally taken to imply increased competition that, even without any change in relative bargaining power, will squeeze sectoral rents and lead to reduced wages in post-globalization bargains. In a closely related fashion, by raising the elasticity of demand for labor, imports can be seen to directly reduce the market power of unions. An alternative argument turns on the expectation that firms/capital are globally more mobile than labor. The existence of an exit option, even if not exercised, changes the relative bargaining power of the firm and the union. Thus, even without an observed increase in trade, unions should do worse in bargains after the cost of globalization of production (via importing, outsourcing, or FDI) fall. Finally, by affecting the return to union membership, the size of unions may decline, causing a further erosion of bargaining power.

Increased inequality, and real deterioration in the labor market outcomes of unskilled workers, is also directly related to changes in demand for welfare state provision. For example, it has been observed that despite increases in the dispersion of earned incomes that, in some countries at least, inequality in post-transfer and post-tax income inequality has *not* grown (e.g., Gottschalk and Smeeding, 1997; Aaberge et al., 2000). This suggests that political pressures have been brought to bear on the generosity of public transfers at a time when earned incomes have become more unequally distributed. From a political economic perspective, the growing inequality of income could be associated with strong compositional effects on the demand for public insurance. In particular, it seems to be the case that the growing size and economic significance of sectors of the economy that pay higher wages for certain types of workers could somewhat paradoxically result in political pressures that lead to higher levels of transfer payments to disadvantaged workers. It has been suggested that this could result from changes in the identity of the median voter (e.g., Alesina and Rodrik, 1994; Persson and Tabellini, 1994; Saint-Paul and Verdier, 1996) or as an optimal response to increased income risk in an increasingly open economy (e.g., Rodrik, 1998). In this paper we consider an alternative account in which self-interested behavior and institutional features of labor determine public insurance policy outcomes. Specifically, we examine how the demand for unemployment benefits may change during periods of trade liberalization, when collective bargaining is more or less centralized.

Where the effect of globalization on unions is taken to be generally negative, the effects on the welfare state are potentially more mixed. On the negative side, scholars such as Steinmo (1994) and Tanzi (1995) argue that increased mobility of capital not only erodes the tax base, reducing the state's ability to fund welfare state programs, but by shifting taxes onto labor, the capacity of the state to redistribute is reduced. In a similar fashion, Garrett (1998) has argued that, by forcing states to turn increasingly to borrowing to fund welfare state programs, the international capital market ends up imposing an increasing premium on large welfare states. In ways that are harder to quantify, but seem *prima facie* plausible, the decreasing cost of the exit option increases the relative power of business in policymaking (Huber and Stephens, 1998). Finally, it has been argued that globalization increases the general credibility of orthodox (i.e., market-oriented) policy advice, thus reducing the plausibility of arguments supporting welfare state expansion and enhancing the credibility of arguments in favor of welfare state retrenchment (Evans, 1997; Krugman, 1999). On the other hand, there are a number of reasons for believing that the sources of pressure for change are, at a minimum, not overwhelming. First, as has been widely noted for some time, the classic, large welfare states developed in the context of considerably more open economies than did the smaller, market conforming welfare states (Katzenstein, 1985; Huber and Stephens, 1998). As Rodrik (1998) has argued, this may be related to increased income risk. Interestingly, Bordo et al. (1999) carry this argument further, suggesting that the presence of sizable welfare states, and Keynesian macroeconomic policy, may have played an important role in providing sufficient indifference to globalization, that policies like support for the GATT/WTO system and the Bretton Woods institutions continued even in the face of recessions that might have had system closing consequences in earlier eras. In addition, current welfare states show considerable heterogeneity in response to the increases in globalization experienced over the last 15 to 20 years (Garrett, 1998; Swank, 2002). Here it has been widely argued that heterogeneity of domestic political, as well as labor market, institutions support heterogeneity of responses to globalization (Calmfors and Driffill, 1988; Garrett, 1998; Swank, 2002).

The next section develops a model in which, when collective bargaining is more centralized, or when unions are relatively more concerned with employment growth than with raising workers' wages, the workers seek to encourage policymakers to raise unemployment benefits. This happens because of the positive effect that higher reservation wages have on negotiated wages. In contrast, if wage and employment levels are negotiated in an extremely decentralized environment in which workers earn higher wages but are exposed to greater degrees of employment risk, then the workers whose employment is at greatest risk ally themselves with employers to lobby for reductions in transfer payments and benefits and the taxes which are necessary to finance them. That is, there is political pressure to decrease both unemployment benefits and taxes, but this tendency is largely reversed during times of greater openness to international competition.

In an era of rapid globalization, labor market deregulation and microeconomic reform, the associated decentralization of collective bargaining results in wages that are more closely aligned with productivity. However, these developments also expose the same workers to greater unemployment risk. Thus, they have an incentive to influence the direction of public insurance policies. There is considerable evidence that unions have played a prominent role in influencing policies that affect the welfare of their members. For example, there is the well-documented support by the trade union movement for higher minimum wages (e.g., Ehrenberg, 1994, pp. 44–45) and their active participation in the politics surrounding NAFTA (Mayer, 1998). In addition, Kau and Rubin (1981) found that US unions use their political contributions in a systematic and coordinated manner. Union campaign contributions are *always* significant in explaining not only voting on minimum wages, but also wage-price controls, benefits for strikers, OSHA (which regulates workplace safety) and CETA (i.e., manpower training programs) appropriations.

4. Indirect Labor Market Effects of Globalization: A Simple Model

Consider a small open economy populated by workers and shareholders. The economy has two sectors, a unionized sector and a non-unionized sector.[6] Our purpose in this section, and the next, is to determine the effects of trade liberalization (our measure of "globalization") on labor market outcomes via its direct effects on the wage bargain and indirect effects working through redistributive policies (e.g., the unemployment benefit).

Production in the Unionized Sector

The concave production technology for a representative firm in the unionized sector is represented by $x = f(n)$, where n is employment. Total profits are simply

$$\pi(n, w; p, t) = pf(n) - (1+t)wn, \tag{1}$$

where w is the wage and $t \in [0, 1)$ is a payroll tax levied on the total wage bill.[7]

The domestic relative output price of the good produced by the unionized sector is

$$p = (1+\tau)p^*, \tag{2}$$

where p^* is the world price and τ is an *ad valorem* tariff. The tariff is assumed to be determined by multilateral trade negotiations in which the small country has negligible bargaining power, and therefore the tariff is taken as given by all domestic agents.

Workers and Shareholders

All individuals in the economy—shareholders, union, and non-union workers—are assumed to have the same preferences over consumption goods. The utility of each individual i is

$$U^i = c^{z^i} + u(c^{x^i}),$$ (3)

where c^{z^i} is consumption of the *numéraire* good produced by the non-unionized sector and c^{x^i} is consumption of the good produced by the unionized sector. $u(.)$ is increasing and concave. Individuals maximize utility subject to their expected income constraint.

The quasilinear form of equation (3) implies that the consumption of c^{x^i} depends only on p. Denoting the aggregate consumption of x by $C(p)$ and aggregate production of x by $X(p)$, the government's tariff revenue is

$$T(p) = \tau p^*(C(p) - X(p)),$$ (4)

where $C(p) - X(p)$ represents aggregate imports of good x.[8]

Union Leadership versus Union Workers

The unionized sector is assumed to have rents to bargain over. The firm and the union leadership, which represents workers, negotiate wages and employment levels. That is, the objectives pursued by a union's leadership and the welfare of individual workers are possibly quite distinct (Pemberton, 1988).

We assume that the union's objective function in bargaining can be represented by the Stone–Geary utility function; i.e.,

$$U(n, w) = (n - m)^\gamma (c^e - c^v)^\delta,$$ (5)

where m represents the number of incumbent union workers, c^e is the income for an employed worker, and c^v denotes the reservation alternative for an unemployed worker.[9]

In the following, we assume that the income for an employed worker is $c^e = w$. During the second stage of the game, we treat c^v as exogenous. For individual workers, c^v reflects the value of not working in the unionized sector. It is affected by the value of leisure time, home or nonmarket production, or the wage in the informal sector of the economy. For the purposes of this paper, we assume that the unemployment benefit or income transfer payable to those not employed in the unionized sector affects c^v.

The values of δ and γ in equation (5) indicate the relative importance of wages and employment in bargaining objectives. Pemberton (1988) interpreted a low value for δ as reflecting a relatively greater weight being placed on the desire for high membership on the part of union leadership *vis-à-vis* the desire for high wages on the part of the median union member.[10] Equation (5) results from interpreting the bargaining objective as deriving from a Nash game played between the union's leadership and the union's median member. The leadership wants a large union (high n), and consequently the lower wages that would achieve this growth or membership objective. The median union member, whose employment is assumed to be secure, is concerned only with maximizing wage rents.

One advantage of the Stone–Geary functional form is that it admits some interesting special cases (Farber, 1986, p. 1061). For example, if $\delta \approx \gamma$ and $m = 0$, then the union's objective is to maximize $U = n(c^e - c^v)$, the rents for employed union members. In this case, it is useful to think of all-encompassing labor market institutions where the bargaining over wages and employment is relatively centralized. When $\gamma = 1$ and $\delta = 0$, the objective is $U = n - m$, to maximize the size of the union. When $\delta = 1$ and $\gamma = 0$, the bargaining objective is $U = c^e - c^v$, the earnings for each of its members over and above their reservation alternative. That is, the union is completely "wage-oriented" in its negotiations with the firm (Carruth and Oswald, 1987). Consequently, the union places no importance on "internalizing" the adverse impact of higher wages on employment levels.

Wage and Employment in the Unionized Sector

We assume that bargaining over wages and employment is efficient and that the choice from the set of efficient contracts is the one that maximizes the symmetric Nash product; i.e.,[11]

$$S(n, w) = U(n, w)\pi(n, w). \tag{6}$$

We assume that the solution lies in the interior of the choice set and that S is strictly concave so that the solution is unique and may be characterized by the following first-order conditions (we suppress arguments where no ambiguity exists and use subscripts to denote partial derivatives):

$$S_w(.) = S(.)[\delta\Delta^{-1} - (1+t)n\pi^{-1}] = 0, \tag{7a}$$

$$S_n(.) = S(.)[\gamma(n-m)^{-1} + (pf_n - (1+t)w)\pi^{-1}] = 0, \tag{7b}$$

where $\Delta = c^e - c^v$ is the economic rent to employed workers. Substituting (7a) into (7b), we obtain the contract curve

$$(\gamma - \delta l)w = \gamma c^v - \frac{\delta l p f_n}{(1+t)}, \tag{8}$$

where $l = (n - m)/n$, $l \in (0, 1]$. From equation (8), and since $f(.)$ is concave, the contract curve has a positive (negative) slope when $\gamma > (<) \delta l$. Note that when $\gamma = 0$, labor is employed until its marginal revenue product equals its marginal cost; i.e., $pf_n = (1 + t)w$. When $\delta = 0$, $w = c^v$ and employment is maximized. In the following we refer to the former case as being equivalent to "decentralized bargaining" because wage and employment outcomes occur along the firm's demand-for-labor curve.[12] Likewise, the latter case is referred to as "centralized bargaining" because wages and employment are determined by the Nash bargaining condition and lie to the right of the firm's demand-for-labor curve.

The following proposition summarizes the comparative static results for wages and employment. For expositional purposes, we consider a production function with constant elasticity of employment, α. (Derivations are provided in the Appendix.)

PROPOSITION 1. $w(c^v, p^*, \tau, t, m, \gamma, \delta)$ and $n(c^v, p^*, \tau, t, m, \gamma, \delta)$. *Suppose that* $\alpha = nf_n f^{-1} > 0$. *Then*

(i) $w_{c^v} > 0, w_{p^*} \geq 0, w_\tau \geq 0, w_t \leq 0, w_m < 0, w_\gamma < 0,$ *and* $w_\delta > 0$;

(ii) $n_{c^v} < 0, n_{p^*} \geq 0, n_\tau \geq 0, n_t < 0, n_m > 0, n_\gamma > 0,$ *and* $n_\delta < 0$.

The sign patterns are quite standard. Higher prices, or import tariffs, for the unionized good increase employment and wages. (The possibility of a zero wage effect for the output price and the payroll tax are byproducts of adopting an isoelastic form for the demand-for-labor curve.) The wage and employment effects of more decentralized wage bargaining and higher values of δ (or lower values of γ) indicate the effect of an increased orientation to the pursuit of higher wages, as opposed to lowering the risk of unemployment. The effects of a higher m, given γ, are equivalent to the effects of a higher value of γ, given m. (Recall that m is the union leadership's threat point in a Nash bargaining game with the median union member. Hence, a higher m strengthens the union leadership's drive for employment growth.)

It is readily apparent that the owners of firms will always lose from any policy that involves increasing c^v. Doing so increases wages and lowers output and labor demand by firms. On the other hand, workers may adopt a variety of positions regarding the desirability of various labor market policies and public insurance programs depending on the size of tax increases needed to finance more generous benefits as well as the nature of their preferences. Specifically, whether workers are likely to support higher unemployment benefits depends on the extent to which payroll tax increases are shifted back onto workers (Ehrenberg, 1994, p. 8), the exposure of workers to unemployment, and the effect of higher reservation wages on negotiated wages. What is clear is that one of the main effects of higher unemployment benefits is to increase the wage pressure by insiders. Further, some authors (e.g., Saint-Paul, 1996) argue that, since incumbent workers are more numerous and better organized than the unemployed, labor institutions are determined by the interests of the employed. In turn, these decisive voters are likely to support policies and labor market institutions that increase the exclusion of outsiders.

5. Equilibrium Unemployment Benefits in a Small Open Economy

In this section, we study the political determination of unemployment benefits. In addition to understanding the effect of different labor institutions on the generosity of benefits, a primary objective is to investigate the relationship between trade liberalization and unemployment benefits.

The Lobby-group Model

The menu auction model of Bernheim and Whinston (1986) provides a useful framework for understanding the interaction between special interest groups and the government.[13] Interest groups are assumed to have organized exogenously and to consist of individuals with similar interests in policy outcomes. Our focus is upon the unemployment benefit, b. Denoting the set of lobby groups by L, political contributions are made by the various groups to an incumbent government in return for preferred labor market policies, $\Lambda^i(b)$, where $i \in L$. These functions relate the political contributions of lobby groups to feasible policy choices.

An incumbent government is assumed to choose b to maximize the weighted sum of aggregate political contributions and aggregate social welfare. The specific form of the government's objective function is

$$V^g(b) = \sum_{i \in L} \Lambda^i(b) + \sum_{j=k,u,n} a^j V^j(b),$$ (9)

where the $V^j, j = k, u, n$, are the gross indirect utility functions for each group of factor owners—capital, incumbent union workers, and non-union workers, respectively. The $a^j \geq 0$ are the "weights" that the government places on each group's social welfare, relative to revenues and political contributions. Equation (9) does not restrict the weights attached to the social welfare of each group in the economy to be equal. For example, $a^u > a^n$ would imply that the government places a higher weight on the welfare of union workers compared to the welfare of non-unionized workers (Rama and Tabellini, 1998; Fredriksson and Gaston, 1999). This particular feature of the model captures ideological or constituency-specific motives behind policymaking, reflecting a view that governments of different political persuasions treat the different groups differently.

Equilibrium unemployment benefits are the outcome of a two-stage game played between the government and the lobby groups.[14] Aggregating the government's welfare and the welfare of each group in society (net of political contributions), the policymaker's choice of b is given by

$$b^* = \text{argmax} \sum_{i \in L} V^i(b) + \sum_{j=k,u,n} a^j V^j(b). \tag{10}$$

Budgetary Considerations

If we restrict our attention to balanced-budget methods of financing higher unemployment benefits, then the revenue available to fund unemployment benefits is given by the sum of payroll taxes and tariff revenues:

$$twn + T(p) = (1-n)b. \tag{11}$$

The effects of a trade liberalization are captured by reductions in τ. This holds true whether τ is an import tariff or subsidy, or an export tax or subsidy. Note that there are two avenues through which a reduction in trade barriers may have effects on unemployment benefits. First, in the case of an export subsidy or an import tariff, a lower τ reduces the internal relative price of the domestic good, thereby directly reducing employment in the protected sector. Second, in the case of an export tax or an import tariff, a lower τ reduces the revenue available to fund increases in benefits. Some authors have pointed to the possibility that the generosity of unemployment benefits, and hence the level of taxation needed to finance it, may well influence trade flows, at least in the short run (e.g., Ehrenberg, 1994). Equation (11) recognizes that, through the effect on government revenues, freer and more open trade will affect the budget used to fund unemployment benefits.

If tariff revenues are not used to fund unemployment benefits, then more generous unemployment benefits need to be matched with higher payroll tax revenues. Since higher benefits have adverse employment effects, this necessitates a higher payroll tax rate.[15] Hence, despite the possibility of beneficial wage effects for some workers, all workers and employers would unambiguously lose from the higher taxes needed to finance more generous benefits. Consequently, a balanced-budget constraint will serve to limit the size of equilibrium unemployment benefits (see below).

Impact of Higher Unemployment Benefits on Expected Income of Workers and Shareholders

Prior to wage and employment negotiations taking place, the income of all of the firm's shareholders is given by equation (1), evaluated at optimal values for w and n. In addition, using equations (2) and (11), and recalling that $C(p)$ is independent of expected income, yields

$$I^k(b) = p^*f(n(b)) - w(b)n(b) - (1 - n(b))b. \tag{12}$$

From the balanced-budget constraint, for a given level of b, it is clear that firms in the unionized sector with higher levels of unemployment are taxed more heavily. In this sense, the financing of unemployment benefits is fully "experience-rated."

The total net income of the group of incumbent union workers, m, is

$$I^u(b) = mw(b). \tag{13}$$

The expected income of $1 - m$ non-unionized workers is

$$I^n(b) = (n(b) - m)w(b) + (1 - n(b))(b + \kappa). \tag{14}$$

The specification for workers assumes that they are risk-neutral and that they maximize expected utility. Note that only when $m = 0$ and $\delta = \gamma$ do the preferences of non-union workers coincide with those of the political leadership of the union. We assume that the income while unemployed for workers is given by $c^v = b + \kappa$, where b is the government-provided benefit or income transfer and κ represents the value of informal sector or nonmarket production (e.g., as in Benhabib et al., 1991).[16]

Before proceeding it is useful to summarize the effects of changes in the generosity of higher unemployment benefits on the indirect utility of factor owners (see the Appendix for details):

$$V_b^k < 0, V_b^u > 0, \text{ and } V_b^n \gtrless 0. \tag{15}$$

Incumbent workers always prefer higher benefits, because their employment is secure and higher unemployment benefits increase the reservation wages of all workers (which, in turn, increase negotiated wages). Naturally, firms unambiguously prefer lower reservation wages. When $l = 1$, it is straightforward to show that

$$V_b^n = \begin{cases} \geq 0 & \text{if } \dfrac{\delta - \gamma - \alpha}{\alpha\delta} \leq v, \\ < 0 & \text{if } \dfrac{\delta - \gamma - \alpha}{\alpha\delta} \in (v, 1), \end{cases} \tag{16}$$

where $v = 1 - n$ is the percentage of the workforce not employed in the unionized sector. A sufficient condition for a higher value of b to have a positive impact on worker welfare is $\gamma + \alpha > \delta$. In fact, this condition implies that the Nash bargaining condition (NBC) has a steeper slope than the union workers' indifference curve (evaluated at (w^*, n^*)).[17] Only when the rents from union bargaining become larger, which may result from very high levels of wage-oriented bargaining, do workers become concerned about the possible unemployment effects of higher levels of b.

Equation (16) also reveals that a sufficiently high probability of employment in the higher-wage and high-rent unionized sector lowers worker demand for public insurance. For example, if the unionized sector suffers falling output prices and higher unemployment, then the demand for higher unemployment benefits will increase. This result differs from a key finding of median voter models in which unemployment benefits are negatively related to unemployment. As Persson and Tabellini (2002, p. 31) note, this seems counterfactual when comparing Europe and the United States. Europe has both higher unemployment and higher unemployment benefits.

Socially Optimal Unemployment Benefits

The presence of a non-lobby group population is important in the context of the Grossman–Helpman model because it admits the possibility that policies shaped by influence-seeking activities are likely to deviate from those chosen by a utilitarian social planner. From equation (10), it is clear that policies will always be socially optimal if the welfare of each group in society is equally weighted and if all groups are politically organized. The socially optimal unemployment benefit is defined as the benefit that maximizes aggregate social welfare (in the absence of any lobbying and political contributions). The utilitarian policymaker assumption is a useful benchmark for discussing the lobby-group model. In this case, b is chosen to maximize

$$\Omega(b) = \sum_{j=k,u,n} V^j(b), \tag{17}$$

subject to the government's balanced-budget constraint. Summing equations (12) to (14), and using equation (11), yields the following maximand:

$$\Omega(b) = p^* f(n(b)) + (1 - n(b))\kappa. \tag{18}$$

The optimal unemployment benefit is simply chosen to maximize the value of market and nonmarket production.[18]

Obviously, if workers are risk-neutral and if nonmarket production has no value (i.e., $\kappa = 0$), then employment in the unionized sector should be maximized and unemployment benefits should never exceed zero (Acemoglu and Shimer, 1999).[19] We summarize the key findings in Proposition 2.

PROPOSITION 2 (Utilitarian policymaker). *Suppose that $\kappa > 0$. Then:*
  (i) *Unemployment benefits are lower when the policymaker chooses balanced-budget or revenue-neutral policies.*
  (ii) *Unemployment benefits are positive only if collective bargaining is centralized.*

First, when a policymaker's balanced-budget constraint binds, unemployment benefits are lower than nonrevenue neutral benefits and transfers. Secondly, a more novel result is that $\gamma > \delta l$ is a necessary condition for the optimal unemployment benefit to be positive. Recall from equation (16) that this condition implies that the bargaining objective places relative greater weight on employment growth and job security. Hence, more centralized bargaining systems are likely to have higher unemployment benefits. Focusing on the effects of liberalizing trade, the key comparative static results are summarized next.

COROLLARY 1 (Open economy). *$b^o(\kappa, p^*, \tau, m, \gamma, \delta)$, where:*
  (i) *$b^o_\kappa > 0$, $b^o_m > 0$, $b^o_\gamma > 0$, and $b^o_\delta < 0$.*
  (ii) *If international competition lowers product prices and raises unemployment, then unemployment benefits are higher; i.e., $b^o_{p^*} \leq 0$.*
  (iii) *The impact of trade liberalization depends on whether tariff revenues are used to fund unemployment benefits. Specifically:*
      (a) *If tariff revenues are not used to fund unemployment benefits, then:*
          1. *in the case of an import tariff or an export subsidy, $b^o_\tau \leq 0$; or*
          2. *in the case of an import subsidy or an export tax, $b^o_\tau \geq 0$.*
      (b) *If tariff revenues are used to partially, or to fully, fund unemployment benefits, then:*

1. *in the case of an import tariff or an export subsidy, $b_\tau^o > 0$; or*
2. *in the case of an import subsidy or an export tax, $b_\tau^o < 0$.*

Part (i) indicates that unemployment benefits are higher when incumbent union workers, whose employment is secure, are more numerous. On the other hand, an aggressive pursuit of wage gains by union leaders, or wage contracts that expose workers to excessive amounts of unemployment risk, are balanced by lower unemployment benefits. The effect of higher values of κ on benefits reflects the increased value of time spent in nonmarket activities relative to time spent on production in the unionized sector.

Part (ii) indicates that, regardless of the method of financing, lower world prices raise unemployment benefits. That is, increased global competition is likely to lead to more generous unemployment benefits. The impact of trade liberalization, on the other hand, depends on whether tariff revenues are used to finance unemployment benefits and whether the unionized sector is protected or "antiprotected" (Vousden, 1990, p. 113).

Part (iii)(a) simply states that, for a small open economy liberalizing its unionized import-competing sector, optimal unemployment benefits will be higher. The lower tariff operates purely as an adverse domestic output price shock for the unionized sector. Of course, as unemployment benefits rise, income tax burdens are greater for workers and shareholders as well. Part (iii)(b) indicates that, when the unionized sector is protected and all tariff revenues are used to fund unemployment benefits, the effect of trade liberalization (assumed to be lower tariffs and lower subsidies) is to reduce the value of unemployment benefits.[20] When the unionized sector is "antiprotected," benefits are increased. The effects of a trade liberalization are therefore twofold. First, lower import tariffs and export subsidies increase competition, which increases unemployment and raises benefits. Second, lower tariff or tax revenues affect the government's budgetary position. In the case of lower import tariffs there is pressure on b to rise due to greater import competition, but there is an offsetting pressure on b to fall due to fiscal concerns.[21]

The Effect of Lobbying Activities

Clearly, how a policymaker weights the welfare of the different groups of factor owners strongly influences the generosity of unemployment benefits. For example, if a higher weight is placed on the welfare of shareholders compared to the welfare of workers, whether organized or not (i.e., $a^k > a^u$ and $a^k > a^n$), then equation (15) implies that benefits are lower than they otherwise would be. That is, this suggests that countries with pro-business governments have lower unemployment benefits than those countries with labor-oriented governments, *ceteris paribus*.

Similarly, to understand the effect that lobbying by interest groups has on the determination of public insurance and other labor market policies, it is important to identify the groups in an economy that are politically organized and actively participate in the political process. If we assume that the political weights attached to each group of factor owners by the policymaker are equal, this is readily seen by rearranging the solution to equation (10) to obtain

$$(1+a)\Omega_b = \sum_{i' \in L} V_b^{i'}. \tag{19}$$

Among others, Rama and Tabellini (1998) show that the policy distortion is proportional to the welfare effect of the policy on the unrepresented group in society.[22]

Clearly, unemployment benefits are set at socially inefficient high (low) levels whenever the left-hand side of equation (19) is negative (positive). This result obtains because of the nonparticipation by groups of factor owners in the political process who, if represented, would press for lower (higher) benefits. Further, the degree of the distortion is decreasing in the relative weight placed on social welfare, a.[23]

The comparative static effects of unequal treatment of groups of factor owners in the lobby group are transparent if we assume that only political contributions matter. Compared to the maximization of social welfare alone, because the government values contributions it weights more heavily the policy preferences of the organized groups that contribute. It seems reasonable to assume that only organized labor and/or capital owners make political contributions. In most OECD countries, non-unionized workers are politically unorganized or sufficiently disenfranchised so as not to lobby (and contribute to) the government for preferred policy outcomes.

Naturally, which groups of factor owners are politically active differs from country to country. In addition, it is not obvious that capital owners would be organized as a lobby in every country.[24] For example, if the unionized firm is foreign-owned and foreign shareholders do not participate politically or form a domestic lobby, then unemployment benefits are set inefficiently high. That is, since the welfare of incumbent union workers is valued more highly, this places upward pressure on benefit levels. To illustrate, the next proposition contains the results for the politically determined benefit, b^*, under the assumption that only organized labor makes political contributions.

PROPOSITION 3 (Lobbying by organized labor). *Suppose that $\kappa > 0$, that $a^j = a$, and that only organized labor lobbies. Then $b^* > b^o$. Further, b^* increases in (i) m, the number of organized workers, and (ii) the elasticity of negotiated wages with respect to unemployment benefits. Further, b^* decreases in (i) a, the government's weight on general welfare, and (ii) the elasticity of employment with respect to unemployment benefits.*

The results are straightforward. In terms of the comparative statics, note for the model we consider in this paper that the demand for higher benefits by incumbent union workers is driven by what Saint-Paul (1996) terms the "wage formation effect." The stronger this wage effect, the higher are unemployment benefits. Likewise, an elastic response of employment to higher benefits would counteract the wage formation effect.

6. Indirect Labor Market Effects of Globalization: Some Empirical Results

To test the main implications of the theory, our empirical analysis proceeds by examining unemployment benefit entitlements both within and between countries (see OECD, 1995 Jobs Study). In particular, we investigate whether openness of the economy and labor market institutions might be responsible for the differences. Amongst other things, in the empirical analysis our goal is to provide insights into policy-related questions that remain largely unresolved. First, is greater openness to trade correlated with the unemployment benefit generosity or stringency? Second, is there a statistical association between the nature of union participation in the economy, government indebtedness, partisan political effects, and unemployment benefits?

Using panel data for 17 OECD countries, we estimate the fixed-effects regression model. The dependent variable in all cases is the OECD's gross benefit replacement rate (BR): the proportion of expected income from work that is replaced by unem-

Table 1. Descriptive Statistics and Summary of Hypotheses

Variable	Label	Hypothesis	Mean	Standard deviation
Benefit replacement rate (%)[a]	•	BR	24.018	14.309
Government gross debt as percentage of GDP (%)[b]	Debt	–	36.295	27.132
Union density (%)[c]	Dentot	+	44.415	19.111
Trade openness[d]	Open	+	58.338	28.003
Political orientation of government[e]	Left	+	2.354	1.533

Notes and data sources:

[a] Replacement rates (i.e., benefits before tax as a percentage of previous earnings before tax) as defined by legislated entitlements averaged across various circumstances in which an unemployed person may be. OECD (courtesy of OECD Social Policy Division).
[b] Consolidated central government gross debt as a fraction of GDP (Franzese, 1998).
[c] Total union membership (less self-employed) weighted by total dependent workforce, European countries from Ebbinghaus and Visser (2000). Data for Australia, Canada, Japan, and US from Golden et al. (1998).
[d] (Total exports of goods and services + total imports of goods and services)/GDP. OECD Main Economic Indicators, online access.
[e] *Left* = 1 if there is right-wing domination in both government and parliament; = 2 if right-wing or center parties make up between 33.3% and 66.6% of government; = 3 if center parties make up 50% or more of government; = 4 if left-wing or center parties make up between 33.3% and 66.6% of government; and = 5 if left-wing parties dominate the government. Woldendorp et al. (1998).

ployment and related welfare benefits.[25] Our model specification considers country fixed-effects and one-period lags of the independent variables, as well as a two-period lag of the dependent variable:[26]

$$BR_{i,t} = \gamma BR_{i,t-2} + \beta' X_{i,t-1} + \theta_i + \varepsilon_{i,t}, \tag{20}$$

where $X_{i,t-1}$ is a vector including measures of openness, political orientation of the government (not lagged), union density, government debt, and a variable constructed by interacting the openness and debt variable; θ_i is the country-specific effect; and $\varepsilon_{i,t}$ is a random disturbance term. These are then stacked for estimation as a panel. Table 1 gives definitions, sources, and predicted signs of the variables in $X_{i,t-1}$.[27] In addition, we consider several variations on sample and specification.[28] The results are reported in Table 2.[29]

Before considering our preferred specification, consider the specification in column (2) of Table 2. This contains the main variables with which we are concerned. As we showed in the previous section, both left-wing governments and widespread coverage of workers by union bargaining are predicted to raise unemployment benefits, and both of these results are clearly present. Our results on these variables are consistent with those in the large empirical literature in comparative political economy focusing on the link between labor market institutions, political orientation, and welfare-state outputs.[30] As suggested by our model, and consistent with the widely remarked link between openness to international trade and size of welfare-state interventions, we find a significant, positive relationship between the trade openness variable and the size of the unemployment benefit. Finally, since the government faces a balanced budget constraint in our model, we introduce a measure of the magnitude of debt as an indicator of how closely the constraint binds. The sign of the coefficient is negative, as predicted,

Table 2. *Determinants of Benefit Replacement Rates, 1963–95 (robust standard errors)*

	(1)	(2) No interaction	(3) Left lagged	(4) Contemporaneous	(5) With Italy
Left	0.260**	0.253**	0.162	0.257**	0.258**
	(0.106)	(0.115)	(0.121)	(0.103)	(0.105)
Union density	0.139***	0.133***	0.139***	0.158***	0.111**
	(0.046)	(0.052)	(0.046)	(0.041)	(0.047)
Openness	0.098***	0.044*	0.098***	0.102***	0.081**
	(0.034)	(0.027)	(0.036)	(0.035)	(0.035)
Government debt	0.043**	−0.015	0.043*	0.047**	0.025
	(0.022)	(0.018)	(0.023)	(0.023)	(0.019)
Openness*Debt*10	−0.007***		−0.007***	−0.007***	−0.006***
	(0.002)		(0.002)	(0.002)	(0.002)
Benefits(−2)	0.797***	0.812***	0.798***	0.782***	0.817***
	(0.072)	(0.072)	(0.072)	(0.066)	(0.079)
R^2	0.932	0.930	0.931	0.933	0.941
Observations	259	259	259	256	274

Notes: Benefits are lagged two years and *Left* is unlagged in all columns, except column (3) where *Left* is lagged one year. All other independent variables are lagged one year, except in column (4) where all variables are contemporaneous with the dependent variable. Column (5) adds Italy to the sample for the column (1) specification. ***,**,* denote significant at 1%, 5%, 10% level, respectively.

but it is not statistically significant. As in all specifications, the standard errors adjust for heteroskedasticity, and our tests reject the null of first- and second-order autocorrelation.

Now consider column (1) of Table 2, which contains the results for our preferred specification. The interpretations of our political orientation and union density variables are the same; but with the introduction of the interaction variable, which is highly significant though quantitatively small, the interpretation of trade openness and government debt become more delicate.[31] Specifically, the values of the coefficients on openness and government debt now vary with each other's levels. That is, they describe conditional relationships, not unconditional ones. In this case, the negative interaction term captures the notion that, at any given level of openness to trade, a standard deviation increase in the government debt to GDP ratio lowers the response of the benefit replacement rate to openness (i.e., the conditional slope) by about 1.1 percentage points (i.e., −0.0007 × 58.338 × 27.132). Having accounted for this relationship, we are concerned that the estimate of a positive relationship between the unemployment benefit and debt may reflect endogeneity problems that will need to be dealt with in future work on this topic. The remaining specifications of the model yield essentially the same results. Consequently, we find the empirical results reported in Table 2 to be quite consistent with the theoretical approach adopted in sections 4 and 5 of this paper.

7. Conclusions

We have argued that standard ways of looking at the link between globalization and labor markets, which consistently find small or zero effects, by focusing on what we have called direct effects, might obscure significant indirect effects. In addition to providing a review of research suggesting the significance of these indirect effects, we have constructed a model in which institutional features of the labor market help to explain observed trends in public insurance policies. That is, where related work has focused on the ways in which trade creates an outside option for domestic capital, we examined the link between trade and welfare-state provision. In our model, when wage bargaining is extremely decentralized, the lobbying influence of unions allied with the lobbying activities of employers encourages policymakers to ease tax burdens and cap increases in unemployment benefits. When the risk of unemployment is lower and collective bargaining is more centralized, workers prefer contracts with high unemployment risk and high wages, and this serves to increase the demand for publicly provided unemployment insurance. We then examined the impact of increased trade (in this case a reduction in the tariff) on the overall equilibrium. Trade has the effect of increasing sectoral unemployment, reducing the power of unions and increasing the demand for welfare-state provision. The particular channel of constraint is the budget deficit. The results of our empirical work are strongly consistent with the main predictions of the model.

We consider the results presented here to be sufficiently strong to support increased study of the indirect effects that are central to our story. We think several extensions are well worth considering. First, our model of lobbying is very simple—only organized labor lobbies and all groups are equally valued by government. Both of these assumptions should be examined. We clearly need to consider either politically active capital or a strong preference for capital in the government's objective function. As we note in section 3, a considerable body of research suggests that political valence (e.g., pro-labor/pro-capital) of the party in power is an important intervening variable in the relationship between globalization and sustainability of welfare states. In addition, it is not at all clear that trade is the empirically most significant force of globalization in determining these indirect effects. Given that the budget constraint plays an essential role here, it seems quite likely that international financial globalization should be considered in greater detail. We hope to pursue both of these in future work.

Appendix

Derivation of Comparative Statics in Proposition 1

Solving equations (7b) and (8) we have

$$w = \frac{(\gamma + \alpha l)c^v}{B} \quad \text{and} \quad \frac{f}{n} = \frac{(\gamma + l)(1 + t)c^v}{Bp},$$

where the elasticity of output is $\alpha = nf_n/f$, $l = (n - m)/n$ and $B = \gamma + \alpha l - (1 - \alpha)\delta l > 0$. It follows that

$$w_{c^v} = \frac{(\gamma + 1)\gamma + (\gamma + l)\alpha l}{y} > 0; \quad n_{c^v} = \frac{-(\gamma + l)Bn}{(1 - \alpha)yc^v} < 0; \quad w_p = \frac{(1 - l)\delta\gamma f}{yn} \geq 0;$$

$$n_p = \frac{(\gamma + 1)B(1 + t)n}{(1 - \alpha)yp} > 0; \quad w_\delta = \frac{w_{c^u}(1 - \alpha)lw}{(\gamma + \alpha l)} > 0; \quad n_d = \frac{-(\gamma + l)nl}{y} < 0;$$

$$w_\gamma = \frac{-(1 - \alpha)\delta lpf}{y(1 + t)n} < 0; \quad n_\gamma = \frac{(1 + \delta)nl}{y} > 0; \quad w_m = \frac{\gamma w_\gamma}{nl} < 0; \quad n_m = \frac{\gamma n_\gamma}{nl} > 0;$$

where $y = (\gamma + l)B + (1 - l)(1 + \delta)\gamma > 0$. Furthermore, it follows that

$$w_{p^*} = \frac{(1+\tau)w_p}{(1+t)} \geq 0; \quad w_\tau = \frac{p^*w_p}{(1+t)} \geq 0; \quad w_t = \frac{-pw_p}{(1+t)^2} \leq 0; \quad n_{p^*} = \frac{(1+\tau)n_p}{(1+t)} \geq 0;$$

$$n_\tau = \frac{p^*n_p}{(1+t)} \geq 0; \quad n_t = \frac{-pn_p}{(1+t)^2} \leq 0.$$

Derivation of Equation (15)

Differentiating equations (12) to (14), using the results listed in the above subsection, and simplifying we have

$$V_b^k = \frac{-[(1-l)\gamma + (\gamma + l)\alpha l]n}{y} < 0, \quad V_b^u = mw_{cu} > 0,$$

$$V_b^n = \frac{[(\gamma + 1)\gamma + (\gamma + l)\alpha l - (\gamma + l)\delta]nl}{y} + (1 - n).$$

Proof of Proposition 2

The solution to the maximization of equation (18) is

$$\Omega_b = (p^*f_n - \kappa)n_b = 0. \tag{A1}$$

When benefits are financed out of general revenues, the policymaker chooses b to maximize

$$\Omega(b) = p^*f(n(b)) + (1 - n(b))(b + \kappa). \tag{A2}$$

The solution is given by

$$\Omega_b = (p^*f_n - \kappa) - b + \frac{(1-n)}{n_b} = 0. \tag{A3}$$

Comparison with equation (A1), and recalling that $n_b < 0$, yields part (i) of the proposition.

Next, use the first-order conditions (equations (7a) and (7b)) and the expression for the balanced-budget constraint (equation (11)) to obtain

$$b^o = \frac{(1-\alpha)\kappa n}{\alpha(\gamma + l)}\left[\frac{(\gamma + \alpha l)(\gamma - \delta l) - Bl\tau}{B + n(1-\alpha)\delta l}\right], \tag{A4}$$

where $B = \gamma + \alpha l - (1 - \alpha)\delta l > 0$. Part (ii) of the proposition follows. $\square$

Derivation of Comparative Statics in Corollary 1

From equation (A1), and using the results from above, the comparative statics in part (i) follow directly. Next, when tariff revenues are not used to finance b, then the policymaker's objective is $\Omega(b) = pf(n(b)) + (1 - n(b))\kappa$, rather than equation (18). Total differentiation of $(pf_n - \kappa)n_b = 0$ yields

$$b_{p*} = \frac{-(1-l)(1+\delta)\gamma c^{v}}{(\gamma+l)Bp*} \leq 0. \tag{A5}$$

Total differentiation of equation (A1) yields

$$b_{p*} = \frac{-(1-l)(1+\delta)\gamma c^{v}}{(\gamma+l)Bp*} \leq 0 \quad \text{and} \quad b_{\tau} = \frac{-n_{\tau}}{n_{b}} > 0. \tag{A6}$$

In the case of an import tariff or an export subsidy, $n_{\tau} > 0$. In the case of an import subsidy or an export tax, $n_{\tau} < 0$. Parts (ii) and (iii) follow.

Proof of Proposition 3

The solution to maximization of equation (19) is

$$a(p*f_{n} - \kappa)n_{b} = -mw_{b}. \tag{A7}$$

Defining $\varepsilon_{w} = bw_{b}/w > 0$ and $\varepsilon_{n} = bn_{b}/n < 0$, equation (A7) can be rewritten as

$$p*f_{n} = \kappa - \frac{(1-l)w\varepsilon_{w}}{a\varepsilon_{n}}. \tag{A8}$$

Comparison with equation (A1), and noting that f_{n} increases in b, yields the proposition. $\qquad\qquad\qquad\qquad\qquad\qquad\qquad\qquad\qquad\qquad\qquad\qquad\qquad\qquad\square$

References

Aaberge, R., T. Wennemo, A. Bjorklund, M. Jantti, P. J. Pedersen, and N. Smith, "Unemployment Shocks and Income Distribution: How Did the Nordic Countries Fare During their Crises?" *Scandinavian Journal of Economics* 102 (2000):77–99.

Acemoglu, D. and R. Shimer, "Efficient Unemployment Insurance," *Journal of Political Economy* 107 (1999):893–928.

Alesina, A. and D. Rodrik, "Distributive Politics and Economic Growth," *Quarterly Journal of Economics* 109 (1994):465–90.

Baldwin, R. and G. Cain, "Shifts in Relative US Wages: the Role of Trade, Technology and Factor Endowments," *Review of Economics and Statistics* 82 (2000):580–95.

Benhabib, J., R. Rogerson, and R. Wright, "Homework in Macroeconomics: Household Production and Aggregate Fluctuations," *Journal of Political Economy* 99 (1991):1166–87.

Bernheim, B. D. and M. D. Whinston, "Menu Auctions, Resource Allocation, and Economic Influence," *Quarterly Journal of Economics* 101 (1986):1–31.

Blank, R. M. and R. B. Freeman, "Evaluating the Connection between Social Protection and Economic Flexibility," in R. M. Blank (ed.), *Social Protection versus Economic Flexibility*, Chicago: University of Chicago Press (1994):21–41.

Bordo, M., B. Eichengreen, and D. Irwin, "Is Globalization Today Really Different than Globalization a Hundred Years Ago?" *Brookings Trade Forum—1999*, Washington, DC: Brookings Institution (1999):1–72.

Calmfors, L., "Centralisation of Wage Bargaining and Macroeconomic Performance: a Survey," *OECD Economic Studies* 21 (1993):161–91.

Calmfors, L. and J. Driffill, "Bargaining Structure, Corporatism and Macroeconomic Performance," *Economic Policy* 6 (1988):14–61.

Carruth, A. A. and A. J. Oswald, "On Union Preferences and Labour Market Models: Insiders and Outsiders," *Economic Journal* 97 (1987):431–45.

Casamatta, G., H. Cremer, and P. Pestieau, "Political Sustainability and the Design of Social Insurance," *Journal of Public Economics* 75 (2000):341–64.

Caves, R., "International Corporations: the Industrial Economics of Foreign Investment," *Economica* 38 (1971):1–27.

Clark, A. and A. J. Oswald, "Trade Union Utility Functions: a Survey of Union Leaders' Views," *Industrial Relations* 32 (1993):391–423.

Danthine, J. P. and J. Hunt, "Wage Bargaining Structure, Employment and Economic Integration," *Economic Journal* 104 (1994):528–41.

Deardorff, A., "Fragmentation across Cones," in S. W. Arndt and H. Kierzkowski (eds.), *Fragmentation: New Production Patterns in the World Economy*, Oxford: OUP (2001):35–51.

Doornik, J., D. Hendry, M. Arellano, and S. Bond, "PcGive, Panel Data Models," in J. Doornik and D. Hendry (eds.), *Econometric Modelling Using PcGive*, Vol. III, London: Timberlake Consultants Ltd (2001).

Ebbinghaus, B. and J. Visser (eds.), *Trade Unions in Western Europe since 1945*, London: Macmillan (2000).

Ehrenberg, R. G., *Labor Markets and Integrating National Economies*, Washington, DC: Brookings Institution (1994).

Evans, P., "The Eclipse of the State: Reflections on Stateness in an Era of Globalization," *World Politics* 50 (1997):62–87.

Farber, H. S., "The Analysis of Union Behavior," in O. Ashenfelter and R. Layard (eds.), *Handbook of Labor Economics*, Vol. 2, New York: Elsevier Science (1986):1039–89.

Feenstra, R., "Integration of Trade and Disintegration of Production in the Global Economy," *Journal of Economic Perspectives* 12 (1998):31–50.

Feenstra, R. and G. Hanson, "The Impact of Outsourcing and High Technology Capital on Wages: Estimates for the US, 1979–1990," *Quarterly Journal of Economics* 114 (1999):907–40.

Franzese, Jr, R. J., "The Political Economy of Public Debt: an Empirical Examination of the OECD Postwar Experience," paper for the Wallis Conference on Political Economy, Northwestern University (1998).

Friedrich, R., "In Defense of Multiplicative Terms in Multiple Regression Equations," *American Journal of Political Science* 26 (1982):797–833.

Fredriksson, P. G. and N. Gaston, "The 'Greening' of Trade Unions and the Demand for Eco-Taxes," *European Journal of Political Economy* 15 (1999):663–86.

———, "Environmental Governance in Federal Systems: the Effects of Capital Competition and Lobby Groups," *Economic Inquiry* 38 (2000):501–14.

Fredriksson, P. G. and J. Svensson, "Political Instability, Corruption and Policy Formation: the Case of Environmental Policy," *Journal of Public Economics* 87 (2003):1383–405.

Freeman, R. B., "War of the Models: Which Labour Market Institutions for the 21st Century?" *Labour Economics* 5 (1998):1–24.

Garrett, G., *Partisan Politics in the Global Economy*, Cambridge: Cambridge University Press (1998).

Gaston, N. and D. Nelson, "Unions and the Decentralisation of Collective Bargaining in a Globalising World," *Journal of Economic Integration* 17 (2002):377–96.

Gaston, N. and D. Nelson, "The Employment and Wage Effects of Immigration: Trade and Labour Economics Perspectives," in D. Greenaway, R. Upward, and K. Wakelin (eds.), *Trade, Investment, Migration and Labour Market Adjustment*, Basingstoke: Palgrave Macmillan, (2002):201–35.

Goldberg, P. K. and G. Maggi, "Protection for Sale: an Empirical Investigation," *American Economic Review* 89 (1999):1135–55.

Golden M., M. Wallerstein, and P. Lange, "Union Centralization Among Advanced Industrial Societies," National Science Foundation (1998).

Gottschalk, P. and T. M. Smeeding, "Cross-national Comparisons of Earnings and Income Inequality," *Journal of Economic Literature* 35 (1997):633–87.

Grossman, G. M. and E. Helpman, "Protection for Sale," *American Economic Review* 84 (1994):833–50.

Hall, H. K. and D. Nelson, "Institutional Structure and the Political Economy of Protection: Administered versus Legislated Protection," *Economics and Politics* 4 (1992):61–77.

————, "The Peculiar Political Economy of NAFTA," manuscript, Murphy Institute of Political Economy (2001).

Haskel, J., B. Kersley, and C. Martin, "Labour Market Flexibility and Employment Adjustment: Micro Evidence from UK Establishments," *Oxford Economic Papers* 49 (1997):362–79.

Helpman, E., "A Simple Theory of International Trade with Multinational Corporations," *Journal of Political Economy* 92 (1984):451–71.

Huber, E. and J. Stephens, "Internationalization and the Social Democratic Model," *Comparative Political Studies* 31 (1998):353–97.

Hymer, S., *The International Operations of National Firms: a Study of Direct Foreign Investment*, Cambridge, MA: MIT Press (1960).

Jones, R. and H. Kierzkowski, "A Framework for Fragmentation," in S. Arndt and H. Kierzkowski (eds.), *Fragmentation: New Production Patterns in the World Economy*, New York: Oxford University Press (2001):17–34.

Katzenstein, P., *Small States in World Markets*, Ithaca: Cornell University Press (1985).

Kau, J. B. and P. H. Rubin, "The Impact of Labor Unions on the Passage of Economic Legislation," *Journal of Labor Research* 2 (1981):133–45.

Kohler, W., "A Specific-factors View on Outsourcing," *North American Journal of Economics and Finance* 12 (2001):31–53.

Koskela, E. and R. Schöb, "Alleviating Unemployment: the Case for Green Tax Reforms," *European Economic Review* 43 (1999):1723–46.

Krugman, P., "Domestic Policies in a Global Economy," *Brookings Trade Forum—1999*, Washington, DC: Brookings Institution (1999):73–93.

Leamer, E., "The Heckscher–Ohlin Model in Theory and Practice," *Princeton Studies in International Finance* 77 (1995).

Martin, J., "Measures of Replacement Rates for the Purpose of International Comparisons: a Note," *OECD Economic Studies* 26 (1996):99–115.

Mayer, F., *Interpreting NAFTA: the Science and Art of Political Analysis*, New York: Columbia University Press (1998).

Organisation for Economic Co-operation and Development (OECD), *Employment Outlook*, Paris: OECD (1997).

Pemberton, J., "A 'Managerial' Model of the Trade Union," *Economic Journal* 98 (1988):755–71.

Persson, T., "Do Political Institutions Shape Economic Policy?" *Econometrica* 70 (2002):883–905.

Persson, T. and G. Tabellini, "Is Inequality Harmful for Growth?" *American Economic Review* 84 (1994):600–21.

————, "Political Economics and Public Finance," in A. J. Auerbach and M. Feldstein (eds.), *Handbook of Public Economics*, Vol. 3, Amsterdam: North-Holland (2002).

Rama, M. and G. Tabellini, "Lobbying by Capital and Labor over Trade and Labor Market Policies," *European Economic Review* 42 (1998):1295–316.

Rodrik, D., "Why Do More Open Economies Have Bigger Governments?" *Journal of Political Economy* 106 (1998):997–1032.

Rowthorn, R. E., "Centralisation, Employment and Wage Dispersion," *Economic Journal* 102 (1992):506–23.

Saint-Paul, G., "Exploring the Political Economy of Labour Market Institutions," *Economic Policy* 23 (1996):263–315.

Saint-Paul, G. and T. Verdier, "Inequality, Redistribution and Growth: a Challenge to the Conventional Political Economy Approach," *European Economic Review* 40 (1996):719–28.

Shleifer, A. and R. W. Vishny, "Corruption," *Quarterly Journal of Economics* 108 (1993):599–617.

Slaughter, M., "What Are the Results of Product–Price Studies and What Can We Learn from Their Differences?" in R. Feenstra (ed.), *The Impact of International Trade on Wages*, Chicago: University of Chicago Press/NBER (2000):129–65.

Steinmo, S., "The End of Redistribution? International Pressures and Domestic Tax Policy Choices," *Challenge* 37 (1994):9–18.

Swank, D., *Global Capital, Political Institutions, and Policy Changes in Developed Welfare States*, Cambridge: Cambridge University Press (2002).

Tanzi, V., *Taxation in an Integrating World*, Washington, DC: Brookings Institution (1995).

Vousden, N., *Economics of Trade Protection*, Cambridge: Cambridge University Press (1990).

Woldendorp J., H. Keman, and I. Budge, "Party Government in 20 democracies: an Update (1990–1995)," *European Journal of Political Research* 33(1) (1998):125–64.

Zweimüller, J. and E. Barth, "Bargaining Structure, Wage Determination, and Wage Dispersion in 6 OECD Countries," *Kyklos* 47 (1994):81–93.

Notes

1. Hall and Nelson (2001) develop a simple, preliminary analysis of this sort.

2. As Gaston and Nelson (2002) argue, the one-sector model used by labor economists has the virtue of providing clear guidance for empirical work, but must introduce the effect of standard globalization shocks (trade, immigration, foreign direct investment) in an essentially ad hoc way. That is, they shift either demand or supply, but there is no essential equilibrium relationship between globalization and the labor market.

3. The surveys of this literature are now almost sufficiently numerous to warrant a survey of their own. We make do with a reference to Slaughter's (2000) survey of work explicitly rooted in the Stolper–Samuelson theorem.

4. Consider a two-good model in which one sector decides to outsource. Either the original sector disappears, producing a three-good model (i.e., the original good unchanged good, and the two new sectors created by splitting the old technology) or a four-good model (if some firms continue to produce the final good under a unified technology). In either case, the dimensionality of both the price vector and the technology matrix must change, rendering standard comparative static methods problematic.

5. See Persson (2002) for a recent discussion with application to macroeconomic policy, and Hall and Nelson (1992) give an early institutional comparative static analysis of trade policy.

6. Rama and Tabellini (1998) refer to these as the "formal" and informal" sectors of the economy.

7. Most OECD countries rely on payroll taxes to fully, or to partially, fund their unemployment insurance systems (Ehrenberg, 1994; Koskela and Schöb, 1999).

8. If aggregate imports are negative, then $\tau > 0$ can be interpreted as an export subsidy. Similarly, if $\tau < 0$, then τ can be interpreted as an import subsidy if aggregate imports are positive, or as an export tax if aggregate imports are negative.

9. Strictly speaking, m denotes the fallback utility level of the union leadership should the sector's employees quit union membership. For example, if the union operates in more than one sector of the economy, it represents union membership in those other sectors (see Pemberton, 1988, and discussion below). In the present context, we assume that there are m incumbent workers employed elsewhere in the organization. We follow Pemberton (1988) and Burda (1997) in assuming that $n > m$, so that $(n - m)$ represents the incremental utility gain to the union leadership from the bargaining agreement.

10. Farber (1986, p. 1063) summarizing his own earlier research on the United Mine Workers states that the union "seems to have placed more weight on employment relative to compensation than rent-maximization would imply." On the other hand, Clark and Oswald (1993) show that unions often care more about wages than employment.

11. It is debatable whether firms and unions negotiate *both* wages and employment or just wages alone. Empirical evidence in favor of efficient bargaining is mixed (Farber, 1986, p. 1067). On the other hand, negotiation over work rules may ensure that bargains are efficient. Notwithstanding, in this paper when unions and firms agree to wage–employment combinations on the firm's labor demand curve is given by the special case $\gamma = 0$.

12. Haskel et al. (1997) show that increasing labor market flexibility in the United Kingdom has resulted in labor input being more closely aligned to the business cycle. This implies that

wage and employment contracts lie closer to the marginal revenue product or demand-for-labor curve.

13. Given our focus on indirect effects of globalization in the context of a politically active union, some form of lobbying model is clearly the preferred political-economy framework. Grossman and Helpman's (1994) implementation of the menu auction model is particularly attractive because it makes the government an active participant in the political process (unlike previous lobbying models) as well as the organized interests (unlike the political-response-function models). However, we are well aware that both political-response-function models and lobbying models with a passive register government yield essentially the same qualitative results.

14. Goldberg and Maggi (1999) emphasize that the Grossman–Helpman formulation is formally equivalent to choosing the unemployment benefit that maximizes the joint surplus of all the parties involved.

15. Since employment is affected by both taxes and unemployment benefits, there are certain permissible values of both t and b for our problem to be well-defined. To illustrate, suppose that tariff revenues are not used to finance benefits, that we have a constant elasticity of production, and that $l = 1$. We require that $bg_n n_t < 1$, where $g(n) = (1 - n)(nw)^{-1}$, which implies that $t(1 + t)^{-1} < (1 - \alpha)(1 - n)$. The condition for the tax rate also ensures that we are on the Laffer-efficient side of the tax revenue function. This requires that the tax elasticity of employment is not "too" elastic; i.e., $n_t t n^{-1} > -1$ (or that $t(1 + t)^{-1} < (1 - \alpha)$).

16. The risk neutrality allows us to focus on the political contestability of unemployment benefits, rather than on the role of benefits as providing insurance, per se. (See also note 19, below.) We also leave aside the issue of whether unemployment insurance benefits might optimally be provided privately, rather than socially; see Casamatta et al. (2000).

17. From equation (7b), assuming $l = 1$, the slope of the NBC is $-(1 - \alpha)wn^{-1}$; and from equation (8), the slope of the indifference curve evaluated at (w^*, n^*) is $-(1 - \alpha)\delta w[(\gamma + \alpha)n]^{-1}$ (using equations (7b) and (8) to simplify). Comparing the two expressions, the NBC has a relatively steeper slope when $\gamma + \alpha > \delta$. In addition, evaluated at (w^*, n^*), the slope of the union leadership's indifference curve has a steeper slope than the worker's indifference curve as long as $\gamma > \delta$; i.e., when the union leaders are relatively more concerned with employment growth than with higher wages.

18. The maximand is the same regardless of whether τ is an export tax or subsidy or an import tariff or subsidy. See note 14.

19. Acemoglu and Shimer (1999) focus on the effects of unemployment benefits on workers' job search behavior. They show that firms may be willing to invest more in high-risk capital if the costs of searching for high-wage/high-unemployment-risk jobs by risk-averse workers are lowered by positive levels of unemployment insurance. An increase in the value of nonmarket time would have similar effects.

20. Such budgetary considerations may provide a theoretical explanation for Blank and Freeman's (1994) argument that some European countries, in the face of increased international competition, tried to reduce the "generosity" of their social programs.

21. In contrast, when an import subsidy is lowered there is pressure on benefits to be reduced due to higher internal prices, but there is also a relaxation of the government's balanced-budget constraint making the payment of more generous benefits possible. (Likewise, there are offsetting effects for export taxes and subsidies.)

22. It should be clear that asymmetric weighting of groups makes for a more complex relationship.

23. Some authors have interpreted a as measuring a policymaker's incorruptibility or the willingness of a government to adhere to welfare-maximizing policies (Shleifer and Vishny, 1993; Fredriksson and Svensson, 2003). However, in the context of pluralist democracies like those of the OECD, which make up our empirical sample, this is clearly a problematic interpretation of public political effort by organized groups.

24. For example, the globalization of capital markets and the increased mobility of capital, coupled with the fact that lobbying and political contributions are costly, may reduce the attractiveness of lobbying for capital owners (Fredriksson and Gaston, 2000). However, this sort of

argument is usually associated with governments being strongly pro-capital as well—i.e., fear of alienating "the capital market" induces governments to adopt market conforming regulation, low rates of capital taxation, etc.

25. The OECD produces these data for odd-numbered years from 1961 to 1999. Martin (1996) provides a detailed description of this variable. The OECD Directorate for Education, Employ-ment, Labour and Social Affairs, Social Policy Division, was kind enough to provide these data.

26. The lag of the dependent variable is a control for first-order autocorrelation. We are con-strained to use a two-year lag because the variable is calculated only biennially.

27. Our sample countries are essentially the high-income OECD countries for which we could get at least 10 years of data: Australia, Austria, Belgium, Canada, Denmark, Finland, France, Germany, Ireland, Italy, Japan, Netherlands, Norway, Sweden, Switzerland, UK, and US. In fact, our preferred specification also excludes Italy as a result of problems with the dependent vari-able (see the annex to Martin, 1996). We initially suspected that there might be problems with the German data as a result of unification, but exclusion of Germany has no qualitative effect, and only very small quantitative effects, on our results.

28. We considered random-effects specifications of all the reported fixed-effects specifications. In addition to the usual problems with interpreting random effects, in all but one case the Hausman test rejected the random-effects specification in favor of the fixed-effects specifica-tion.

29. The reported estimates were produced in PcGive, using the panel data models module (Doornik et al., 2001). We checked the results by estimating the models in TSP and EViews with no significant differences in results. That is, although these packages use somewhat different cor-rections to the standard errors, the qualitative and quantitative differences in significance were small.

30. See the discussions in Garrett (1998) and Swank (2002).

31. See Friedrich (1982) for an extended discussion of the use of interaction terms and their interpretation.

Chapter 4

Aspects of International Fragmentation

Wilhelm Kohler

1. Introduction

The traditional view of internationalization rests on a clear distinction between *produced* commodities and *primary* factors. According to this view, the principle of international arbitrage operates on goods prices via international exchange of goods, based on a given and well-defined underlying value-added process. In addition, it operates on factor prices—directly via international factor movements, and indirectly via the factor-price effects of trade. However, recent developments appear to challenge this view. Improvements in communications technology as well as reductions of formal and technical barriers to trade gave rise to a new vehicle of internationalization where international arbitrage cuts value-added processes into ever smaller slices produced in different locations (Jones and Kierzkowski, 1990; Harris, 1995). This blurs the distinction between commodity markets and trade on the one hand, and factor movements on the other. What we observe, then, is an international fragmentation of value-added processes which have hitherto been carried out in an integrated way within certain countries. A term often used synonymously is "international outsourcing," indicating that single components of a value-added process are shifted to foreign sources where they can be carried out at lower cost. As will become evident below, the phenomenon should not simply be seen as trade in established markets for intermediate goods. The defining feature is that firms are engaged in "fine-tuning" the locational pattern of increasingly fragmented production processes to the international pattern of (unequal) factor prices. In contrast to traditional trade theory, a certain value-added process then no longer takes place under a uniform set of factor prices, but draws on different factor markets for different fragments. The theoretical challenge is to analyze the driving forces and effects of this *process* of increasing international fragmentation. It is quite obvious that this goes beyond extending trade theory to include trade on *established* markets of existing intermediate goods, which is hardly new, and indeed a largely accomplished task. Essentially, international fragmentation extends the realm of international arbitrage into new ground by "atomizing" production processes. This may give rise to *new* markets, or the emergence of *multinational firms*. In either case, the phenomenon we are looking at will often appear more like a "regime shift" than a continuous process, which requires new tools of analysis (Markusen, 2002).

There is a sizable body of literature demonstrating the empirical significance and theoretical implications of international fragmentation in the recent episode of economic globalization.[1] In an early paper, Jones and Kierzkowski (1990) pointed out that international fragmentation should be beneficial in that it enhances the gains from trade. Krugman (1995) strikes a somewhat less optimistic tone, arguing that it may contribute to the decline of wages for low-skilled labor in industrialized countries. This claim has been further substantiated, both theoretically and empirically, by Feenstra and Hanson (1996, 1997, 1999). However, there is no clear-cut theoretical result supporting the view that international fragmentation will generally harm low-skilled labor in industrial countries, in absolute terms or relative to high-skilled labor. Thus, Arndt (1997, 1999) argues that labor may benefit, relative to capital, from outsourcing in the US–Mexican context, while papers by Venables (1999), Deardorff (2001a,b), and Jones and Kierzkowski (2001a,b) point to a multiplicity of possible factor price effects from fragmentation. In Kohler (2003), I made an effort to derive general results identifying the common forces at work in all of these cases.

For the policymaker, international fragmentation sometimes arises in a pretty fearsome way in that certain regions all of a sudden face the spectre of losing whole components of value-added chains in certain industries which they may perceive as cornerstones of their economies. There will often be a temptation to "do something about it," particularly with respect to local labor markets. In search of an adequate policy response, it is important to distinguish between *efficiency* (or welfare) aspects and *distributional* aspects of international fragmentation. A crucial question relevant on both accounts relates to employment. If labor which is set free due to outsourcing remains permanently unemployed, there is a clear case for a defensive policy stance, even from an efficiency point of view, trying in one way or another to prevent or restrict outsourcing. But whether such unemployment is permanent is not exogenous to policy. Much depends on labor market institutions, hence policy should not simply equate jobs lost to outsourcing with a rise in unemployment and a loss in output. The relevant question to ask is whether, under given labor market institutions, alternative employment of the resources set free through outsourcing generates value-added which fully compensates for the value-added that is lost to outsourcing. If the answer is yes, then the economy (or region) as a whole gains.

This paper looks into this question, assuming a perfect labor market and using the well-known specific-factors model pioneered by Jones (1971). That model is well established as a powerful workhorse to address distributional issues. As will become apparent below, it proves a very valuable tool also for the aforementioned efficiency question, while retaining its distributional insights. The setup is one where international fragmentation is driven by a foreign location advantage due to relatively cheap labor. I will show that if international fragmentation takes place without any element of nonconvexity in production, then it causes an efficiency gain which is analogous to the so-called immigration surplus of inward migration. However, contrary to immigration, and in contrast to a widespread view on globalization, with outsourcing there is no positive relationship between the magnitude of that gain and the amount of pain that comes in the form of potentially troublesome income distribution. Instead, the larger the gain, the more moderate the redistribution effect. I will then show that, even under a well-functioning labor market bar of any rigidities, outsourcing may cause an efficiency loss, if technology features a specific form of nonconvexity. The nonconvexity considered is one where the specific factor used in the disintegrated component of value-added is a *fixed input*. I shall identify the crucial conditions responsible for whether or not the negative welfare result obtains. Among the surprising results, I find that these conditions are more likely to be met if the wage gap between the domestic and the foreign economy is small. This is in contrast to the often held view that outsourcing poses a particular threat if this gap is large. However, the smaller this gap, the more likely will outsourcing cause the domestic wage rate to even fall below the foreign wage rate. I shall analyze international fragmentation as a two-stage game, whereby in stage one firms decide on where to locate their specific asset, and in stage two they choose optimal employment of domestic and foreign labor. The model endogenously determines the domestic wage rate and the share of domestic firms choosing a fragmented production mode.

2. Basic Model of International Fragmentation

A defining feature of international fragmentation is that it allows firms to draw on cheaper foreign factors for certain fragments of their value-added process. Outsourcing such fragments to foreign factor markets makes production less costly and should, therefore, mandate higher returns to domestic factors as a whole. However, the reallocation of domestic factors attendant upon such outsourcing will normally imply unequal domestic factor price effects, and under certain conditions it may also imply an overall welfare loss. This section sets the stage for the analysis by first characterizing a general equilibrium for a case where fragmentation is a technological possibility, but does not arise for a lack of economic incentives. Introducing such incentives in the form of lower costs of international fragmentation gives rise to a new domestic equilibrium, the details of which depend on the precise circumstances under which fragmentation takes place. Subsequent sections will explore these details and investigate the welfare and distributional aspects of international fragmentation by means of a comparative static analysis of the two equilibria.

Fragmentation is easier in some sectors than in others. Suppose, therefore, that the domestic economy features two sectors, each using mobile labor and specific capital, and each facing a given price for its output on perfectly competitive world markets. By assumption, fragmentation is possible only in sector 1 where technology is described by the following separable production function:

$$Y^1 = Y^1[F_A^1(L_A^1, \overline{K}_A^1), F_B^1(L_B^1, \overline{K}_B^1)], \tag{1}$$

where F_A^1 and F_B^1 denote two fragments, and L and K denote labor and capital. Production in sector 2 satisfies $Y^2 = Y^2(L^2, \overline{K}^2)$. I assume, to start with, that all production functions are concave. Nonconvexities in sector 1 will be considered in the next section.[2] A bar indicates exogenously given quantities, capital stocks are sector-specific, and in sector 1 also specific to individual fragments.

Treating good 2 as the *numéraire*, and using $\overline{p}^1$ to denote the relative price of good 1 and w for the domestic wage rate, employment in the two industries is governed by the following first-order conditions, where subscripts $j = A, B$ and L denote partial derivatives:

$$w = \overline{p}^1 Y_j^1[F_A^1(L_A^1, \overline{K}_A^1), F_B^1(L_B^1, \overline{K}_B^1)] \times F_{jL}^1(L_j^1, \overline{K}_j^1), \quad j = A, B \tag{2}$$

$$w = Y_L^2(L^2, \overline{K}^2). \tag{3}$$

These conditions require the usual equality between the wage rate and the marginal value-productivity of labor in all possible employments. Notice that the two fragments in sector 1 are treated separately in (2). Since we shall not consider changes in final goods prices, we may assume for simplicity that $\overline{p}^1 = 1$.

The two conditions (2) can be solved for L_A^1 and L_B^1 to yield two labor demand curves $L_A^1 = V_A^1(w, \overline{K}_A^1, \overline{K}_B^1)$ and $L_B^1 = V_B^1(w, \overline{K}_A^1, \overline{K}_B^1)$. These give profit-maximizing employment of labor in the two fragments of sector 1 as functions of the *common* wage rate and the fragment-specific capital stocks. They are downward-sloping in w, of course, and increasing in *both* capital stocks. Using $V^2(w, \overline{K}^2)$ for the labor demand curve in sector 2, we obtain the equilibrium wage rate w^* from

$$\overline{L} = V_A^1(w, \overline{K}_A^1, \overline{K}_B^1) + V_B^1(w, \overline{K}_A^1, \overline{K}_B^1) + V^2(w, \overline{K}^2), \tag{4}$$

where $\overline{L}$ denotes domestic labor endowment. I now write $V^1(w, \overline{K}_A^1, \overline{K}_B^1) = V_A^1(w, \overline{K}_A^1, \overline{K}_B^1) + V_B^1(w, \overline{K}_A^1, \overline{K}_B^1)$ for overall labor demand by industry 1 under *integrated* production, the term "integrated" meaning that both fragments are produced drawing on the *same* (domestic) labor market. In other words, the equilibrium wage rate w^* relates to a case where there is *no* international fragmentation of production. I shall use η_j^1 and η^2 to denote the elasticities of V_j^1 and V^2 with respect to w. Inserting w^* back into the first-order conditions (2) and (3), we obtain equilibrium employment levels $L^{1*} = L_A^{1*} + L_B^{1*}$ and $L^{2*} = \overline{L} - L^{1*}$.

The situation is depicted in the usual way by Figure 1, where the possibility of fragmentation is brought to the fore by drawing V_B^1 with its origin placed at L_A^{1*}. Equilibrium output in industry 1 is measured, in value terms, by the area $A^1BL^{1*}O^1$ or, equivalently, by the sum of areas $A^1B_A^1L_A^{1*}O^1$ (value generated by fragment A) and $A_B^1BL^{1*}L_A^{1*}$ (value generated by fragment B). It should be borne in mind, however, that each of the two marginal product schedules V_j^1 is subject to the other fragment being available in the optimal amount. This makes the case fundamentally different from a simple three-sector model.

I now turn to *international fragmentation*, assuming that outsourcing is restricted to fragment B. It is quite obvious from the introduction that international fragmentation bears a close resemblance to multinational firms, or foreign direct investment of the *vertical* type. Indeed the conceptual framework often used in the theory of multinational firms serves quite well to describe the nature and driving force of what I mean by the *process* of international fragmentation in this paper. The framework involves the celebrated trinity of ownership advantage, location advantage, and internalization advantage.[3] I assume that $\overline{K}_B^1$ confers an *ownership* advantage to domestic firms. We interpret $\overline{K}_B^1$ as a capital stock, but it could actually be any asset conferring such an ownership advantage (Markusen, 2002). The crucial point is that such an advantage rules out any foreign production of fragment B, independent of domestic sector 1 firms. Moreover, international fragmentation requires that the asset $\overline{K}_B^1$, or its services, be transferred to fragment B production facilities abroad. In other words, fragmentation arises with foreign direct investment.

I assume that there is a neighboring country which enjoys a *location* advantage with respect to fragment B, based on a relatively low wage rate. I do not model this neighboring economy explicitly, but simply assume that its wage rate is given. Moreover, I assume that there are prohibitive barriers to labor migration. For the initial equilibrium described above, I assume that additional costs of transport and communication involved in cross-border vertical fragmentation of production nullify this location advantage, whence fragmentation does not take place. The easiest interpretation is to assume that all such costs arise in the form of additional labor. Thus, assuming that foreign production of fragment B requires $1 + t$ units of labor for each effective unit of labor input, an effective location advantage for international fragmentation arises if, due to a fall in t, we observe $w^f = w^n(1 + t) < w^*$, where w^n is the given wage rate in

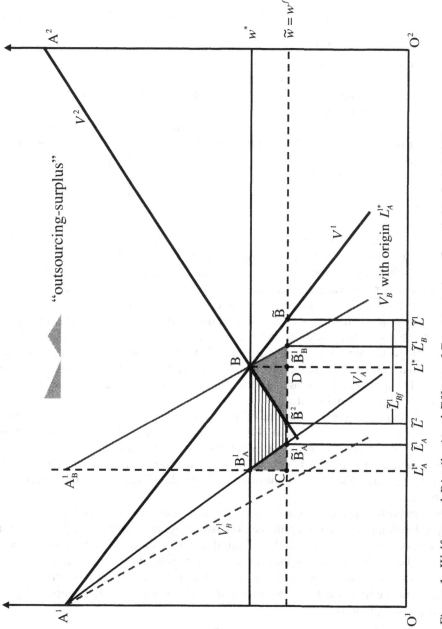

Figure 1. Welfare and Distributional Effects of Fragmentation; Case 1: No Indivisibility

the neighboring country.[4] It should be noticed that fragment B is part of a two-stage production process, deriving its economic value from production according to $Y^1[F_A^1(L_A^1, \overline{K}_A^1), F_B^1(L_B^1, \overline{K}_B^1)]$. Fragmentation, thus, is of the vertical type where low international barriers work in favor of a foreign location advantage, as opposed to horizontal FDI.[5] It is important that the ownership advantage of domestic firms only applies in relation to the neighboring country. Therefore, despite this advantage, domestic firms behave competitively on the world market where they face a given price for good 1. Put differently, the domestic and the neighboring foreign country are jointly small on world markets. Moreover, although one could make the stages of production explicit, it does not make any fundamental difference for our analysis whether we look at fragment B as a "downstream" or "upstream" activity.[6]

The location advantage still leaves open whether fragmentation is carried out by means of arm's-length transactions with foreign subcontractors, or internally within domestic firms' own hierarchies. For our purposes, this doesn't really matter, but as pointed out by Markusen (2002, p. 20), transferring assets relevant for the ownership advantage at arm's length will typically run the risk of "asset dissipation." This, in turn, confers an advantage to *internalization* and it seems reasonable to assume that fragmentation occurs with the emergence of multinational firms. But, as I said, the crucial element of the present approach is the ownership advantage as such, and not internalization.

With $w^f < w^*$, returns to fragment-B-type capital K_B^1 may obviously be increased by vertical fragmentation. Profit-maximizing firms will start investing part of their given assets $\overline{K}_B^1$ in the neighboring country, thereby shifting from integrated production to production under vertical fragmentation. What does the new equilibrium look like? Comparing this equilibrium with the case where the costs of fragmentation nullify the location advantage, what are the welfare and distribution effects of vertical fragmentation? In this section, I address these questions for the case where $F_B^1(L_B^1, \overline{K}_B^1)$ is concave. In particular, what I rule out is any indivisibility with respect to assets $\overline{K}_B^1$, meaning that vertical fragmentation may take place by outsourcing arbitrarily small amounts of fragment B. The subsequent section will look at a case where $\overline{K}_B^1$ is subject to a specific type of indivisibility.

I use a tilde to indicate equilibrium values under vertical fragmentation. As firms in sector 1 can now procure fragment B by drawing on foreign labor for a given wage rate $w^f < w^*$, it is clear that $\tilde{w} < w^*$. It seems that the distributional implication of vertical fragmentation is almost trivial: labor loses and capital owners in sector 1 gain. However, exploring the new equilibrium in more detail reveals further interesting insights.

A first important point to note is that, even if vertical fragmentation is not subject to any indivisibility, it need not pull the domestic wage rate all the way down to w^f. In other words, outsourcing is a rather limited form of indirect integration of labor markets. This is due to technology in sector 1 which implies that outsourcing of fragment B also affects domestic labor demand for fragment A. With vertical fragmentation, employment in the two fragments of sector 1 is governed by the following two equations:

$$w = Y_A^1[F_A^1(L_A^1, \overline{K}_A^1), F_B^1(L_B^1, \overline{K}_B^1)] \times F_{AL}^1(L_A^1, \overline{K}_A^1), \tag{5}$$

$$w^f = Y_B^1[F_A^1(L_A^1, \overline{K}_A^1), F_B^1(L_B^1, \overline{K}_B^1)] \times F_{BL}^1(L_B^1, \overline{K}_B^1). \tag{6}$$

Notice that these equations do *not* imply that domestic labor faces different wages in equilibrium. The point is that L_B^1 must not be equated with *domestic* employment. Indeed, only if the equilibrium wage rate $\tilde{w}$ is equal to w^f will equilibrium employment $\tilde{L}_B^1$ partly also involve domestic employment. Conversely, if $\tilde{w} > w^f$, then $\tilde{L}_B^1$ will entirely be *foreign* labor. A case where $\tilde{w} < w^f$ is, of course, ruled out in equilibrium since firms would face an incentive to replace domestic for foreign employment at the margin on fragment B. If such replacement can only occur subject to indivisibilities pertaining to the fragment B asset $\overline{K}_B^1$, then things are different, as we shall see in the subsequent section.

Whether or not the case $\tilde{w} > w^f$ arises depends on general-equilibrium interactions with sector 2 where employment is still governed by condition (3). It is convenient to work with reduced-form labor demand functions derived from (5) and (6). Solving these equations for L_A^1 we obtain

$$\tilde{L}_A^1 = \tilde{V}_A^1(w, w^f, \overline{K}_A^1, \overline{K}_B^1), \tag{7}$$

which gives *domestic* employment levels in fragment A for alternative domestic wage rates w, always assuming optimal response of employment (whether domestic or foreign) on fragment B at the wage rate w^f, which can in turn be described by the corresponding solution of (5) and (6) for L_B^1:[7]

$$\tilde{L}_B^1 = \tilde{V}_B^1(w, w^f, \overline{K}_A^1, \overline{K}_B^1). \tag{8}$$

Notice that $\tilde{V}_{Aw^f}^1 < 0$, since a higher foreign wage rate lowers foreign employment and thus the marginal productivity of domestic labor in fragment A. For a similar reason, $\tilde{V}_{Bw}^1 < 0$. Defining $\omega = w^f/w^* - 1$ as the percentage *wage gap* between the two neighboring economies, the condition under which vertical fragmentation leads to a wage rate $\tilde{w} > w^f$ may be approximated by

$$L_A^{1*}\eta_A^1\omega + L^{2*}\eta^2\omega > L_B^{1*}, \tag{9}$$

where a star indicates employment levels in the initial equilibrium, and where η_A^1 and η^2 are elasticities of V_A^1 and V^2, as defined above, evaluated at w^*.[8] The left-hand side gives the additional employment arising in fragment A of industry 1 and industry 2, if the domestic wage rate were to fall down to w^f. If this is larger than the employment lost due to outsourcing, then domestic labor market equilibrium requires $\tilde{w} > w^f$. Notice that by construction of our argument $\omega < 0$, and assuming normal labor demand schedules η_A^1 and η^2 are also negative. Condition (9) may be rewritten as

$$|\omega|^{-1} < \frac{L_A^{1*}}{L_B^{1*}}|\eta_A^1| + \frac{L^{2*}}{L_B^{1*}}|\eta^2|. \tag{10}$$

If this condition is met, then outsourcing, or the international division of labor on the level of fragments, is complete. For given labor demand elasticities, the wage gap must exceed a critical level for this to arise. Conversely, for a given wage gap, if labor demand elasticities in the "non-outsourcing" activities and their initial employment levels, relative to the incipient employment loss from outsourcing, are sufficiently large, then the domestic wage rate will not fall all the way down to w^f, and there will be no domestic employment in fragment B.[9] Notice that it is only when the domestic economy loses all of fragment B entirely that some of the initial wage gap remains. This may seem counterintuitive to the layman, but it is what trade theory leads us to expect: complete vertical specialization is consistent with a wage difference, while incomplete specialization implies wage equalization.

Notice also that incomplete vertical specialization also implies that foreign direct investment (FDI) is similarly incomplete, with part of $\bar{K}_B^1$ invested abroad and the rest domestically. The condition which governs this margin requires that the rental obtained on both types of investment must be the same. With homothetic technology, the shares of domestic employment and domestic investment in fragment B are the same.

Figure 1 depicts a case where condition (10) is violated and where, therefore, the vertical fragmentation equilibrium features $\tilde{w} = w^f$. Domestic employment in fragment A is at $\tilde{L}_A^1$, while sector 2 employs $\tilde{L}^2$ (measured from O^2), both at the equilibrium wage rate $\tilde{w} = w^f$. Total employment in fragment B is equal to the difference between overall labor use by sector 1 firms, $\tilde{L}^1$ (measured from O^1), and $\tilde{L}_A^1$. Of this labor use, also measured by $\tilde{L}_B^1$ (with origin at L_A^{1*}), $\tilde{L}_{Bf}^1$ is foreign labor, while $\tilde{L}_B^1 - \tilde{L}_{Bf}^1$ is domestic labor, whereby it is evident that $\tilde{L}_B^1 - \tilde{L}_{Bf}^1 + \tilde{L}_A^1 + \tilde{L}^2 = \bar{L}$ (full employment).

Figure 1 allows us to identify the *welfare effect* of vertical fragmentation. We must first note that domestic labor suffers an income loss equal to $(w^* - \tilde{w})\bar{L}$, all of which ends up as additional income to capital owned by domestic firms. In addition, however, domestic capital owners gain on inframarginal units of reallocated domestic labor, and on foreign labor. More specifically, the labor initially set free through outsourcing, once reallocated towards alternative domestic use, generates additional value-added in fragment A equal to the area $B_A^1\tilde{B}_A^1\tilde{L}_A^1L_A^{1*}$, and additional output in industry 2 equal to the area $B\tilde{B}^2\tilde{L}^2L^{1*}$. In addition, domestic and foreign labor taken together generate additional value-added in fragment B, measured by the area $B\tilde{B}_B^1\tilde{L}_B^1L^{1*}$.[10] Netting out the labor income which is lost on previous production of fragment B (and which does not show up as redistributed income to capital)—i.e., subtracting $B_A^1BL^{1*}L_A^{1*}$— we arrive at a net welfare gain to the domestic economy which is measured by the compound shaded triangles indicated in Figure 1. The welfare gain is somewhat less straightforward to measure diagrammatically, if outsourcing is complete and $\tilde{w} > w^f$, but essentially similar logic can be applied to establish a clear welfare gain also in this case.

This analysis is reminiscent of the well-known immigration surplus (Borjas, 1999). After all, outsourcing in this model is an indirect way of drawing on foreign labor. It is well known that the immigration surplus arises if foreign labor is employed according to a downward-sloping marginal product curve and is paid its marginal product.[11] In our case, what guarantees a "vertical fragmentation surplus" comparable to the immigration surplus is the presence of specific factors. There is an important difference, however. While the immigration surplus approaches zero if the domestic labor demand schedule becomes flat, as in the case of Rybczynski-type domestic re-allocation, the outsourcing surplus arising here is the larger, the larger the elasticities of labor demand in the alternative domestic employment of labor. This is readily seen from Figure 1, where the overall shaded area increases in size, if the slopes of V_A^1 and V^2 fall in absolute value. The difference is easily explained. The immigration surplus as usually portrayed assumes an exogenously given labor inflow, with wages adjusting endogenously. Here, we assume an exogenous wage differential $w^* - w^f$ to start with, and the quantity adjustments (extent of outsourcing as well as domestic labor reallocation) follow endogenously.

Putting the results obtained so far into a broader perspective, we can identify an important message. It is widely acknowledged that globalization may hold significant efficiency gains, but there is equally widespread concern that such gains may be associated with painful redistribution. Moreover, it is often argued that the larger the gains, the larger the pains.[12] Somewhat surprisingly, outsourcing in the present context is a form of globalization where this tension does not arise. Indeed, it is evident from Figure 1 that the larger the gain from international outsourcing, the *lower* the redistribution effect in the form of lower wage income. Suppose, for instance, that labor demand in sector 2 is perfectly elastic. Taking the nonfragmentation equilibrium with w^* as a reference point, the vertical fragmentation equilibrium then implies $\tilde{w} = w^*$, with $\tilde{L}_A^1 = \tilde{V}_A^1(w^*, w^f, \overline{K}_A^1, \overline{K}_B^1)$ and $\tilde{L}^2 = \overline{L} - \tilde{L}_A^1$. Moreover, there will be complete outsourcing of fragment B with foreign labor use equal to $\tilde{L}_B^1 = \tilde{V}_B^1(w^*, w^f, \overline{K}_A^1, \overline{K}_B^1)$. There is no domestic wage depression from international fragmentation. At the same time, in a figure analogous to 1, our logic finds that the welfare gain rises to include the full rectangle B_A^1BDC, plus a triangle corresponding to $B\tilde{B}_B^1D$, with the point $\tilde{B}_B^1$ shifted to the left, reflecting employment along the schedule $\tilde{V}_B^1(w^*, w^f, \overline{K}_A^1, \overline{K}_B^1)$ instead of $V_B^1(w^f, \overline{K}_A^1, \overline{K}_B^1)$. From this extreme case it is easily seen that in this model, contrary to widespread belief about globalization effects, the redistribution effects from international fragmentation are the *lower*, the *larger* are the efficiency gains.[13]

3. Indivisibility and "Discrete Outsourcing"

The preceding analysis has an odd feature: if outsourcing is incomplete in the vertical fragmentation equilibrium, then *all* firms in sector 1 produce fragment B both at home and abroad. This is odd because the driving forces behind *vertical* FDI normally assumed in the theory of multinational firms are such that the equilibrium involves a coexistence of different types of firms—purely domestic firms and vertical multinationals, say—but no firms doing the same stage both at home and abroad. The reason, of course, is the assumed presence of scale economies. The FDI literature often stipulates some variant of fixed cost on the plant-level and/or the firm-level, and then determines the equilibrium number of different types of firms by assuming a free-entry zero-profit equilibrium (Markusen, 2002). In this section, I shall reinterpret the above model towards the presence of fixed cost. However, instead of assuming free entry, I assume a given number n of domestic firms and look at the question of how these firms respond to a fall in the costs of vertical fragmentation by allocating their fixed assets for fragment B at home or abroad. At the firm level, then, outsourcing will always be complete—if the firm goes for fragmentation at all. But the industry as a whole may well exhibit both, purely domestic firms and firms producing in a fragmented manner. I denote the number of fragmented firms by n^f and their fraction by $v \equiv n^f/n$. I will show that, from an economy-wide perspective, the two most important consequences of allowing for fixed costs are (a) that vertical fragmentation induced by lower effective foreign cost of labor may lower domestic welfare, and (b) that the domestic wage rate may fall below the foreign wage rate.

Suppose that production of fragment B, whether carried out at home or abroad, requires a fixed amount $\overline{k}_B^1$ of capital which is specific to sector 1 and fragment B. As indicated above, $\overline{k}_B^1$ could also be interpreted as some other asset whose service is required to support production of fragment B with a variable input of labor. The important point is that it confers an ownership advantage to domestic firms.[14] Given the presence of this asset, the marginal productivity of labor is diminishing, giving rise to downward-sloping labor demand functions for each firm. In order to link the analysis to the previous section, I assume that $n\bar{k}_B^1 = \bar{K}_B^1$, where all firms are symmetric. Moreover, I assume that the marginal productivity of labor in terms of fragment B can be described by a function $F_{Bl}^1(\bar{k}_B^1, l_B^1)$, where l_B^1 denotes firm-level employment.

Fixed costs imply a nonconvex technology, and this begs the question of whether perfect competition remains a reasonable assumption. I assume that the fixed cost involved in fragment B is not "too large," relative to overall cost and world demand, so that a long-run, free-entry equilibrium of the world market features a sufficiently large number of firms, worldwide, for each of them to perceive a given world price for its final output. Moreover, to start with, I assume that industry-1 firms have no market power on the domestic labor market where they compete with industry 2. We will, however, see that vertical fragmentation may confer a certain amount of market power on firms in sector 1.

The Single-firm Case

We first look at the easiest case where $n = 1$, starting out with an appropriate reinterpretation of Figure 1. Employment in fragment A is at $\tilde{B}_A^1$ while, due to the underlying indivisibility of the relevant asset $\bar{k}_B^1$, the firm produces *all* of fragment B abroad, with a profit-maximizing *foreign* labor input equal to the distance $\tilde{B}_A^1\tilde{B}$. Since industry 2 is at point $\tilde{B}^2$, there is *excess supply* on the domestic labor market equal to $\tilde{B}_A^1\tilde{B}^2$, which pulls the domestic wage down to an equilibrium value $\tilde{w} < w^f$. As the wage falls below w^f, the firm increases its domestic labor demand according to the schedule $\tilde{V}_A^1$, defined in (7), and its foreign labor demand on fragment B moves from $\tilde{B}$ to $\tilde{E}^1$, in line with $\tilde{V}_{Bw}^1 \cdot dw$, where $\tilde{V}_B^1$ is defined in (8) above. Notice that all *domestic* labor is paid a *uniform* wage rate $\tilde{w}$, but the domestic firm pays a higher wage rate for foreign labor. Shouldn't this be an incentive for the domestic firm to withdraw, or abstain, from international fragmentation? The answer is no, if the firm anticipates that by investing its asset $\bar{k}_B^1$ at home would immediately move the economy back to B, where its profits are clearly lower. In a sense, since vertical fragmentation is an option to a single firm, and since it may only take place in discrete amounts, this firm obtains "quasi-market-power" on the domestic labor market in that it can influence the domestic wage rate. Market power is, however, limited, since there are only two possible outcomes, $\tilde{w}$ and w^*, from which this firm can choose.

In the case depicted by Figure 2, this scenario of vertical fragmentation involves an overall *welfare loss* for the home economy. The reason is that there is a triangular loss, in addition to the positive welfare triangles familiar from Figure 1. Domestic labor which is reallocated from domestic production of fragment B to fragment A and industry 2, respectively, generates less value-added than it did before. Prior to this reallocation, it has received income equal to the rectangle $B_A^1BL^{1*}L_A^{1*}$. Now, its income has fallen to $C'D'L^{1*}L_A^{1*}$ which is equal to $(L^{1*} - L_A^{1*})\tilde{w}$. The difference is not completely offset by the immediate cost-savings effect of outsourcing measured by the area B_A^1BDC, plus the additional capital income generated on inframarginal labor now employed in industry 2 and fragment A, equal to the sum of the areas $B\tilde{E}_A^1D'$ and $B_A^1\tilde{B}_A^1\tilde{E}_A^1C'$. International fragmentation is beneficial only if the triangle $\tilde{B}_A^1\tilde{B}^2\tilde{E}_A^1$ is smaller in size than the compound triangular gain identified in the simpler case above.

Such a loss can, however, arise only if condition (10) is violated. Another way to look at this condition which may shed more light on the issue is to use employment shares $\lambda_A^1 = L_A^{1*}/(L_A^{1*} + L^{2*})$ and $\lambda^2 = 1 - \lambda_A^1$ for all those activities that—for whatever reason—

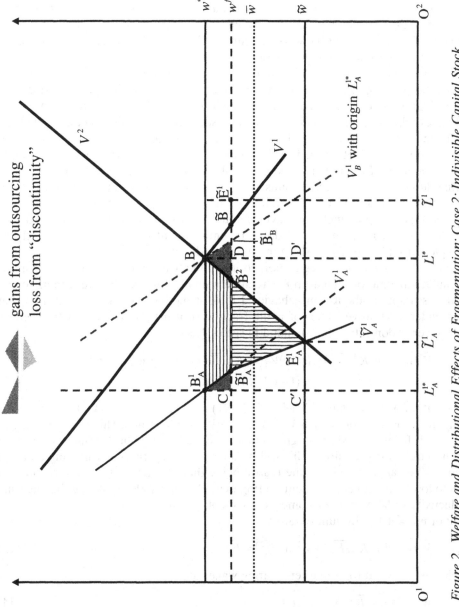

Figure 2. Welfare and Distributional Effects of Fragmentation; Case 2: Indivisible Capital Stock

are not amenable to outsourcing. In our case these "non-outsourcing activities" are sector 2 and fragment A of sector 1. Condition (10) can then be reformulated to

$$\frac{(L_A^{1*} + L^{2*})(w^* - w^f)}{w^* L_B^{1*}} > \frac{1}{\lambda_A^1 |\eta_A^1| + \lambda^2 |\eta^2|}. \tag{11}$$

The left-hand side of (11) measures the "would-be-cost-effect" of the wage gap if applied to the initial levels of the "non-outsourcing activities," relative to the initial wage cost of the "outsourcing activity" which is fragment B in sector 1. The right-hand side is simply the inverse of the weighted sum, in absolute terms, of labor demand elasticities of the "non-outsourcing activities."

There is an important general lesson from this analysis. Policy discussions often concentrate on the wage gap $w^* - w^f$ as a measure of the threat that globalization may pose to high-wage countries. The present analysis reveals that this is potentially misleading. Conditions (10) and (11) equivalently state that, other things equal, a welfare loss for the domestic economy is less likely, if this wage difference is large. Nor is the redistribution effect determined by this gap, as is most easily recognized by simply altering the level of w^f in Figure 2, keeping all else constant. The welfare loss is rising, but the domestic wage effect remains unaltered. The intuition for this result is quite straightforward. Due to the indivisibility pertaining to $\bar{k}_B^1$, an arbitrarily small wage gap—with a correspondingly low savings potential from fragmentation—can act as a valve for a heavy incipient loss of domestic employment which will subsequently be re-employed subject to diminishing marginal productivity.[15]

If $n > 1$, then issues of strategic interaction are likely to arise in the process of international fragmentation, at least if n is relatively small. However, before turning to any specific assumption about firm behavior, I look at the labor market equilibrium that arises under alternative values of v, the fraction of firms producing in a fragmented mode. Overall domestic labor demand in sector 1 is

$$\tilde{V}^1(w, w^f, v, \bar{K}_A^1, \bar{K}_B^1) \equiv (1-v)V_A^1(w, \bar{K}_A^1, \bar{K}_B^1) + v\tilde{V}_A^1(w, w^f, \bar{K}_A^1, \bar{K}_B^1)$$
$$+ (1-v)V_B^1(w, \bar{K}_A^1, \bar{K}_B^1). \tag{12}$$

By definition of $\tilde{V}_A^1$ we have $\tilde{V}_A^1(w^f, w^f, \bar{K}_A^1, \bar{K}_B^1) = V_A^1(w^f, w^f, \bar{K}_A^1, \bar{K}_B^1)$. Obviously, $\tilde{V}^1$ is falling in w.[16] Moreover, if $V_B^1 > \tilde{V}_A^1 - V_A^1$, then $\tilde{V}_A^1$ is falling in v. This condition necessarily holds for $w < w^f$, where fragmented firms have lower labor demand on fragment A than purely domestic firms. This will be the case we are primarily looking at. For a given v, $\tilde{V}^1$ is falling also in w^f, the reason being that a higher w^f leads all fragmented firms to lower foreign employment on fragment B, thereby also reducing the marginal productivity of labor in their domestic fragment A plant.

Labor market equilibrium requires

$$\tilde{V}^1(w, w^f, v, \bar{K}_A^1, \bar{K}_B^1) + V^2(w, \bar{K}^2) = \bar{L}, \tag{13}$$

which can be solved for a market-clearing wage rate

$$\tilde{w} = \tilde{w}(w^f, v, \bar{K}_A^1, \bar{K}_B^1, \bar{K}^2, \bar{L}). \tag{14}$$

The function $\tilde{w}$ is obviously increasing in all capital stocks, while falling in $\bar{L}$ and v. Somewhat counterintuitively, it is falling in w^f, the reason being that, for a given v, $\tilde{V}^1$ is falling in w^f, as argued above. This should, however, not be interpreted as a complementarity relationship between foreign and domestic labor *in general equilibrium*. We have not yet established a general equilibrium. The crucial point is that, given the foreign wage rate w^f, the equilibrium value of v depends on the domestic wage rate $\tilde{w}$. More specifically, in addition to (14) an equilibrium requires that the share of fragmented firms v be such that, given the discrepancy between $\tilde{w}$ and w^f, no firm faces an incentive to switch from one regime (domestic integration) to the other (vertical fragmentation).

Notice that, strictly speaking, v cannot be seen as a continuous variable, unless the number of firms n is very large. Moreover, given the underlying indivisibility of $\bar{k}_B^1$, $\tilde{V}^1$ varies in discrete and potentially large jumps as v varies, with associated jumps in the domestic wage rate that clear the labor market in line with (13). I shall return to this problem below. Here, we may note that, since V^2 is continuous in w, there is a *unique* wage rate that satisfies (13) for each possible value of v.

Multiple Firms: the Non-cooperative Equilibrium

Some of the possible equilibria for $n > 1$ are easily identified. Suppose, for instance, that the elasticities $|\eta_A^1|$ and $|\eta^2|$ are large enough for condition (10) to be met. In terms of Figure 2, this implies that the V_A^1 and the V^2 schedules intersect at a wage rate above w^f. In such a case, a domestic wage rate equal to w^f would be associated with excess demand on the domestic labor market, even if all firms are fragmented, $v = 1$, and even more so if $v < 1$. Therefore, equilibrium implies $v = 1$ and $\tilde{w} > w$. All firms produce in fragmented mode and have no incentive to change their strategy. This equilibrium is identical in all respects to the one arising with a perfectly divisible asset. Indivisibility simply doesn't matter, irrespective of the number of firms present in sector 1.

The more interesting case to look at is one where condition (10) is violated, say because labor demand in the "non-outsourcing activities" is relatively inelastic. Then, a case where all firms are fragmented would give rise to a domestic wage rate $\tilde{w} < w^f$. If n is large, such that an individual domestic firm is unaware of its "quasi-market-power" on the domestic labor market, then it treats the domestic wage rate $\tilde{w}$ as given, independent of its own choice of regime. Taking the symmetry assumption to its extreme, if $\tilde{w} < w^f$, all firms simultaneously revert to an integrated production mode which gives rise to a domestic wage rate w^*. But $w^* > w^f$ constitutes an incentive for fragmentation, and we observe an oscillating equilibrium between $\tilde{w}$ and w^f. Obviously, this is not a realistic scenario, as it involves repeated shifts from one regime to the other without firms ever learning about the wage effect of these shifts. The more realistic and interesting case, therefore, is one where firms anticipate the wage effects attendant upon shifting from one regime to the other.

If domestic firms, cognizant about these wage effects, behave in a cooperative manner, then we are effectively back to the case of a single firm described above. In the non-cooperative case, we must make some assumption about the form of *strategic interaction*. I assume that each firm takes all other firms' choice of regime (domestic integration versus international fragmentation) as given and considers whether changing its own strategy increases its profits. The case is perhaps best modeled as a *two-stage decision*. In *stage one*, firms decide on whether to invest their assets $\bar{k}_B^1$ to serve domestic or foreign production of fragment B. In *stage two*, integrated firms choose their profit-maximizing employment levels according to $V_A^1(w, \bar{K}_A^1, \bar{K}_B^1)/n$ and $V_B^1(w, \bar{K}_A^1, \bar{K}_B^1)/n$, while fragmented firms employ domestic labor according to $\tilde{V}_A^1(w, w^f, \bar{K}_A^1, \bar{K}_B^1)/n$ and foreign labor according to $\tilde{V}_B^1(w, w^f, \bar{K}_A^1, \bar{K}_B^1)/n$. I shall now explore a *subgame-perfect equilibrium* where each firm anticipates a wage rate $\tilde{w}$ according to (14) to prevail in stage two, when making its investment decision in stage one. In other words, in stage two firms behave competitively in the domestic labor market. Equilibrium thus requires that no firm (whether integrated or fragmented) may expect to increase its profit by shifting to the other regime, taking into account the effect that this shift would have on the domestic wage rate according to (14).

As noted above, the only interesting case remaining to look at is one where condition (10) is violated, and $\tilde{w} \leq w^f$ for some interior value of v between 0 and 1. The crucial point is under what conditions such a case is supported as a subgame-perfect equilibrium as described above. This requires that a representative fragmented firm faces no incentive to exploit the domestic wage advantage by returning its asset $\bar{k}_B^1$ back to the home economy, thus becoming a purely domestic firm, while at the same time a representative domestic firm has no incentive to become fragmented.

We now look at an arbitrary value of $\tilde{w} \leq w^f$. If a fragmented firm shifts to a purely domestic production mode, moving fragment B back to the home economy, it will bid up the domestic wage rate according to (14), and it will do so by a discrete amount, due to the indivisibility of $\bar{k}_B^1$. This hurts the firm in its domestic production of fragment A. On the other hand, since $\tilde{w} \leq w^f$, the firm will benefit from lower wage cost on fragment B. If the domestic wage increase is not too high, then overall wage cost per unit of output may be reduced, and the expected return-specific capital increased, by a "return-shift" of assets $\bar{k}_B^1$ back to the home economy. I use ω^r to denote the critical wage increase in percentage terms. In other words, if the domestic wage increase to be expected from a "return-shift" is lower than ω^r, then a representative fragmented firm would have an incentive to do so. Obviously, ω^r is the higher, the larger the domestic wage advantage to start with; i.e., the lower the ratio $\tilde{w}/w^f$.

Discrete changes notwithstanding, I proceed by approximating the cost-effects from wage changes relying on the familiar "cost-shares calculus." Using $\tilde{\theta}_j^1$ to denote the share of fragment j in the unit cost of good 1, and $\tilde{\theta}_{jL}^1$ for the labor share in the unit cost of fragment j, respectively, of a fragmented firm, I define $\tilde{\varphi}_j^1 = \tilde{\theta}_j^1 \tilde{\theta}_{jL}^1$ as the corresponding fragment-A labor share in the unit cost of good 1. A completely analogous definition holds for φ_j^1 with respect to a purely domestic firm. The difference between $\tilde{\varphi}_j^1$ and φ_j^1 is due to fragmented firms paying w^f on foreign procurement of fragment B, while domestic firms pay $\tilde{w}$ for domestic labor on both fragments. Elasticities of substitution will determine whether $\tilde{\varphi}_j^1$ is larger, smaller, or equal to φ_j^1, if $\tilde{w} < w^f$. For log-linear technologies, we have $\tilde{\varphi}_j = \varphi_j^1$. This seems like an innocuous assumption for the subsequent analysis.

The critical wage increase ω^r is then determined by

$$\varphi_A^1 \omega^r - \varphi_B^1 \left[1 - \frac{\tilde{w}}{w^f}(1+\omega^r) \right] = 0. \tag{15}$$

The bracketed term gives the percentage difference between the foreign wage and the wage rate the firm anticipates it will pay on fragment B upon the "return-shift". Notice that by assumption $\tilde{w}/w^f < 1$. Condition (15) can be rewritten as

$$\omega^r = \frac{\varphi_B^1}{\varphi_A^1 + \varphi_B^1(\tilde{w}/w^f)}\left(1 - \frac{\tilde{w}}{w^f} \right). \tag{16}$$

Conversely, if a purely domestic firm shifts to vertical fragmentation, it suffers from a higher foreign wage rate on fragment B, $w^f > \tilde{w}$. It may still want to do so, however, if it expects a sufficiently strong wage reduction from a higher v according to (14). Thus, from a purely domestic firm's perspective, there is a critical wage effect, below which a regime shift towards outsourcing fragment B implies an expected reduction in wage-cost per unit of output. Expressed in percentage terms, we denote this critical level by ω^o, and it is determined by

$$\varphi_A^1 \omega^o + \varphi_B^1\left(\frac{w^f}{\tilde{w}} - 1\right) = 0. \tag{17}$$

The first term gives the benefit from a lower domestic wage, while the second term gives the cost effect from paying a higher foreign wage on fragment B. Notice that $\omega^o < 0$ if $\tilde{w}/w^f < 1$, as assumed. We now look at the absolute value of the wage effect, rewriting condition (17) as

$$|\omega^o| = \frac{\varphi_B^1}{\varphi_A^1}\left(1 - \frac{\tilde{w}}{w^f}\right)\frac{w^f}{\tilde{w}}. \tag{18}$$

If the domestic wage reduction caused by a domestic firm outsourcing its fragment B exceeds $|\omega^o|$ in absolute terms, then outsourcing would increase the return to $\underline{k}_B^1$ and the firm would have an incentive to do so. Since by assumption $w^f/\tilde{w} > 1$, the right-hand side of (18) is larger than the right-hand side of (16). Assume for a moment that the two types of firms have symmetric views on the wage effects of a regime shift; i.e., the wage effect from a domestic firm becoming fragmented is the same, in absolute terms, as the wage effect from a fragmented firm becoming a purely domestic one.[17] Then, if a fragmented firm faces an incentive to move back, there cannot at the same time be an incentive for an integrated firm to move fragment B offshore. By complete analogy, if a domestic firm faces an incentive to become fragmented, then (18) is necessarily violated, so fragmented firms face no incentive to switch to integrated production.

Figure 3 depicts the two conditions (16) and (18), with ω^r and $|\omega^o|$, respectively, plotted on the vertical, and $\tilde{w}/w^f$ on the horizontal axis. Without loss of generality, we may assume $w^f = 1$, so that we may directly read $\tilde{w}$ off the horizontal axis. From the

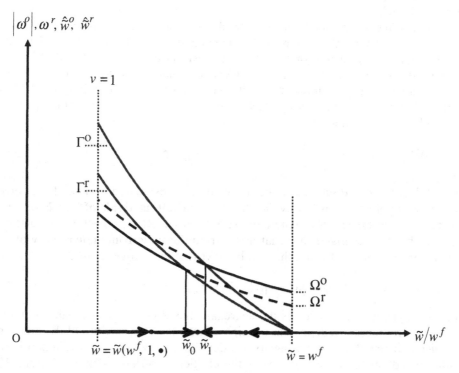

Figure 3. Indivisibility and Stable Interior "fragmentation equilibrium"

above discussion, it follows that both lines are downward-sloping and convex. The intuition for line $\Gamma^r(\tilde{w}/w^f)$ representing (16) is as follows. Given $\tilde{w}/w^f < 1$, a fragmented firm pays a higher foreign wage rate and may, therefore, consider moving fragment B back to the domestic economy. However, while the firm thus saves on fragment B wage cost, it will at the same time expect to be negatively affected on fragment A, because it bids up the domestic wage by adding a discrete amount of domestic labor demand on fragment B. The lower $\tilde{w}/w^f$, the larger the savings effect on fragment B, the more room, therefore, for the firm to "accommodate" an expected wage increase. Obviously, the line intersects with the horizontal axis at $\tilde{w}/w^f$. Moreover, there is a lower bound on $\tilde{w}/w^f$ determined by $v = 1$, where all n firms are fragmented. A similar intuition holds for the line $\Gamma^o(\tilde{w}/w^f)$ representing (18). A purely domestic firm has the advantage of a lower domestic wage rate on fragment B, but may still consider investing its asset k_B^1 abroad, since this lowers the domestic wage rate, with an ensuing cost-savings effect on fragment A. The lower $\tilde{w}/w^f$, the larger the disadvantage from becoming fragmented, the higher therefore the domestic wage effect, in absolute value, which is necessary to compensate for this in terms of a lower wage on fragment A. As with $\Gamma^r(\tilde{w}/w^f)$, the line $\Gamma^o(\tilde{w}/w^f)$ intersects with the horizontal axis at $\tilde{w}/w^f = 1$, and from the above discussion, we know that $\Gamma^o(\tilde{w}/w^f) > \Gamma^r(\tilde{w}/w^f)$ for $\tilde{w}/w^f < 1$, which is the range we are looking at. Obviously, if there are costs of shifting from one regime to the other, the two lines are farther apart.

To proceed with the analysis, I now turn to the expected wage effects from regime shifts, assuming that each firm considers shifting *alone*. An obvious, if extreme, assumption is that each firm fully internalizes (14) when deriving the wage effect. I approximate the wage effect relying on elasticities of the labor demand schedules appearing in (13) and (12). I denote the relative wage effect attendant upon an isolated "return-shift" by $\hat{\tilde{w}}^r$, while the wage effect from an isolated shift to outsourcing is denoted by $\hat{\tilde{w}}^o$.

The direct effect on domestic labor demand from a single firm's regime shift of type r is $\Delta^r V^1 = (V_A^1 - \tilde{V}_A^1 + V_B^1)/n$, where all labor demands are evaluated at $w = \tilde{w}$ for the given foreign wage rate w^f. For the other shift we have $\Delta^o V^1 = -\Delta^r V^1$. Moreover, if $\tilde{w} < w^f$ as assumed, then $\Delta^r V^1 > 0$. $\Delta^r V^1$ is the discrete analogue to $\tilde{V}_v^1 dv$ in (12). According to the labor-market equilibrium condition (13), the market-clearing wage effect of a regime shift of type r, $\Delta^r w$, taking place at $\tilde{w}$ with the corresponding value of v from (14), can be approximated by

$$(\tilde{V}_w^1 + V_w^2)\Delta^r w + \Delta^r V^1 + \frac{1}{n}(V_{Aw}^1 - \tilde{V}_{Aw}^1 + V_{Bw}^1)\Delta^r w = 0, \tag{19}$$

where all labor demand schedules and derivatives are evaluated at $\tilde{w}$ (and the corresponding value of v). This is simply the change in the left-hand side of (13). Notice the third term which takes into account the second-order effect, reflecting the discrete nature of the labor demand shift that arises from the underlying indivisibility of k_B^1. Using labor demand elasticities, this can be rewritten in relative terms as

$$[\eta + \eta_A^1(v_A^1 - \tilde{v}_A^1) + \eta_B^1 v_B^1]\hat{\tilde{w}}^r = -[(v_A^1 - \tilde{v}_A^1) + v_B^1], \tag{20}$$

where $\hat{\tilde{w}}^r \equiv \Delta^r w/\tilde{w}$, and η indicates the aggregate elasticity of domestic labor demand $\tilde{V}^1 + V^2$ with respect to w, defined as a weighted average of elasticities of the different labor demand schedules according to the definition of $\tilde{V}^1$ in (12), evaluated at $\tilde{w}$. As introduced above, η_A^1 and η_B^1 denote the elasticities of labor demand V_A^1 and V_B^1, respectively, with respect to w. Notice that all elasticities are negative with normal labor demand. Equation (20) assumes for simplicity that $\eta_A^1 = \tilde{\eta}_A^1$. And finally, lower-case letters indicate the share of a representative firm's labor demand in overall domestic employment, for instance $v_A^1 \equiv V_A^1/n\overline{L}$ (analogously for $\tilde{v}_A^1$ and v_B^1). Thus, $(v_A^1 - \tilde{v}_A^1) + v_B^1 = \Delta'V^1/\overline{L}$. Solving (20), we obtain

$$\hat{\hat{w}}^r = -\frac{(v_A^1 - \tilde{v}_A^1) + v_B^1}{\eta + \eta_A^1(v_A^1 - \tilde{v}_A^1) + \eta_B^1 v_B^1} > 0, \tag{21}$$

where the inequality follows from $v_A^1 > \tilde{v}_A^1$ (assuming $\tilde{w}/w^f < 1$) and the assumption of downward-sloping labor demand schedules.

It is now relatively straightforward to see that an isolated regime switch of type o entails a wage effect equal to

$$\hat{\hat{w}}^o = \frac{(v_A^1 - \tilde{v}_A^1) + v_B^1}{\eta - [\eta_A^1(v_A^1 - \tilde{v}_A^1) + \eta_B^1 v_B^1]} < 0, \tag{22}$$

where the inequality follows in line with the above, additionally assuming that the second-order effect (second term in the denominator) does not dominate the first-order effect. Looking at the wage effect in absolute terms, we have

$$\left|\hat{\hat{w}}^o\right| = -\frac{(v_A^1 - \tilde{v}_A^1) + v_B^1}{\eta - [\eta_A^1(v_A^1 - \tilde{v}_A^1) + \eta_B^1 v_B^1]} > \hat{\hat{w}}^r > 0. \tag{23}$$

That is, a regime switch of type o implies a wage effect of a larger magnitude than does a shift of type r, due to the second-order effect which works in opposite directions for the two shifts. This is because in the above analysis elasticities of labor demand operate on a level of demand equal to $\tilde{V}_w^1 + V_w^2 + \Delta'V^1$ for a shift of type r, and on a lower level $\tilde{V}_w^1 + V_w^2 - \Delta'V^1$ for a shift of type o. Hence, the magnitude of the equilibrating wage adjustment is larger for an o-type shift than for an r-type shift.

To complete the analysis, we may now ask how $\hat{\hat{w}}^r$ and $|\hat{\hat{w}}^o|$ vary with $\tilde{w}/w^f$. In line with the above, we restrict ourselves to $\tilde{w}/w^f < 1$. The direct labor demand effect of a regime shift, $\Delta'V^1 = |\Delta^oV^1|$, is falling in $\tilde{w}/w^f$. The larger the demand shift, the larger, *ceteris paribus*, the magnitude of the ensuing wage effect. Hence, we expect two down-ward-sloping schedules $|\hat{\hat{w}}^o| = \Omega^o(\tilde{w}/w^f)$ and $\hat{\hat{w}}^r = \Omega^r(\tilde{w}/w^f)$. Although there are also indirect effects operating through potential changes in the elasticities appearing in the denominators of (23), it appears reasonable to assume that the direct effect is domi-nating.[18] Figure 3 depicts the two schedules, again restricted to the range $\tilde{w} < w^f$.

A general equilibrium requires that a wage rate from (14) satisfies

$$\left|\hat{\hat{w}}^o\right| = \Omega^o(\tilde{w}/w^f) \leq \Gamma^o(\tilde{w}/w^f), \tag{24}$$

$$\hat{\hat{w}}^r = \Omega^r(\tilde{w}/w^f) \geq \Gamma^r(\tilde{w}/w^f). \tag{25}$$

The first condition states that the wage rate must be such that a representative domes-tic firm has no incentive to shift towards an outsourcing strategy, while the second condition states that for the same wage rate a representative fragmented firm has no incentive for returning in order to become a purely domestic firm.

While the schedules Ω^r and Ω^o as such are defined for any domestic wage rate, it is important to see that, in line with (14), it is changes in v that give rise to alternative values of $\tilde{w}$ along the horizontal axis. The model jointly determines the equilibrium wage rate and the fraction of fragmented firms v. But as I have emphasized above, given the underlying indivisibility of assets $\bar{k}_B^1$, we cannot treat v as a continuous variable. Thus, if we take into account the discrete nature of v in (14), then only a limited number of points along the horizontal axis in Figure 3 are relevant. However, at each point there is a unique value of both Ω^o and Ω^r, as well as Γ^o and Γ^r. There is, of course, a lower bound for the wage rate which is reached with $v = 1$, which is equivalent to the single-firm case described above. Figure 3 clearly indicates the possibility of an equilibrium with $\tilde{w} < w^f$ also for the case where $n > 1$. The next subsection explores some features of this equilibrium.

Existence, Uniqueness, and Adjustment

Although the above analysis does not include any explicit adjustment mechanism, Figure 3 indicates adjustment taking place if (24) or (25) is violated. For any wage rate $\tilde{w}$ above $\tilde{w}_1$ domestic firms shift to outsourcing, while for $\tilde{w} < \tilde{w}_0$ fragmented firms shift to an integrated production in the domestic economy. Will there always *exist* an equilibrium with a unique value of v, and a unique value of $\tilde{w}$, given that v cannot adjust continuously? From Figure 3, it cannot be ruled out that there is no relevant equilibrium point according to (14) within the interval $[\tilde{w}_0, \tilde{w}_1]$. Indeed, if the schedules Ω^o and Ω^r are sufficiently far apart, this interval is empty. The difference between these two schedules is, however, only due to the second-order effect (see above), and I henceforth rule out this case. But even in the case depicted, the interval may not contain any of the relevant points corresponding to (14). In such a case no equilibrium with a unique v exists. Intuitively, as fragmented firms approach $\tilde{w}_0$ from the left, they would eventually come to a "return-shift" which increases the domestic wage beyond $\tilde{w}_1$. Conversely, if domestic firms approach $\tilde{w}_1$ from the right, a further shift towards outsourcing would depress $\tilde{w}$ below $\tilde{w}_0$. One could explore this case further into the possibility of equilibria in mixed strategies. However, as with the oscillating equilibrium in the non-cooperative case mentioned above, this is a questionable interpretation, as it ignores the cost of shifting from one regime to the other. In terms of Figure 3, such costs would increase the vertical distance between the two schedules Ω^o and Ω^r, thus also increasing the interval $[\tilde{w}_0, \tilde{w}_1]$ and making this case seem somewhat unlikely.

However, a large interval $[\tilde{w}_0, \tilde{w}_1]$ begs the question of *multiplicity* in that there may be more than one labor-market-clearing value $\tilde{w}$ within this interval. This issue can be resolved by stipulating a specific adjustment process. If one assumes that firms are purely domestic to start with, then a process of increasing fragmentation approaches the equilibrium domestic wage rate from above (or the right in Figure 3). The opposite, perhaps less convincing, assumption would be that fragmented firms increasingly return fragment B to the home economy, in which case the equilibrium wage rate is reached from below.

Any outsourcing shift, by depressing the domestic wage rate, increases both $v_A^1 - \tilde{v}_A^1$ and v_B^1. In turn, this increases the direct labor demand effect of a further shift, and thus $|\tilde{w}^o|$ according to the schedule Ω^o. But so does the critical level $|\omega^o|$ according to Γ^o. The slopes in Figure 3 imply that this latter effect always dominates, such that the *adjustment process* leads to a unique interior equilibrium. Suppose, however, that the effect of an outsourcing shift on $|\tilde{w}^o|$ dominates that on $|\omega^o|$, and analogously for the "return-shift." Then, the slopes of the Ω schedules are steeper than the Γ schedules, as drawn in Figure 4. To the left of $\tilde{w}_0$, outsourcing shifts would further enhance the case for outsourcing, and conversely for "return-shifts" to the right of $\tilde{w}_1$. This suggests the possibility of *unstable* interior equilibria. Notice, however, that for $\tilde{w}/w^f = 1$ the Γ lines always intersect with the horizontal axis, while the Ω lines are clearly posi-

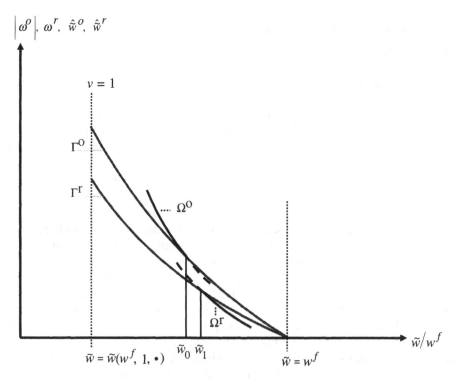

Figure 4. Indivisibility and Stable Interior "fragmentation equilibrium"

tive. Hence, barring the aforementioned problems related to discontinuity, there is a stable interior equilibrium close to $\tilde{w}/w^f = 1$. This, in turn, implies that, in the case depicted in Figure 4, there must actually be multiple intersections between the Ω and the Γ lines. However, the interesting point emerging from this analysis is that even in a multiple-firm case without collusion, there may be an equilibrium with $v = 1$.

A final point worth mentioning is that, in any interior equilibrium, fragmented firms have lower profits (or capital rental) than purely domestic firms. By assumption, all firms share the same technology, but domestic firms enjoy a lower (domestic) wage on fragment B than fragmented firms who use foreign labor.[19] This raises the question of why any firm would choose an outsourcing strategy in stage one, knowing that the equilibrium features a coexistence of both strategies, with higher profits for the strategy of integrated production. One can rely on at least two different interpretations of the equilibrium when trying to answer this question. The first is a probabilistic interpretation, as often suggested for equilibria where symmetric agents find different "treatments." The model determines the equilibrium *share* of fragmented firms, but leaves open whether a specific firm will end up as a domestic or a fragmented firm, which can then be seen as the outcome of a draw. Of course, indeterminacy on the individual level will disappear if a specific form of asymmetry between firms is introduced. For instance, there may be an asymmetry among firms, unrelated to their fundamental technology, which determines a well-specified sequencing of firm decisions on choosing their production regime. In view of the above discussion on uniqueness, this could be combined with an assumption about a specific starting point, in which case the position of *individual* firms is determined endogenously. I do not, however, explore this any further in this paper.

4. Remarks on the Potential Welfare Loss

When discussing the single-firm and the cooperative case in Figure 2, we have noted the possibility of a welfare loss from fragmentation. This possibility is upheld in the non-cooperative multiple firm case, if the equilibrium wage rate $\tilde{w}$ is sufficiently below w^f. From the preceding analysis, we can identify some of the forces determining the equilibrium magnitude of $w^f - \tilde{w}$. Other things equal, the vertical position of the Ω lines are important. This is most easily pinned down by looking at $\Omega^o(1) = -v_B^1/(\eta - \eta_B^1 v_B^1)$ and $\Omega^r(1) = -v_B^1/(\eta + \eta_B^1 v_B^1)$, where $v_B^1 = V_B^1(w^f, \overline{K}_A^1, \overline{K}_B^1)/n\overline{L}$. In other words, the share of an individual firm's fragment B labor demand in overall labor endowment, evaluated at $w = w^f$, relative to the aggregate domestic labor demand elasticity, plays an important role. The welfare loss is more likely if this share is large.

For a given vertical position of the Ω lines, the relative slopes of the Ω and Γ lines are important. In particular, the flatter the Γ lines, the more likely a welfare loss. In particular, if φ_B^1/φ_A^1 is small, then the slope of Γ^o in Figure 3 is relatively small and—other things equal—the equilibrium value of $w^f - \tilde{w}$ is large. Indeed, as noted above, there may be intersection points where the Ω^o line is steeper than the Γ^o line, in which case the equilibrium may even involve $v = 1$, as in the single-firm case discussed above.

There is a further subtle issue of interpretation relating to the vertical position of the Ω lines which, as we have just seen, is important for whether a welfare loss from fragmentation obtains. When identifying the possibility of such a loss by means of Figure 2, the reference equilibrium was one where the domestic labor market is characterized by perfect competition. One may now argue that a case where $\Omega^o(1)$ and $\Omega^r(1)$ are large is also a case where a single domestic firm in industry 1 is large enough to have market power on the domestic labor market. If so, it questions the validity of a competitive reference equilibrium against which to evaluate the welfare effects of fragmentation. It should be noticed, however, that the relevant magnitude is the size of a domestic industry 1 firm *relative* to the overall labor demand elasticity η. More importantly, one should bear in mind the two-stage nature of the decision-making that underlies this analysis, as well as the discontinuity involved in stage one. Specifically, stage one by definition always involves *discrete variations* in labor demand, whereby firms look at alternative cases where their fragment B capital stocks $\bar{k}_B^1$ are invested domestically, or abroad. By way of contrast, in stage two, once the investment decision has been made, labor demand is always a matter of a truly *marginal* decision, where firms are less likely to perceive themselves as having influence on the domestic wage rate.

This is not to deny the possibility that the kind of indivisibility underlying the analysis may lead to market power of industry-1 firms on the domestic labor market. If that is the case, then the reference equilibrium for evaluating international fragmentation involves a *distortion* in the domestic labor market to start with, implying that too much labor is employed in industry 2, and too little in industry 1 where the wage rate is below the marginal productivity of labor. In a globalization scenario where lower costs of international fragmentation cause international outsourcing there will, then, be first-order welfare effects which I have not covered in the above analysis. A full-fledged analysis of this case is beyond the scope of the present paper, but it is important to bear in mind this complication when interpreting the results.

How does the welfare loss from fragmentation in this model relate to other cases where international division of labor is not beneficial to all countries involved? First, there is no terms-of-trade effect involved, and there is no offsetting gain in the foreign economy. Indeed, under the assumptions made, the foreign economy neither gains nor loses from fragmentation. Second, there is no distortion at the margin to start with, which would explain the welfare loss as a second-best phenomenon. Third, the loss is also not of the Graham-type where in the presence of scale economies a country ends up "at the wrong" end of international specialization. The crucial point is that participation in the international division of labor may only take in *discrete* steps, rather than *marginally*. If this option arises for a relatively small number of firms, then it affords them "quasi-market-power" on the domestic labor market, with the potential of a welfare loss. Without jumping too far, the analysis suggests that trade theory, with its tendency to portray internationalization under conditions where agents move in infinitesimally small steps, may ignore important consequences of the real world where, in some areas at least, globalization involves certain discontinuity of adjustment.

One may finally wonder about the empirical relevance of a case where international outsourcing to a low-wage foreign country leads to a domestic wage rate which is below the foreign wage rate. But this is easily resolved by remembering that wage rates in this context are wage rates for comparable *efficiency units*, and even if $\tilde{w} < w^f$ the wage rate for a *natural unit* of labor may well continue to be higher domestically than abroad.

5. Concluding Remarks

In concluding, I should like to offer a few remarks on how this analysis should be interpreted, given the assumptions made. The underlying assumption is that labor markets are sometimes pretty regional in nature, with a high degree of labor mobility between a relatively small number of industries within a small region, but with very low mobility across such regions, despite potentially sizable wage differences. This seems a reasonable assumption particularly in the European context, where outsourcing then seems an interesting option for firms to arbitrage on wage differences across small labor markets. The purpose of this paper is to offer a framework of analysis which juxtaposes the efficiency and distributional effects arising from such arbitrage. Although the paper has stopped way before suggesting specific policy measures, a number of important insights have emerged.

The analysis confirms the *a priori* intuition that domestic labor initially employed in those value-added fragments lost to foreign regions will always lose, while other factors gain. As to the efficiency effect of fragmentation, the crucial question emphasized by the above analysis is whether or not the resources set free through outsourcing will find alternative employment where they generate value-added which is equal to what they have earned before. Thus, one must look at what outsourcing implies for the activities that remain in the domestic region. It is often argued that these activities will in some sense benefit from the cost advantage that comes with outsourcing. This paper has focused on exactly this linkage, assuming that mobile domestic labor is employed alongside sector-specific factors, and exploring the effect of outsourcing on labor demand for the remaining domestic part of production.

The analysis reveals that, potentially unwelcome distributional implications notwithstanding, a region that loses some fragment of its domestic value-added through outsourcing will reap a welfare gain, provided such outsourcing does not involve any nonconvexity in technology. The welfare gain identified has a close resemblance to the well-known "immigration surplus." However, the relationship between the "outsourcing surplus" and redistribution is the opposite of the usual story: the larger the gain, the lower the pain of redistribution.

If international fragmentation is subject to the presence of fixed assets that can be deployed (or serve production) either at home or abroad, then outsourcing is a discrete event, with important consequences for welfare. The cost-savings linkage to domestic activities notwithstanding, labor which is set free through outsourcing may not generate sufficient value-added in its alternative domestic use for fragmentation to be welfare-enhancing. This holds true even under otherwise optimal factor market institutions ruling out distortions or unemployment. The crucial point is that, to reap the gains from lower foreign wages, firms have to move in discrete steps, if outsourcing involves alternative deployment of indivisible assets, like capital.

The paper has modeled such discrete shifts between domestic and fragmented modes of production as a two-stage game, where stage 1 involves deploying indivisible assets either at home or abroad, and stage 2 involves profit-maximizing labor demand at home and abroad. The option of outsourcing affords domestic firms "quasi-market-power" on the domestic labor market, even if they behave competitively in stage 2. The resulting fragmentation equilibrium may be such that international fragmentation which is caused by lower costs of outsourcing may involve a welfare loss. The analysis has identified specific conditions that are important for whether or not such a loss arises.

Whether or not these conditions are fulfilled in specific instances of fragmentation is an empirical matter. The above analysis should, thus, be a valuable guide to future empirical research on outsourcing. Moreover, future theoretical work should focus on cases where the reference equilibrium features labor market distortions that may arise from the kind of indivisibility emphasized in this paper.

References

Arndt, Sven W., "Globalization and the Open Economy," *North American Journal of Economics and Finance* 8 (1997):71–9.

——, "Globalization and Economic Development," *Journal of International Trade and Economic Development* 8 (1999):309–18.

Arndt, Sven W. and Henryk Kierzkowski (ed.), *Fragmentation: New Production Patterns in the World Economy*, Oxford: Oxford University Press (2001).

Borjas, George, "The Economic Analysis of Immigration," in Orley Ashenfelter and David Card (eds.), *Handbook of Labor Economics*, Vol. 3A, Amsterdam: Elsevier (North-Holland) (1999):1697–760.

Deardorff, Alan V., "Fragmentation Across Cones," in Sven W. Arndt and Henryk Kierzkowski (eds.), *Fragmentation: New Production Patterns in the World Economy*, Oxford: Oxford University Press (2001a).

——, "Fragmentation in Simple Trade Models," *North American Journal of Economics and Finance* 12 (2001b):121–37.

Feenstra, Robert C., "Integration of Trade and Disintegration of Production in the Global Economy," *Journal of Economic Perspectives* 12 (1998):31–50.

Feenstra, Robert C. and Gordon H. Hanson, "Foreign Investment, Outsourcing and Relative Wages," in Robert C. Feenstra et al. (eds.), *Political Economy of Trade Policy: Essays in Honor of Jagdish Bhagwati*, Cambridge, MA: MIT Press (1996):89–127.

——, "Foreign Direct Investment and Relative Wages: Evidence from Mexico's Maquiladoras," *Journal of International Economics* 42 (1997):371–93.

——, "The Impact of Outsourcing and High-technology Capital on Wages: Estimates for the United States, 1979–1990," *Quarterly Journal of Economics* 114 (1999):907–40.

Harris, Richard G., "Trade and Communication Costs," *Canadian Journal of Economics* 28 (1995):46–75.

Hummels, David, Dana Rapoport, Jun Ishii, and Key-Mu Yi, "Vertical Specialization and the Changing Nature of World Trade," *Federal Reserve Bank of New York Economic Policy Review* (June 1998):79–99.

Hummels, David, Jun Ishii, and Key-Mu Yi, "The Nature and Growth of Vertical Specialization in World Trade," *Journal of International Economics* 54 (2001):75–96.

Irwin, Douglas A., "The United States in a New Global Economy? A Century's Perspective," *American Economic Review, Papers and Proceedings* 86 (1996):41–6.

Jones, Ronald W., "A Three-factor Model in Theory, Trade, and History," in Jagdish N. Bhagwati et al. (eds.), *Trade, Balance of Payments and Growth: Essays in Honor of Charles Kindleberger*, Amsterdam: Elsevier (North-Holland) (1971):3–21.

——, *Globalization and the Theory of Input Trade*, Cambridge, MA: MIT Press (2000).

Jones, Ronald W. and Henryk Kierzkowski, "The Role of Services in Production and International Trade: a Theoretical Framework," in Ronald W. Jones and Anne O. Krueger (eds.), *The Political Economy of International Trade*, Oxford: Basil Blackwell (1990):31–48.

——, "A Framework for Fragmentation," in Sven W. Arndt and Henryk Kierzkowski (eds.), *Fragmentation: New Production Patterns in the World Economy*, Oxford: Oxford University Press (2001a).

——, "Globalization and the Consequences of International Fragmentation," in Guillermo A. Calvo et al. (eds.), *Money, Capital Mobility, and Trade: Essays in Honor of Robert A. Mundell*, Cambridge, MA: MIT Press (2001b).

Kohler, Wilhelm, "A Specific Factors View on Outsourcing," *North American Journal of Economics and Finance* 12 (2001):31–53.

——, "The Distributional Effects of International Fragmentation," *German Economic Review* 4 (2003):89–120.

Krugman, Paul, "Growing World Trade: Causes and Consequences," *Brookings Papers on Economic Activity* (1995):327–77.

Markusen, James R., *Multinational Firms and the Theory of International Trade*, Cambridge, MA: MIT Press (2002).

Rodrik, Dani, *Has Globalization Gone Too Far?* Washington, DC: Institute for International Economics (1997).

——, "Symposium on Globalization in Perspective: an Introduction," *Journal of Economic Perspectives* 12 (1998):3–8.

Venables, Anthony J., "Fragmentation and Multinational Production," *European Economic Review* 43 (1999):935–45.

Notes

1. For empirical studies, see Irwin (1996), Feenstra and Hanson (1996, 1997, 1999), Feenstra (1998), Hummels et al. (1998, 2001), and several chapters in Arndt and Kierzkowski (2001). In this literature, the terms "fragmentation," "outsourcing," "international disintegration of production," or "vertical specialization" sometimes have different meanings, but for the present purpose I use them interchangeably.

2. Equation (1) stipulates a "smoother" technology than is often assumed in the literature on fragmentation and multinational firms. The advantage of this approach is that we may rely on methods of calculus to a larger extent than would otherwise be the case. The underlying technology here is similar to that in Kohler (2001), but I explore a different and somewhat richer set of conditions under which outsourcing takes place.

3. See Markusen (2002) for a modern treatment of this conceptual framework.

4. The theory of the vertical multinational firm usually assumes that the location advantage is based on different factor intensities of different stages of production (Markusen, 2002). Assuming that outsourcing is restricted to fragment B can be interpreted along such lines, although for simplicity I do not model it explicitly.

5. Markusen (2002) demonstrates in a comprehensive analysis that the recent upsurge of *foreign direct investment* is predominantly horizontal in nature, if looked at from a worldwide perspective. But he explicitly acknowledges the importance of vertical FDI for many countries and industries. On the other hand, one frequently finds studies claiming and documenting the

particular significance of intermediates in recent *trade* developments; see Jones, (2000) and several of the studies mentioned in the introduction.

6. One could, for instance, treat fragment A as an upstream semifinished good which may be shipped abroad where fragment B involves further processing and assembly. The final good may then be shipped back to the sales departments in the home country.

7. If we compare these schedules with V_A^1 and V_B^1 which both rule out vertical fragmentation, we observe that $\tilde{V}_A^1(w, w^f, \overline{K}_A^1, \overline{K}_B^1) > V_A^1(w, \overline{K}_A^1, \overline{K}_B^1)$ and $\tilde{V}_B^1(w, w^f, \overline{K}_A^1, \overline{K}_B^1) < V_B^1(w^f, \overline{K}_A^1, \overline{K}_B^1)$ if $w > w^f$, with equality obtaining if $w = w^f$. Conversely, if $w < w^f$, we have the opposite inequalities, but this case of course begs the question of why fragment B is not moved back to the domestic economy. I shall return to this in the next subsection.

8. Applying a discrete wage difference to labor demand elasticities which need not be constant involves an approximation. Moreover, since $V_A^1(w^f, \overline{K}_A^1, \overline{K}_B^1) = \tilde{V}_A^1(w^f, w^f, \overline{K}_A^1, \overline{K}_B^1)$, the change from $V_A^1(w^*, \overline{K}_A^1, \overline{K}_B^1)$ to $\tilde{V}_A^1(w^f, w^f, \overline{K}_A^1, \overline{K}_B^1)$ may be approximated by $L_A^{1*}\eta_A^1\omega$.

9. A similar thrust is also emerging from the general analysis of distributional effects in Kohler (2003), where it is shown that the factor price effects are importantly driven by the production characteristics of the domestic "non-outsourcing" activities.

10. Note that the distance $\tilde{L}_A^1\tilde{L}^1$ is equal to the distance $L_A^{1*}\tilde{L}_B^1$.

11. There are several ways in which this may arise, an important point being whether the mix of factor inflows is any different from the mix of domestic endowment (Borjas, 1999). Notice, however, that Rybczynski-type internal factor reallocation may allow the domestic economy to employ additional labor at a constant marginal productivity, in which case no surplus will arise. It is interesting to compare this to the general result on distributional effects from fragmentation derived in Kohler (2003), where the factor intensity pattern of outsourcing *relative to the domestic endowment* similarly plays a key role.

12. See Rodrik (1998) who emphasizes that gains from trade require restructuring and that restructuring is likely to have distributional impacts. Moreover, he argues that "if the distributional impacts have been small, the net gains have been small in all likelihood as well." In Rodrik (1997), he reports on estimates indicating that $5 of income get redistributed for every $1 of net welfare gains from trade.

13. It should be noted, however, that even in the extreme case above, although there is no domestic wage depression, there is still redistribution in that incomes to capital owners in sector 1 have risen. This is a case where a redistribution effect is present, but it satisfies the criterion of Corden's "conservative social welfare function."

14. The interpretation of fixed costs can be one of *firm-level* or *plant-level* scale economies. In the former case, the underlying assumption is that the firm may geographically separate the asset and the plant, but where the asset can serve *only one plant*—either domestic or foreign. In the latter case the asset itself must be transferred to the foreign plant. Assumptions like these are often made to separate theoretical paradigms for vertical and horizontal FDI (Markusen, 2002), but since the present model is entirely geared towards vertical fragmentation anyway, the reader is free to choose whatever may seem a more satisfactory interpretation.

15. A similar thrust also emerges from the general analysis of distributional effects in Kohler (2003), where it is shown that the factor price effects are importantly driven by the production characteristics of the domestic "non-outsourcing activities."

16. Equation (12) formulates labor demand in such a way that there is a firm relation to the previous section and to Figures 1 and 2.

17. Whether or not such symmetry prevails will be discussed below.

18. For constant labor demand elasticities, the denominator of (23) is increasing in absolute value in $\tilde{w}/w^f$, which would imply that $|\tilde{w}^o|$ can be seen as a downward-sloping function $\Omega^o(\tilde{w}/w^f)$. However, even if labor demand elasticities are constant, η varies with $\tilde{w}/w^f$ through an associated variation in v. Without digging deeper, we cannot rule out an upward-sloping schedule $\Omega^o(\tilde{w}/w^f)$. For (21), the denominator is falling in $\tilde{w}/w^f$, hence even for constant elasticities the slope of $\Omega^r(\tilde{w}/w^f)$ is ambiguous.

19. Domestic labor, of course, receives a uniform wage rate in all domestic employment.

Chapter 5

Outsourcing, Foreign Ownership, and Productivity: Evidence from UK Establishment-level Data

Sourafel Girma and Holger Görg

1. Introduction

"Outsourcing" can be loosely defined as the contracting out of activities that were previously performed within a firm, to subcontractors outside the firm.[1] It appears to be becoming more widespread and is attracting increasing attention in the popular business press as well as in the academic literature. For example, the *Financial Times* asserts: "Subcontracting as many non-core activities as possible is a central element of the new economy" (31 July 2001, p. 10). Also, a recent article on car manufacturers in *The Economist* points out: "The whole industry is disintegrating (or becoming less vertical) as vehicle assemblers try to outsource more and more of what they once did for themselves" (23 February 2002, p. 99). There is plenty of anecdotal evidence that this is not limited to the car industry but is also observed in other manufacturing sectors.

Outsourcing (or fragmentation) has also affected the pattern of international trade. For example, Hummels et al. (2001) found that outsourcing (or vertical specialization in their parlance) accounted for 22% of US exports in 1997, and for 30% of the growth in the US export share of merchandise GDP between 1962 and 1997. Görg (2000) reported that, between 1988 and 1994, around 20% of US exports to the EU were for inward processing; that is, they are exported to the EU for processing and subsequent export outside the EU.

Various aspects of the trend to outsourcing have been discussed in the literature. A large literature, starting with the seminal paper by Coase (1937) and including more recent papers by Grossman and Hart (1986), Bolton and Whinston (1993), and Grossman and Helpman (2002a,b), examines theoretically a firm's decision of whether to produce inhouse or to outsource. At the heart of this literature are issues concerned with transaction costs and, in particular, incomplete contracts leading to either vertical integration or specialization. Lyons (1995) provided an empirical application to evaluate the importance of transaction costs theory for firms' outsourcing decisions.

More recently, the trade-related aspects of outsourcing have attracted increasing attention. Trade-theoretic models such as those of Deardorff (2001), Jones and Kierzkowski (2001), and Kohler (2001) examine the effects of trade in "fragmented products" on countries' patterns of specialization and resulting implications for factor prices. On the empirical side, papers by Feenstra and Hanson (1996, 1999) and Hijzen et al. (2004) have analyzed the effect of international outsourcing on relative wages and labor demand using industry-level data for the US and UK, respectively. In line with traditional HOS trade theory, these authors find that international outsourcing (moving low-skill-intensive production to low-skill-abundant countries) leads to increased demand and increases in the wage premium for high-skilled workers in the US and the UK. Egger and Egger (2001) investigated the effect of outsourcing on the productivity of low-skilled labor in the EU using industry-level data. They found that increases in outsourcing have a negative effect on low-skilled labor productivity in the short run, but a positive effect in the long run.

In this paper we are not concerned with the international trade dimension to outsourcing. Rather, we investigate empirically an establishment's decision to outsource and the subsequent effect of outsourcing on productivity of that establishment. We do not distinguish between international and domestic outsourcing since we are interested in the establishment's characteristics that determine outsourcing. We therefore consider it immaterial as to whether the activities are outsourced to firms abroad or in the domestic economy. Also, as we are interested in the subsequent effect on productivity for the outsourcing establishment, it should not matter whether outsourcing takes place internationally or domestically. All we may assume is that the firm will minimize transaction costs when outsourcing activities to any subcontractor.

This paper uses establishment-level data for UK manufacturing industries for the empirical analysis. It contributes in a number of ways. This is, to the best of our knowledge, the first study to analyze the establishment-level determinants of outsourcing using data for the UK.[2] Second, the analysis of the effect of outsourcing on productivity of the establishment is an innovation.[3] Third, we investigate whether there are differences in the determinants of outsourcing, and productivity effects of outsourcing, between domestic establishments and foreign-owned establishments which can be assumed to be part of a larger multinational company.[4]

We focus our analysis on establishments in three broad UK manufacturing sectors: chemicals, mechanical and instrument engineering, and electronics.[5] Foreign-owned firms are important players in all three sectors, accounting for about 12–19% of total employment in the sectors (Griffith and Simpson, 2003, Table 4). We examine these three sectors separately as one may expect at least some heterogeneity in the use of outsourcing and, perhaps more importantly, differences in the impact of outsourcing on productivity across these sectors.

The data used in this paper are available from the Annual Respondents Database (ARD) which is described in more detail in the next section. Section 3 then examines the determinants of outsourcing at the level of the establishment, while section 4 presents the results of our analysis of productivity effects of outsourcing. Section 5 summarizes our main findings and concludes.

2. Data Description and Summary Statistics

For the empirical estimations, this paper draws on the Annual Respondents Database (ARD) provided by the Office for National Statistics. The ARD consists of individual establishments' records that underlie the Annual Census of Production and the data used cover the period 1980 to 1992. As Barnes and Martin (2002) provide a useful introduction to the dataset, we include only a brief discussion of some of the features of the data that are relevant to the present work. For each year the ARD consists of two files. What is known as the "selected file" contains detailed information on a sample of establishments that are sent inquiry forms. The second file comprises the "non-selected" (nonsampled) establishments, and only basic information such as employment, location, industry grouping, and foreign ownership status is recorded. Some 14,000–19,000 establishments are selected each year, based on a stratified sampling scheme. The scheme tends to vary from year to year, but during the period under consideration the sample included all establishments with more than 100 employees plus a selection of smaller ones.

In the ARD, an establishment is defined as the smallest unit that is deemed capable of providing information on the Census questionnaire. Thus a "parent" establishment reports for more than one plant (or "local unit" in the parlance of ARD). For selected multiplant establishments, we have aggregate values only for the constituent plants. Indicative information on the number of plants is available in the "nonselected" file. In the sample period considered in this paper (1980–92), about 95% of the establishments that are present in these industries are single-plant firms. In the actual sample we used for the econometric estimation this figure is around 80%. Hence, most of the data used are actually plant-level data.

The focus of this paper is on outsourcing activities of an establishment. While there has been some empirical research in this area, there does not appear to be a standard definition of what constitutes outsourcing. For example, papers in the empirical trade literature (e.g., Feenstra and Hanson, 1996, 1999; Hijzen et al., 2004) define outsourcing essentially as trade in intermediate products. This appears as a rather wide measure of "outsourcing," especially at the level of the establishment. Abraham and Taylor (1996) define it more narrowly as various activities, namely, contracting out of machine maintenance services, engineering and drafting services, accounting services, computer services, and janitorial services. Our definition includes the first two categories but not the latter three. We define as outsourcing the "cost of industrial services received" by an establishment. This includes activities such as processing of inputs which are then sent back to the establishment for final assembly or sales, maintenance of production machinery, engineering or drafting services, etc. Note that "nonindustrial services" such as accounting, consulting, cleaning, or transportation are not part of that definition.

Outsourcing can be seen as a substitute for inhouse production and may therefore, in the short run, lead to a reduction in the total wage bill. In some sense the cost of outsourcing is therefore equal to the opportunity wage that would have occurred to inhouse employees if the services had not been contracted out. We therefore decided to calculate an indicator of an establishment's propensity to outsource as an outsourcing intensity equal to the cost of industrial services received relative to the total wage bill of the establishment. Some summary statistics for this measure for the three broad manufacturing industries are presented in Table 1. Note that the average outsourcing intensity in the electronics sector is considerably lower than in chemicals and engineering, although the standard deviation is also considerably higher. We also find that the mean outsourcing intensity for foreign-owned establishments appears to be higher than that for domestic-owned establishments in the same sector.

Figures 1–3 plot the development of outsourcing intensity by sector. Figure 3 in particular indicates that the propensity to outsource in the electronics sector has increased sharply since 1989/90, leaving it at about the same rate as in the other two sectors at the end of the period under consideration. Hence, the lower means in Table 1 can be attributed to the very low levels in the early 1980s. This recovery appears to have been mainly due to domestic establishments where we see a considerable growth in outsourcing since 1989. However, we also find that the outsourcing intensity in

Table 1. Mean Outsourcing Intensity by Sector (standard deviation in parentheses)

Sector	All	Foreign	Domestic
Chemicals	0.138	0.161	0.128
	(0.279)	(0.256)	(0.343)
Engineering	0.140	0.161	1.136
	(0.360)	(0.288)	(0.226)
Electronics	0.091	0.097	0.090
	(0.554)	(0.458)	(0.599)

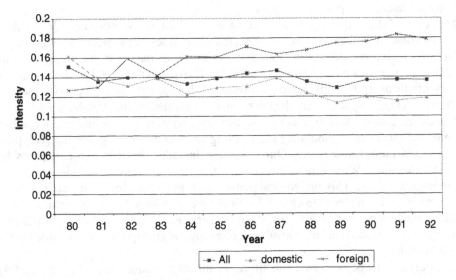

Figure 1. Outsourcing Intensity: Chemicals

foreign-owned establishments has increased over the total period 1980 to 1992, although there has been a slight decrease since 1989.

3. Determinants of Outsourcing

This section investigates what determines firms' use of outsourcing. Abraham and Taylor (1996) postulate that there are three general considerations that may affect firms' decisions in that regard, namely, wage costs savings, output cyclicality, and economies of scale.

Firms may try to cut costs by contracting-out activities to firms that operate with lower costs (i.e., offer lower wages to their employees). For outsourcing abroad, this may be the case if market wages are lower in the foreign country due to the abundance of labor. Even if firms outsource in the domestic economy this argument may still hold if, for example, a unionized firm pays wages higher than what it would otherwise choose to pay. Even if a firm is not unionized, a firm may still pay high wages

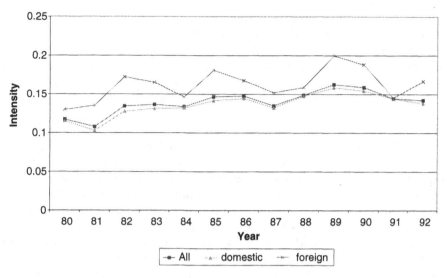

Figure 2. Outsourcing Intensity: Mechanical Engineering

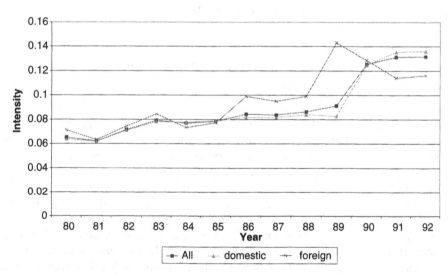

Figure 3. Outsourcing Intensity: Electronics

due to paying "efficiency wages" (e.g., Weiss, 1991) to its employees. In this case, while it might be sensible to pay efficiency wages to the firm's "core" workforce, there may be other more peripheral activities for which the extra payments are not justified. These activities could easily be contracted out to low-wage producers.[6,7]

If the firm's output is subject to heavy seasonal or cyclical fluctuations it may revert to outsourcing in order to smoothe the workload for the core workforce. Some firms might choose to even the workload by assigning peak-period tasks to outside contractors. Other firms might decide to reduce outsourcing during slow periods by having work performed inhouse that would otherwise have been assigned to outside contractors. Hence, fluctuations in output may affect the use of outsourcing either positively or negatively, depending on the preferences of the firm.

The third reason put forward by Abraham and Taylor for the use of outsourcing is economies of scale for specialized services. It may not be optimal for small or medium-sized enterprises to provide for themselves a full range of support services.

We postulate that one can also expect the nationality of ownership of a firm to matter for its use of outside contractors. Foreign establishments, which are by definition part of a multinational company, can be expected to use higher levels of technology than purely domestic firms, due to their having access to firm-specific assets (e.g., Markusen, 1995). The use of high technology may lead to the contracting-out of activities, in particular low-tech activities. Also, if the foreign establishment is part of a vertical multinational there will be specialization of activities and, by definition, outsourcing of activities to vertically linked plants within the same multinational. Such specialization of activities may be less for purely domestic firms.[8] Furthermore, given that they are embedded in an international production network through their relationship with the parent and other affiliates abroad, they may be expected to have different strategies for dividing inhouse and outsourced production, and may have better access to external providers of services than do purely domestic firms. Hence, we would expect that foreign firms have higher propensities of outsourcing than domestic firms.[9]

In order to test for the importance of these determinants, we estimate empirically variants of the following equation:

$$outs_{it} = \beta_0 + \beta_1 w^s_{it-1} + \beta_2 w^{us}_{it-1} + \beta_3 un_{jt-1} + \beta_4 size_{it-1} + \beta_5 foreign_{it} + \dots$$
$$+ D_j + D_t + D_r + dv_{jt} + \varepsilon_{it}, \tag{1}$$

where *outs* is measured as the log of the cost of industrial services received by establishment i at time t. The regressors w^s and w^{us} are the log of wage rates for skilled and unskilled workers, respectively, while *un* captures the degree of unionization in the four-digit industry j, calculated using data from the *New Earnings Survey*. These variables are included to capture the "cost saving" motive for outsourcing. Given our discussion above, we would expect high-wage firms to do more outsourcing than other firms. Also, firms in highly unionized sectors may prefer outsourcing as union work rules may act to increase costs, even if wages are no different in unionized and non-unionized firms.[10] The *size* variable is the log of establishment size measured in terms of employment and is included to control for the economies-of-scale effect. Based on this reasoning we would expect smaller firms to be more intensive users of outsourcing. However, given that our dependent variable is measured in absolute terms, the size variable controls for the fact that large firms may do more outsourcing (in absolute terms) than smaller firms. *Foreign* is an ownership dummy equal to one if the establishment is foreign owned and zero otherwise. As pointed out above, we would expect this variable to have a positive coefficient if foreign firms are more intensive users of outsourcing. Furthermore, sectoral time dummies (dv_{jt}) are also included to control for the effect of cyclical or seasonal variations in output in the four-digit industries. Finally, we include four-digit sector (D_j), time (D_t), and region (D_r) dummies in equation (1).

Equation (1) is estimated for each of the three broad sectors separately using ordinary least-squares (OLS) estimation. We allow for heteroskedasticity of the error term,

Table 2. Determinants of Outsourcing: OLS Regression in Levels

Dependent variable: log of industrial services received	(1) chem I	(2) chem II	(3) engin I	(4) engin II	(5) electr I	(6) electr II
$size_{t-1}$	1.542	1.587	1.521	1.578	1.754	1.767
	(0.060)***	(0.067)***	(0.047)***	(0.048)***	(0.046)***	(0.050)***
skilled $wage_{t-1}$	0.837	0.814	0.399	0.378	0.392	0.384
	(0.216)***	(0.226)***	(0.163)**	(0.162)**	(0.137)***	(0.138)***
unskilled $wage_{t-1}$	0.028	0.006	0.117	0.148	0.068	0.065
	(0.152)	(0.174)	(0.049)**	(0.057)***	(0.058)	(0.063)
foreign dummy	0.665	0.433	0.612	0.574	0.309	0.144
	(0.139)***	(0.233)*	(0.120)***	(0.140)***	(0.144)**	(0.185)
foreign* $size_{t-1}$		−0.183		−0.404		−0.097
		(0.119)		(0.147)***		(0.120)
foreign* skilled $wage_{t-1}$		0.042		0.330		0.069
		(0.268)		(0.102)***		(0.129)
foreign* unskilled $wage_{t-1}$		0.103		−0.083		0.015
		(0.270)		(0.055)		(0.114)
union			1.218	1.121		
			(1.368)	(1.363)		
Constant	−5.731	−5.667	−3.999	−4.175	−10.001	−10.041
	(2.510)**	(2.484)**	(1.969)**	(1.948)**	(2.901)***	(2.911)***
Observations	6,917	6,917	23,555	23,555	12,552	12,552
F-test		1.31		3.49**		0.52
R^2	0.32	0.32	0.20	0.21	0.26	0.26

Notes: Heteroskedasticity–autocorrelation consistent standard errors in parentheses. Regressions include four-digit sector, time, region, and sectoral time dummies. Union variable in (1), (2), (5), and (6) is dropped due to multicollinearity with the sectoral time dummies. F-test is for joint significance of three interaction terms. ***, **, and *: significant at 1%, 5%, and 10% levels, respectively.

as well as an unspecified correlation between error terms within establishments, but not across establishments. This allows for the possibility that there may be unobserved establishment-specific effects which are correlated with the regressors but which we do not explicitly account for in the empirical model. The estimation results for the three sectors are presented in Table 2.

In line with our prior expectations, we find that high wages are positively correlated with outsourcing, which concurs with the hypothesis that high-wage establishments are more prone to outsource in order to reduce costs. The distinction between skilled and unskilled wages shows that the larger effects seem to stem from the former, rather than the latter part of labor costs. For example, for the engineering sector (column 4) we find that the elasticity of outsourcing with respect to skilled wages is 0.38, while the elasticity for the unskilled wage rate is 0.15. The rate of unionization can be included only for the engineering sector, where the coefficients turn out to be positive, albeit statistically insignificant. Large firms also outsource more than small firms—in all cases, the elasticity is between 1.5 and 1.8. This may reflect a pure size effect—large firms produce higher levels of output and therefore have more activities, in absolute terms, to outsource than do smaller firms.

We now turn to the importance of nationality of ownership for the use of outsourcing. As pointed out above, we would expect foreign firms to be more intensive users of outsourcing. As can be seen from columns 1, 3, and 5, this result is borne out by the data for all three manufacturing sectors. Controlling for size, labor costs, and cyclicity of production, foreign-owned establishments use more outsourcing than domestic establishments.

A reasonable question to ask is whether the determinants of outsourcing are systematically different for the former compared to the latter as well. In other words, do the slope coefficients on the regressors differ between foreign and domestic establishments? To investigate this issue we interact all establishment-level regressors (wage and size variables) with the ownership dummy and rerun the augmented specification of equation (1). The results are reported in columns 2, 4, and 6 of Table 2.

We test for the joint significance of the three interaction terms using an F-test. The test statistics suggest that, for the chemicals and electronics sectors, we cannot reject the hypothesis that the interaction terms are jointly equal to zero. Hence, we do not find systematic differences in the determinants of outsourcing between foreign and domestic establishments in these sectors. It is different in the engineering sector, where the interaction terms are jointly significant. We still find that the ownership dummy is statistically significant and positive, suggesting that foreign firms use more outsourcing. What differs also between the foreign and domestic groups of establishments is the effect of the other regressors included in the equation. The size effect is reduced substantially for foreign establishments, with the elasticities being 1.58 for domestic firms and 1.18 for foreign firms. Also, the elasticity of outsourcing with respect to skilled wages is larger for foreign than domestic establishments (0.71 vs 0.38).

Two criticisms could be directed at equation (1). First, if there are time-invariant establishment-specific effects that are not captured in the explanatory variables but that are correlated with them, then our estimation may produce biased and inconsistent estimates. In other words, if the error term included in equation (1) equals $\varepsilon_{it} = v_i + u_{it}$, then a simple OLS regression is problematic. In order to take this into account, we relate the change in the outsourcing variable to changes in the wage and size variables, thus purging the establishment-specific effect v_i in the levels specification. However, we still include *foreign* and *un* in levels, as we are interested in establishing whether foreign firms or more unionized sectors experience higher growth of outsourcing than others. Second, if there is persistence in the outsourcing decision then we may expect that the decision to outsource in period t is related to the level of outsourcing in the previous period $t - 1$. To allow for such temporal correlation between outsourcing in t and $t - 1$, we include the lagged level of outsourcing also in the equation. Hence, our alternative specification is described by the following equation:

$$\Delta(outs_{it}) = \beta_0 + \beta_1 \Delta(w^s_{it-1}) + \beta_2 \Delta(w^{us}_{it-1}) + \beta_3 un_{jt-1} + \beta_4 \Delta(size_{it-1}) + \ldots$$
$$+ \beta_5 foreign_{it} + \beta_6 outs_{it-1} + D_j + D_t + D_r + dv_{jt} + \varepsilon_{it}. \qquad (2)$$

The results of estimations of this equation using data for the three manufacturing sectors separately are presented in Table 3. Note that the lagged level of outsourcing is highly statistically significant and negative in all cases, suggesting that there is indeed

Table 3. Determinants of Outsourcing: First-differences with Lagged Level of Outsourcing

Dependent variable: log of industrial services received	(1) chem I	(2) chem II	(3) engin I	(4) engin II	(5) electr I	(6) electr II
$outs_{t-1}$	−0.346	−0.345	−0.353	−0.353	−0.327	−0.327
	(0.021)***	(0.021)***	(0.010)***	(0.010)***	(0.012)***	(0.012)***
$\Delta size_{t-1}$	0.211	0.264	−0.131	−0.132	0.156	0.162
	(0.309)	(0.325)	(0.125)	(0.126)	(0.152)	(0.157)
$\Delta skilled\ wage_{t-1}$	0.414	0.344	0.002	−0.005	−0.081	−0.071
	(0.270)	(0.281)	(0.089)	(0.089)	(0.143)	(0.144)
$\Delta unskilled\ wage_{t-1}$	−0.006	0.052	0.151	0.184	−0.050	−0.069
	(0.149)	(0.184)	(0.054)***	(0.064)***	(0.051)	(0.055)
foreign dummy	0.501	0.490	0.581	0.584	0.385	0.390
	(0.083)***	(0.085)***	(0.063)***	(0.065)***	(0.081)***	(0.084)***
foreign* $\Delta size_{t-1}$		−0.130		0.015		−0.045
		(0.213)		(0.134)		(0.160)
foreign* $\Delta skilled\ wage_{t-1}$		0.266		0.096		−0.113
		(0.247)		(0.103)		(0.118)
foreign* $\Delta unskilled\ wage_{t-1}$		−0.185		−0.118		0.145
		(0.239)		(0.074)		(0.072)**
union			−0.796	−0.821		
			(1.524)	(1.527)		
Constant	4.804	3.482	4.120	4.131	5.776	5.788
	(1.090)***	(1.257)***	(0.777)***	(0.778)***	(1.981)***	(1.979)***
Observations	5,707	5,707	18,428	18,428	10,095	10,095
F-test		0.41		0.98		1.41
R^2	0.21	0.21	0.20	0.20	0.18	0.18

Notes: See Table 2.

temporal correlation in outsourcing; i.e., present outsourcing is heavily influenced by previous outsourcing. Inclusion of the lagged level leads to most of the explanatory variables being statistically insignificant. However, most importantly from our point of view, the finding that foreign establishments outsource more than domestic ones, *ceteris paribus*, is robust to the inclusion of the lagged level of outsourcing.

4. Productivity Effects of Outsourcing

Having analyzed the determinants of outsourcing, we now turn to investigate whether outsourcing leads to an improvement in establishments' performance. More specifically we analyze whether outsourcing has a positive effect on productivity, measured in terms of labor or total factor productivity (TFP), of the establishment that decides to outsource the activities.

In a recent paper, Ten Raa and Wolff (2001) argued that TFP growth in manufacturing industries is positively related to an increased use of outsourcing, defined as inputs purchased from services industries. Their empirical evidence is based on industry-level data using US input/output tables to calculate the importance of outsourcing. The effects of outsourcing for service industries have also been investigated recently. Fixler and Siegel (1999) argued that outsourcing has played a major role in the growth of the services sector. Their empirical evidence, based on industry-level data for the US, suggests that outsourcing has led to short-run reductions in service sector productivity, but that there have been positive effects in the long run. Our paper is, to the best of our knowledge, the first study to investigate with establishment-level data the effects of outsourcing on productivity in the establishment undertaking the outsourcing.

As argued in the previous section, one of the reasons for outsourcing may be to economize on labor costs. An increase in outsourcing may lead directly to a reduction of employment, while keeping output constant, so having an immediate effect on labor productivity. Our investigation of this issue is based on the following equation of labor productivity augmented by a measure of outsourcing intensity at the level of the establishment:[11]

$$\Delta y/l_{it} = \alpha_0 + \alpha_1 \Delta k/l_{it} + \alpha_2 \Delta m/l_{it} + \alpha_3 outint_{it} + D_t + D_r + \varepsilon_{it}, \tag{3}$$

where y is output, l is labor, k is capital, m is material inputs, D_t and D_r are time and regional dummies, respectively, and ε is an error term. The outsourcing intensity *outint* is calculated as the value of industrial services received divided by total wage costs, as in section 2.[12] In order to see whether there are different productivity effects of outsourcing for foreign and domestic firms, we allow α_3 to vary for the two nationality groups. Outsourcing may affect not only the productivity of labor but also that of other factors of production if it leads to an adjustment of the production process. In order to capture these productivity effects, we also examine whether outsourcing affects TFP growth.[13] Both labor and total factor productivity equations are estimated in levels as well as first-differences.

A major econometric concern with the above equation is that there may be a potential endogeneity problem; i.e., there may be unobserved covariates that are correlated with productivity and outsourcing intensity that may be driving the results. For example, it might be the case that highly productive establishments are more skill-intensive and therefore more likely to use outsourcing to shift the production of low-skill-intensive components outside the firm. In order to take account of this possibility, we instrument for outsourcing intensity with the past level of outsourcing intensity, the growth rates and lagged values of establishment size, skilled and unskilled wages. We use the robust form of Sargan's test of over-identifying restrictions to examine the null hypothesis that the correlation between the instrumental variable candidates and the error terms in the productivity equation is zero—a necessary condition for the validity of the instrumental-variables regression approach. Depending on the particular sector and equation in question (TFP or labor productivity; levels or differences), instruments which are found to be invalid are dropped from the specification.

We are also careful to assess the strength of the relationship between the instruments and the potentially endogenous regressors. It has been noted in the econometric literature (e.g., Staiger and Stock, 1997) that when the partial correlation between the instruments and the endogenous variable is low, instrumental-variables regression is biased in the direction of the OLS estimator. Staiger and Stock recommend that the F-statistics (or equivalently the p-values) from the first-stage regression be routinely reported in applied work. The F-statistic tests the hypothesis that the

Table 4. Labor Productivity and Outsourcing: Instrumental Variables Estimates

	Chemicals sector		Electronics sector		Engineering sector	
	Levels	First differences	Levels	First differences	Levels	First differences
Capital intensity	0.020	0.004	−0.049	0.026	0.028	−0.000
	(2.84)***	(0.47)	(1.07)	(1.52)	(2.83)***	(0.01)
Material inputs	0.773	0.732	0.991	0.551	0.587	0.531
intensity	(20.40)***	(13.78)***	(5.63)***	(5.49)***	(15.75)***	(17.16)***
Outsourcing	0.174	0.135	−0.468	−0.410	0.491	0.002
intensity	(6.61)***	(1.28)	(1.13)	(1.63)	(4.63)***	(0.38)
Outsourcing	0.019	0.009	0.009	0.014	0.076	0.047
intensity*	(1.65)*	(0.84)	(0.24)	(0.63)	(2.25)**	(3.34)***
foreigndummy						
Exogeneity test	0	1	0.995	1	0.239	0
(p-value)						
F (first-stage)	18.71	0.19	2.46	0.51	29.1	51.46
{p-value}	(0)	(0.9912)	(0.022)	(0.847)	(0)	(0)
Sargan	0.377	0.602	0.351	0.237	0.543	0.202
{p-value}						
Observations	6,115	6,115	10,882	10,882	18,793	13,245
Number of plants	1,133	1,133	2,184	2,184	4,376	4,376

Notes: Regressions include time and region dummies. Heteroskedasticity-consistent standard errors in parentheses. The test of exogeneity is a Hausman test which examines the null hypothesis that there is no statistically significant difference between the OLS and IV estimates. ***, **, and *: significant at 1%, 5%, and 10% levels, respectively.

instruments should be excluded from the first-stage regressions (i.e., the relevance of the instruments). The idea here is that when the F-statistic is small (or the corresponding p-value is large), the instrumental variable estimates and the associated confidence interval are unreliable.

Tables 4 and 5 present the empirical estimates from the labor productivity and TFP equations, respectively. Again we estimate the model separately for the three manufacturing sectors. As might be expected, the estimates display some heterogeneity across sectors.

Turning to labor productivity first and focusing on the specification in levels, it can be seen from Table 4 that, for the chemical and engineering sectors, outsourcing is positively related with labor productivity. It does not seem to exert any influence on the productivity path of plants in the electronics sector, however. The elasticity of labor productivity with respect to outsourcing is about three times higher in the engineering than in the chemicals sector. Furthermore, this productivity effect of outsourcing is more pronounced in the sample of foreign-owned establishments as indicated by the positive coefficients on the interaction terms.

The first-difference specification does not yield strong results. Labor productivity and outsourcing growth rates appear to be correlated in foreign establishments within the engineering sector. This lack of robust correlation may be due to the weakness of the instrumental-variable candidates, which are too weak as evidenced by the low

Table 5. TFP and Outsourcing: Instrumental Variables Estimates

	Chemicals sector		Electronics sector		Engineering sector	
	Levels	First differences	Levels	First differences	Levels	First differences
Outsourcing intensity	0.087 (4.89)***	0.257 (1.70)*	−0.645 (1.51)	0.054 (0.41)	0.346 (4.63)***	0.158 (2.24)**
Outsourcing intensity* foreign dummy	0.019 (2.22)**	0.026 (1.22)	−0.004 (0.10)	−0.011 (1.63)	0.078 (3.12)***	0.449 (2.60)***
Exogeneity test (*p*-value)	0.01	0.991	1	1	0.499	0.4627
F (first-stage) {*p*-value}	67.25 (0)	1.44 (0.139)	1.83 (0.089)	0.32 (0.924)	34.49 (0)	38.91 (0)
Sargan {*p*-value}	0.155	0.496	0.652	0.133	0.127	0.060
Observations	6,115	5,068	10,882	8,723	18,793	13,245
Number of plants	1,133	896	2,184	1,638	4,376	2,941

Notes: See Table 4.

F-statistics from the first-stage regressions for the chemicals and electronics sectors.[14] In the absence of other instrumental-variable candidates or a "natural experiment" for the outsourcing variable, it does not seem appropriate to draw firm conclusions about the effect of outsourcing on productivity based on the first-differenced specifications.

Table 5 reports the results of the TFP estimations. The level of TFP seems to respond to changes in the outsourcing intensity, again in the chemical and engineering sectors. This is particularly pronounced for foreign establishments. TFP adjusts faster to outsourcing in the engineering sector, particularly in foreign establishments. From the first-differenced estimation there is also evidence of a positive relationship between TFP growth and the changes in the degree of outsourcing for the engineering sector. For the other two sectors, the low *F*-statistics from the first-stage regressions may again indicate the weakness of the instruments used, which may explain the lack of a significant correlation between outsourcing and TFP.

The econometric estimates reported in the above tables give some idea as to the relationship between outsourcing and productivity, and the statistical significance of this association. What, then, is the economic significance of outsourcing in the establishment-level productivity trajectory? As a first attempt towards answering this question, we calculate the implied change in productivity resulting from the change in outsourcing intensity,[15] and relate it to the actual productivity growth observed in the data. Table 6 reports the results from this experiment.

Consistent with the reported point estimates, outsourcing played a more important role in the engineering sector: nearly a quarter of the observed change in *total factor productivity* and almost 15% of the change in *labor productivity* in domestic plants is attributed to the change in outsourcing intensity. The effects on foreign firms' productivity are much smaller—0% and 7%, respectively. Of course, to the extent that the outsourcing variable captures the effect of some omitted variable, the figures in

Table 6. *Contribution of Outsourcing to Productivity Growth: Median Values across Establishments*

	Chemicals sector		Engineering sector	
	Actual yearly growth rate	Implied % contribution of outsourcing	Actual yearly growth rate	Implied % contribution of outsourcing
Labor productivity				
Domestic	2.17%	4.7%	1.6%	14.7%
Foreign	3.06%	2.4%	2.66%	6.8%
TFP				
Domestic	−0.6%	1.1%	−0.1%	24.4%
Foreign	0%	0%	−0.1%	0%

Note: The implied change in productivity due to outsourcing is obtained by multiplying the point estimates of the elasticity of productivity with respect to outsourcing by the actual change in outsourcing intensity in the data. The estimates are obtained from the models in levels.

Table 6 might overstate the importance of outsourcing. Nonetheless these "back-of-envelope" calculations are indicative that the role of outsourcing in enhancing productivity, at least in the engineering sector, is likely to be economically significant.

5. Conclusions

This paper has presented an empirical analysis of "outsourcing" using establishment-level data for UK manufacturing industries. Our results suggest that high wages are positively related to outsourcing, so that the cost-saving motive is important. We also find that foreign-owned firms have higher levels of outsourcing than domestic establishments. In the productivity analysis, we find that an establishment's outsourcing intensity in the chemical and engineering sectors is positively related to its productivity. This relationship appears to be more pronounced in foreign-owned establishments.

Appendix: TFP Estimation

Using log values, we write the production function as $y_{it} \equiv f(l_{it}^s, l_{it}^u, k_{it}, m_{it}, TFP_{it})$, where y is output and there are four factors of production: skilled labor (l^s), unskilled labor (l^u), materials or cost of goods sold (m), and capital stock (k). For estimation purposes we employ a first-order Taylor approximation and write the production function as

$$y_{it} = \beta_0 + \beta_s l_{it}^s + \beta_u l_{it}^u + \beta_k k_{it} + \beta_m m_{it} + TFP_{it}. \tag{A1}$$

TFP is assumed to follow the following AR(1) process:

$$TFP_{it} = \rho TFP_{it-1} + \delta D_t + f_i + v_{it}, \tag{A2}$$

where D is a common year-specific shock, f is a time-invariant firm-specific effect, and v a random error term. Note that we do not simply model productivity as a fixed effect, as that would imply that TFP differences are fixed, and there is no role for technology diffusion (convergence).

Recently the fundamental assumption of pooling individual times-series data has been questioned. Pesaran and Smith (1995) demonstrated that standard GMM estimators of dynamic panel models lead to invalid inference if the response parameters are characterized by heterogeneity. They argue that one is better off averaging parameters from individual time-series regressions. This is not feasible here since the individual firm's time-series data are not of adequate length. However, we take some comfort from a recent comparative study by Baltagi and Griffin (1997) which concludes that efficiency gains from pooling are likely to more than offset the biases due to individual heterogeneity. Baltagi and Griffin especially point out the desirable properties of the GLS-AR(1) estimator, and we use this estimator to obtain estimates of the factor elasticities, and derive TFP as a residual term. We estimate equation (4) for each of the four-digit SIC80 industries available in our sample.

References

Abraham, K. G. and S. K. Taylor, "Firms' Use of Outside Contractors: Theory and Evidence," *Journal of Labor Economics* 14 (1996):394–424.

Arndt, S. and H. Kierzkowski (eds.), *Fragmentation: New Production Patterns in the World Economy*, Oxford: Oxford University Press (2001).

Baltagi, B. H. and J. M. Griffin, "Pooled Estimators versus their Heterogeneous Counterparts in the Context of the Dynamic Demand for Gasoline," *Journal of Econometrics* 77 (1997):303–27.

Barnes, M. and R. Martin, "Business Data Linking: an Introduction," *Economic Trends* no. 581 (2002):34–41.

Bolton, P. and M. D. Whinston, "Incomplete Contracts, Vertical Integration, and Supply Assurance," *Review of Economic Studies* 60 (1993):121–48.

Coase, R., "The Nature of the Firm," *Economica* 4 (1937):386–405.

Deardorff, A. V., "Fragmentation in Simple Trade Models," *North American Journal of Economics and Finance* 12 (2001):121–37.

Egger, H. and P. Egger, "International Outsourcing and the Productivity of Low-skilled Labor in the EU," working paper 152/2001, Austrian Institute of Economic Research (WIFO), Vienna (2001).

Feenstra, R. C. and G. H. Hanson, "Globalization, Outsourcing, and Wage Inequality," *American Economic Review Papers and Proceedings* 86 (1996):240–5.

———, "The Impact of Outsourcing and High-technology Capital on Wages: Estimates for the United States, 1979–1990," *Quarterly Journal of Economics* 114 (1999):907–40.

Fixler, D. J. and D. Siegel, "Outsourcing and Productivity Growth in Services," *Structural Change and Economic Dynamics* 10 (1999):177–94.

Görg, H., "Fragmentation and Trade: US Inward Processing Trade in the EU," *Weltwirtschaftliches Archiv* 136 (2000):403–21.

Görg, H. and A. Hanley, "Does Outsourcing Increase Profitability?" working paper 2003/01, Nottingham University Business School (2003).

Görzig, B. and A. Stephan, "Outsourcing and Firm-level Performance," discussion paper 309, DIW Berlin (2002).

Greenhalgh, M., M. Gregory, and A. Ray, "The Changing Structure of UK Production, Trade and Employment: an Analysis using Input–Output Tables," Applied Economics discussion paper 70, University of Oxford (1999).

Griffith, R. and H. Simpson, "Characteristics of Foreign-owned Firms in British Manufacturing," in R. Blundell, D. Card, and R. Freeman (eds.), *Creating a Premier League Economy*, Chicago: Chicago University Press (2003).

Grossman, G. M. and E. Helpman, "Outsourcing in a Global Economy," NBER working paper 8728 (2002a).

———, "Integration versus Outsourcing in Industry Equilibrium," *Quarterly Journal of Economics* 117 (2002b):85–120.

Grossman, S. J. and O. D. Hart, "The Costs and Benefits of Ownership: a Theory of Vertical and Lateral Integration," *Journal of Political Economy* 94 (1986):691–719.

Hijzen, A., H. Görg, and R. C. Hine, "International Outsourcing and the Skill Structure of Labour Demand in the UK," *Economic Journal* (2004): forthcoming.

Holmes, T. J., "Localization of Industry and Vertical Disintegration," *Review of Economics and Statistics* 81 (1999):314–25.

Hummels, D., J. Ishii, and K.-M. Yi, "The Nature and Growth of Vertical Specialization in World Trade," *Journal of International Economics* 54 (2001):75–96.

Jones, R. W. and H. Kierzkowski, "A Framework for Fragmentation," in S. Arndt and H. Kierzkowski (eds.), *Fragmentation: New Production Patterns in the World Economy*, Oxford: Oxford University Press (2001).

Kohler, W., "A Specific Factors View on Outsourcing," *North American Journal of Economics and Finance* 12 (2001):31–53.

Lyons, B. R., "Specific Investment, Economies of Scale, and the Make-or-Buy Decision: a Test of Transaction Cost Theory," *Journal of Economic Behavior and Organization* 26 (1995):431–43.

Markusen, J. R., "The Boundaries of Multinational Enterprises and the Theory of International Trade," *Journal of Economic Perspectives* 9(2) (1995):169–89.

Pesaran, M. H. and R. Smith, "Estimating Long-run Relationships from Dynamic Heterogeneous Panels," *Journal of Econometrics* 68 (1995):79–112.

Staiger, D. and J. H. Stock, "Instrumental Variables Regression with Weak Instruments," *Econometrica* 65 (1997):557–86.

Swenson, D. L., "Firm Outsourcing Decisions: Evidence from US Foreign Trade Zones," *Economic Inquiry* (2000):175–89.

Ten Raa, T. and E. N. Wolff, "Outsourcing of Services and the Productivity Recovery in US Manufacturing in the 1980s and 1990s," *Journal of Productivity Analysis* 16 (2001):149–65.

Turok, I., "Inward Investment and Local Linkages: How Deeply Embedded is 'Silicon Glen'?", *Regional Studies* 27 (1993):401–17.

Weiss, A., *Efficiency Wages*, Princeton, NJ: Princeton University Press (1991).

Notes

1. This phenomenon, which we refer to as outsourcing, may also be termed "make or buy decision" (Grossman and Helpman, 2002b), "vertical disintegration" (Holmes, 1999), "fragmentation" (Arndt and Kierzkowski, 2001), "vertical specialization" (Hummels et al., 2001), to mention but a few synonyms.

2. Greenhalgh et al. (1999) documented that there is an increase in contracting-out of services in the UK. Our approach is closely related to the paper by Abraham and Taylor (1996) who analyze the determinants of outsourcing using plant-level data for the US. However, they do not distinguish between domestic and foreign-owned establishments. A related paper by Swenson (2000) examines the decision to import intermediates for firms located in US foreign-trade zones, paying particular attention to the effect of changes in international prices on imported inputs.

3. There are a few papers that look at the effects of outsourcing on manufacturing (Ten Raa and Wolff, 2001) or service-sector (Fixler and Siegel, 1999) productivity using industry-level data. Also, in related papers, Görzig and Stephan (2002) and Görg and Hanley (2003) look at the relationship between outsourcing and profitability, using film-level data.

4. Note that with the data available we are not able to identify UK multinationals.

5. More precisely, using SIC 1980 classifications, chemicals is SIC 25, mechanical and instrument engineering (hereafter referred to as engineering) includes SIC 32 and SIC 37, and electronics includes SIC 33 (manufacture of office machinery and data processing equipment) and SIC 34 (electrical and electronic engineering).

6. This argument implies that firms cannot pursue different wage strategies, paying high (efficiency) wages to core workers and lower wages to other workers. This may be due to unionization, or to internal equity considerations.

7. Outsourcing may also be undertaken to save on costs other than wages or to provide access to better technology, more favorable regulations, etc. Unfortunately, we cannot from our data measure such other determinants and therefore cannot include them in the empirical analysis.

8. Although it may be similar for domestic establishments which are part of a UK multinational. Unfortunately, we are not able to observe UK multinationals in our dataset.

9. The fact that multinationals have been found to import more of their intermediate inputs than domestic firms (e.g., Turok, 1993) gives some preliminary support for this assumption.

10. On the other hand, as a referee pointed out to us, unions may attempt to prevent outsourcing in order to safeguard jobs, which would have a negative effect on outsourcing.

11. We assume that the intensity of outsourcing shifts the technology parameter of the underlying production.

12. Note that we do not simply measure outsourcing as use of intermediate inputs (m) in the production function.

13. See the Appendix for a description of how TFP is calculated.

14. Notice that these instruments are valid according to the Sargan test, however.

15. The point estimates from the equations in levels are used to this end. We confine our analysis to establishments with more than five years of data.

Chapter 6

Two Dimensions of Convergence: National and International Wage Adjustment Effects of Cross-border Outsourcing in Europe

Peter Egger and Michael Pfaffermayr

1. Introduction

The driving forces of international factor price convergence and the international distribution of income have attracted a lot of interest in the last decades. International trade in final goods, especially, but also trade in intermediate goods resulting from cross-border outsourcing of production processes, are seen as forces towards factor price equalization between the developed and the less-developed economies. Nowadays, researchers widely agree upon the notion that trade in goods per se does not provide a sufficient explanation for the change in factor prices (Krugman, 1995; Feenstra and Hanson, 2001). However, the changing *composition* of trade, and the growing importance of *intermediate input trade* in particular, seems much more important in both theory and evidence; see Feenstra and Hanson (2001) for an overview.

Baier and Bergstrand (2001) derived simulation results from a stylized computable general-equilibrium model. Using reasonable parameter estimates, they found that intermediate goods trade (outsourcing) might account for about one-sixth of the growth of world trade between 1960 and 1990. Hummels et al. (2001, p. 15) find that "vertical specialization accounts for up to 30% of world exports."

There are at least two theoretical arguments for trade in intermediate goods to take place and, thereby, to affect factor prices. First, the theoretical outsourcing literature predominantly investigates the effects on the national skilled to unskilled workers' wage differential or the reward of capital relative to labor (Arndt, 1997; Deardorff, 2001; Feenstra and Hanson, 2001; Jones and Kierzkowski, 2001; Kohler, 2001, 2003). In these models, outsourcing is defined as the vertical splitting of the production process across borders according to comparative advantage, resulting in an inherent difference in the labor intensity of intermediate goods exports and imports. For instance, capital-abundant economies outsource labor-abundant production stages, whereas labor-abundant countries outsource capital-abundant fragments, and both components are traded. Accordingly, the exploitation of specialization gains through outsourcing may foster international factor price equalization. Deardorff (2001, p. 135) concludes that, if there are some impediments to factor price equalization (e.g., transportation costs, tariff or nontariff barriers to trade, etc.), outsourcing may drive factor price equalization to "the extent that factor prices are not equalized internationally without outsourcing." Jones and Kierzkowski (2001, p. 31) mention that depending on the extent of dissimilarity in factor endowment proportions outsourcing may "bring factor prices closer together," but generally "almost anything can happen." Kohler (2003) derives similar conclusions in his higher dimensional analysis of outsourcing effects, which contains the models of Arndt (1997) and Feenstra and Hanson (1996, 1997) as special cases. In the now standard models of outsourcing, the equalization of wages *within* countries is assumed (through the perfect mobility of labor between sectors) and the equalization of wages *between* countries is a likely, and empirically highly relevant, outcome.

Second, if there is Ethier-type specialization (Ethier, 1982), the productivity of final goods producers increases with the (horizontal) splitting of the production chain per se due to external scale economies. Countries then engage in intermediate goods trade to take advantage of a larger available variety of components rather than of exploiting comparative advantage in the production of fragments. However, this model does not imply factor intensity differences in the intermediate goods production between economies. If this type of specialization becomes technologically or economically feasible for exogenous reasons, Ethier demonstrates that factor prices equalize under free trade.

In the short run, the lack of labor mobility between sectors within a country due to national barriers to mobility (e.g., because of industry-specific knowledge of workers) and adjustment costs may impede the effects of outsourcing (or intermediate goods imports) on incomes to take place immediately. It is a stylized fact that wages vary systematically across industries with capital-intensive industries paying higher wages, and that this phenomenon is quite persistent over time (Krueger and Summers, 1988). However, in the steady state, one would expect that the rewards of different factors (capital and labor) grow at the same rate and wage differentials between industries within a country as well as between countries—if they exist at all—do not change. But even in the long run, average wage rates may differ across industries because a different mix of skilled and unskilled workers is used (e.g., due to worker quality variation even within skill groups).

The available empirical evidence on the consequences of cross-border outsourcing at the industry level for both the US and Europe mainly supports the Heckscher–Ohlin view: Feenstra and Hanson (1999, 2001), Greenaway et al. (1999), Egger and Egger (2001), and others identify a clear positive impact of outsourcing on the skilled-to-unskilled wage and/or employment ratio in high-wage countries. Feenstra and Hanson (1997) provide evidence that outsourcing raises the skilled-to-unskilled wage ratio in both the North (the US) and the South (Mexico).

So far, there seems to be no evidence on the impact of intermediate goods trade on the convergence of real wages in a large cross-section of industries and economies. This paper tries to fill this gap and assesses the effects of intermediate goods trade on the convergence of real wages both *within* and *between* countries in a unified empirical framework. We propose an empirical model to assess the impact of intermediate goods trade in these two dimensions using two-digit manufacturing industry-level data of the 15 EU members and 5 CEEC (Czech Republic, Hungary, Poland, Slovenia, and Slovak Republic) covering the period 1993 to 2000. Given that in the steady state wage differentials are constant, intermediate goods trade may be expected to affect the speed of convergence, but not to induce differences in steady-state growth rates. Therefore, we start from a traditional β-convergence model as proposed by Barro and Sala-i-Martin (1995), which is designed to analyze dynamic adjustment processes with one-way cross-sectional units (e.g., countries, regions, firms). However, to decompose the intermediate goods trade effect into its within- and between-countries component, we account for the "two-way" character of the cross-sections and specify a bivariate system of differential equations, which drives the country-by-industry evolution of real wage rates.

According to our main empirical results, *between*-country convergence dominates the adjustment of real wage rates and intermediate goods trade facilitates *international* factor price equalization in Europe. Moreover, outsourcing accelerates convergence *within* the EU-15 member countries, while it does not lead to convergence *within* the CEEC, where interindustry wage differentials tend to persist.

The next section introduces the concept of the two dimensions of convergence, while section 3 discusses the database, the econometric specification, and the estimation results. The last section summarizes the main findings and concludes.

2. Two Dimensions of Convergence

To measure the speed of convergence of real wages *between countries* and *within countries* (across industries), we propose an extension of the standard β-convergence equation. Specifically, we hypothesize that the speed of convergence differs between the within-country (between industries) dimension (b_1) and the between-country dimension (b_2). If $b_1 < b_2$, the overall catching-up in real wage rates between countries dominates. If, on the other hand, $b_1 > b_2$ the interindustry wage rate differentials disappear quickly, but overall catching-up between countries is slow.

For a typical industry i in country c, convergence requires that the growth rate of a country's real wage rate be negatively proportional to its initial level (Barro and Sala-i-Martin, 1995). Formally, the log-linearization around the steady state is given by the following system of linear first-order differential equations:

$$\frac{d\omega_{ic}(t)}{dt} - \frac{d\omega_{.c}(t)}{dt} = -b_1[\omega_{ic}(t) - \omega_{.c}(t)], \tag{1}$$

$$\frac{d\omega_{.c}(t)}{dt} - \frac{d\omega^*(t)}{dt} = -b_2[\omega_{.c}(t) - \omega^*(t)], \tag{2}$$

$$\frac{d\omega^*(t)}{dt} = g. \tag{3}$$

$\omega_{ic}(t) = \ln w_{ic}(t)$ is the log of the real wage rate of industry i in country c, and $\omega_{.c}(t) = (1/I)\Sigma_{i=1}^{I}w_{ic}(t)$, where I denotes the number of industries. $\omega^*(t)$ denotes the log of the "worldwide" steady state of the real wage rate at time t with assumed constant growth rate g. Equation (2) states that the difference between a country's real wage growth ($d\omega_{.c}(t)/dt$) and the steady-state growth rate ($d\omega^*(t)/dt$) is higher, the higher the distance of the average log real wage rate of country $c(\omega_{.c}(t))$ from its steady-state counterpart ($\omega^*(t)$) at time t. Equation (1) implies that the real wage rate in industry i grows faster, the more it lags behind the average country-wide real wage rate. For simplicity, we assume that a single industry is too small to influence the country average. Hence, the system is only an approximation of the true, by far more compli-cated, system, where the real wages of all industries show up on the right-hand side of (1). Solving this system of differential equations results in the following equation for a period of length T:

$$\omega_{ic}^T = e^{-b_1 T}(\omega_{ic}^0 - \omega_{.c}^0) + e^{-b_2 T}(\omega_{.c}^0 - \omega^{0,*}) + \omega^{T,*}. \tag{4}$$

Equation (3) implies that the steady-state real wage rate in logs is defined by $\omega^*(t) = gt + \omega^{0,*}$, with $\omega^{0,*}$ as the exogenously given steady-state log wage rate at time 0. Subtracting the initial value ω_{ic}^0 from both sides of (4), rearranging terms, dividing by T, and adding an i.i.d. error term u_{it}, we get a natural extension of the traditional convergence equation for the annual average growth rate of real wages in industry i over a period of length T:

$$\frac{1}{T}(\omega_{ic}^T - \omega_{ic}^0) = g - \frac{1}{T}(1 - e^{-b_1 T})(\omega_{ic}^0 - \omega_{.c}^0) - \frac{1}{T}(1 - e^{-b_2 T})(\omega_{.c}^0 - \omega^{0,*}) + u_{it}. \tag{5}$$

β-convergence is a necessary, however not sufficient, condition for convergence. Therefore, we additionally look at σ-convergence and investigate whether the standard deviation of real wage rates decreased over time, again both *within* and *between* countries. Formulating the system (1)–(3) in discrete time, substituting (2) and (3) in (1), and adding a random i.i.d. error-term, which is uncorrelated with the right-hand-side variables, gives:

$$\omega_{ic}^t = \beta_1(\omega_{ic}^{t-1} - \omega_{.c}^{t-1}) + \beta_2(\omega_{.c}^{t-1} - \omega^{t-1,*}) + \omega^{t,*} + u_{it}, \tag{6}$$

where $\beta_1 = 1 - b_1$ and $\beta_2 = 1 - b_2$. The standard deviation of ω_{ic}^t can be easily calculated, when assuming that the overall mean of the real wage rate approximately corresponds to the steady state: $(1/IC)\Sigma_{c=1}^C \Sigma_{i=1}^I \omega_{ic}^t = \omega_{..}^t = \omega^{t,*}$, where C denotes the number of countries, and IC is the overall number of (country-by-industry) observations. Since $\omega_{..}^t = (1/IC)\Sigma_{c=1}^C \Sigma_{i=1}^I \omega_{ic}^t = (1/IC)\Sigma_{c=1}^C \beta_1(\omega_{.c}^{t-1} - \omega_{.c}^{t-1}) + (1/C)\Sigma_{c=1}^C \beta_2(\omega_{.c}^{t-1} - \omega^{t-1,*}) + \omega^{t,*} = \omega^{t,*}$, we have

$$\sigma_t^2 = \frac{1}{IC}\sum_{c=1}^C \sum_{i=1}^I (\omega_{ic}^t - \omega_{..}^t)^2 + \sigma_u^2$$

$$= \frac{1}{IC}\sum_{c=1}^C \sum_{i=1}^I [\beta_1(\omega_{ic}^{t-1} - \omega_{.c}^{t-1}) + \beta_2(\omega_{.c}^{t-1} - \omega^{t-1,*})]^2 + \sigma_u^2$$

$$= \frac{1}{IC}\sum_{c=1}^C \sum_{i=1}^I [\beta_1^2(\omega_{ic}^{t-1} - \omega_{.c}^{t-1})^2 + 2\beta_1\beta_2(\omega_{ic}^{t-1} - \omega_{.c}^{t-1})(\omega_{.c}^{t-1} - \omega^{t-1,*})$$

$$+ \beta_2^2(\omega_{.c}^{t-1} - \omega^{t-1,*})]^2 + \sigma_u^2$$

$$= \beta_1^2 \sigma_{t-1,W}^2 + \beta_2^2 \sigma_{t-1,B} + \sigma_u^2, \tag{7}$$

where $\sigma_{t,W}^2 = (1/IC)\Sigma_{c=1}^C \Sigma_{i=1}^I(\omega_{ic}^t - \omega_{.c}^t)^2$ and $\sigma_{t,B}^2 = (1/C)\Sigma_{c=1}^C(\omega_{.c}^t - \omega^{t,*})^2$.

Hence, there are three principal opportunities to estimate the parameters of the two dimensions of convergence in real wage rates. First, we can use (5) to estimate the speed of convergence in a cross-section of industries and countries. Second, one can estimate (6) in a panel with industry, country, and time variation using the procedure proposed by Arellano and Bond (1991). Third, one could look at σ-convergence based on a regression of (7). Since the time-series dimension of our data is rather short, the latter is not feasible. Rather, we follow Carree and Klomp (1997) and test whether the variance of real wage rates (σ_t^2, $\sigma_{t,W}^2$, and $\sigma_{t,B}^2$) decreased over the period 1993 to 2000.

We test below whether the speed of convergence depends on the volume of intermediate goods trade as a percentage of gross production (intermediate goods trade: o_{ic}). Its impact may differ *within* and *between* countries and also between the CEEC and the EU-15. Note, we rule out the possibility that the *level* of intermediate goods trade exerts any impact on the steady-state *growth* of wage rates. Rather, we assume that it affects only the *level* and the corresponding *transition* path. Hence, the wage growth effects of intermediate goods trade are assumed to be transitory. The rationale is the analogy to the impact of exogenous, labor-augmenting technical progress on the level of labor productivity in a Solow–Swan-type neoclassical growth model.

3. Data and Estimation Results

Data

Our data comprise 14 manufacturing industries, which are slightly higher aggregated than NACE two-digit ones. For simplicity, we refer to them as two-digits. The real wage data for the EU countries are taken from New Cronos Products (EUROSTAT). The CEEC wages are kindly provided by the Vienna Institute for International Economic Studies (WIIW). Wages are expressed in constant prices and US dollars using 1995 as the base year. For the EU countries, we have to estimate part of the year 2000 values from production data using a fixed industry-by-country within estimator. All wages are deflated by country-specific GDP-deflators and expressed in 1995 dollars, and we calculate average growth rates in line with the bulk of the convergence literature.

To construct the intermediate goods trade variable, we use data on bilateral intermediate goods trade volumes at the five-digit Standard International Trade Classification level from UNO's Broad Economic Categories (Fontagné et al., 1996) and aggregate them to obtain NACE two-digit manufacturing industry input trade volumes of each country with the EU and the CEEC. We aggregate each country's bilateral trade in intermediate goods with the EU and CEEC as the destination countries. For example, the intermediate goods trade measure of a specific German NACE two-digit manufacturing industry is the sum of Germany's exports and imports of intermediate goods of this industry to all other EU countries and the CEEC, and similarly for all other economies in the sample. In this way, we capture the impact of the overall volume of intermediate goods trade on the convergence of real wage rates and treat all countries symmetrically. We express two-digit industry input trade volumes as a percentage of a country's gross production to obtain a (wide) measure of the country-specific European (intra-sample) level of cross-border outsourcing of production. A couple of missing values are interpolated, especially for Greece. In the regressions below, the initial value refers to 1993.

Starting from significantly lower wage rates after the fall of the Iron Curtain and the first step of systemic transformation, real wages grew substantially faster (by 1.3 percentage points per annum) in the 5 CEEC than in the 15 EU members. Intermediate goods imports in terms of gross production grew by approximately 1.3 percentage points per annum faster in the EU countries between 1993 and 2000, compared to the CEEC. This pattern is largely due to the increase in imports of manufacturing inputs originating from the EU countries themselves.

Econometric Specification

We estimate (5), allowing outsourcing to affect the adjustment process (i.e., the speed of adjustment) to the steady-state real wage rate both within and between countries. The associated β-convergence regression reads as follows:

$$\Delta\omega_{ic} = \gamma_0 + \gamma_1\tilde{\omega}_{ic}^0 + \gamma_2\tilde{\omega}_{ic}^0 o_{ic}^0 D_{EU} + \gamma_3\tilde{\omega}_{ic}^0 o_{ic}^0 D_{CEEC}$$
$$+ \gamma_4\omega_{.c}^0 + \gamma_5\omega_{.c}^0 o_{ic}^0 D_{EU} + \gamma_6\omega_{.c}^0 o_{ic}^0 D_{CEEC} + u_{ic},$$

$$\Delta\omega_{ic} = \frac{\ln w_{ic}^t - \ln w_{ic}^0}{T},$$

$$\tilde{\omega}_{ic}^0 = (\omega_{ic}^0 - \omega_{.c}^0),$$

$$o_{ic}^0 = \frac{(\text{intermediates goods trade volume})_{ic}^0}{(\text{gross production})_{ic}^0}.$$

(8)

This means that we parameterize $-(1/T)(1 - e^{-b_1 T})$ as $\gamma_1 + \gamma_2 o_{ic}^0 D_{EU} + \gamma_3 o_{ic}^0 D_{CEEC}$ and $-(1/T)(1 - e^{-b_2 T})$ as $\gamma_4 + \gamma_5 o_{ic}^0 D_{EU} + \gamma_6 o_{ic}^0 D_{CEEC}$. D_{EU} takes the value 1 if a country belongs to the EU and 0 otherwise, and $D_{CEEC} = 1 - D_{EU}$ is the CEEC dummy. According to the discussion above, we allow European cross-border outsourcing to exert a different impact on the convergence *within* countries (i.e., between industries within a country: γ_2, γ_3) than *between* countries (γ_5, γ_6). Furthermore, outsourcing may affect the EU economies (γ_2, γ_5) and the CEEC (γ_3, γ_6) differently. γ_0 is the common steady-state growth of real wages. In this form, the specification implies *unconditional convergence*. Similar to previous work, we account for the other determinants of convergence by the direct effects of the initial levels (γ_1, γ_4). In a second specification, we add industry dummies to control for other unobserved industry-specific determinants of the steady-state growth of real wages. (See Carree et al. (2000) for a similar approach.) The resulting long-run differences in real wage growth rates may arise from shifts in the skill composition and, *inter alia*, also from short-run asymmetric business cycle effects. This specification implies *conditional convergence*.

As discussed in Quah (1993), β-convergence is not sufficient to guarantee overall convergence to a common steady state. Therefore, additional evidence on the distribution of real wages must be considered to assess the information obtained from the above regressions. Convergence to a single-peaked distribution supports results from β-convergence regressions. In our application, convergence of the real wage distribution (conditional on fixed industry effects) to a single peak is empirically supported and β-convergence analysis is informative.

Given single-peakedness, we further look at the distribution of wages and compute the associated variance of real wages across both countries and industries to see whether the distribution of real wages has significantly collapsed over time. As mentioned above, the small time dimension of our data does not allow us to run a σ-convergence regression. In our case, the dispersion of real wages is falling since 1995. This process is driven by convergence of wages between economies rather than *within* them. According to the t_2-statistic by Carree and Klomp (1997), differences in real wage rates *between* countries were significantly larger in 1993 than in 2000 ($t_2 = 64.2$, $p = 0.00$). Also the *overall* decrease in the variance is significant ($t_2 = 33.8$, $p = 0.00$). However, *within* the typical economy we observe a slightly increasing dispersion between industries.

Estimation Results

Comparing the results between the conditional and the unconditional convergence regression in Table 1, we find that the hypothesis of a common steady state across industries is rejected. This points to long-run differences in real wage growth rates across industries common to all countries and/or short-run asymmetric business cycle effects not explicitly addressed in the theoretical models discussed above. Nevertheless, the resulting point estimates of the convergence parameters are relatively similar, with some important exceptions.

The econometric evidence suggests that intermediate goods trade in the EU has speeded up the pace of adjustment to the industry steady state *within countries*. All estimated *between-country* conditional convergence parameters are significantly different from zero, and we find that outsourcing tends to foster convergence of both the CEEC (i.e., convergence *from below*) and the EU-15 member countries (on average, convergence *from above*). The difference in the CEEC and the EU marginal effects of the initial values (evaluated at the relevant means of intermediate goods trade) is significant regarding both convergence within countries (according to the *F*-test of $a - b = 0$ in Table 1) and overall convergence (according to the *F*-test of $(a + c) - (b + d) = 0$ in Table 1). Also the difference between the marginal effects of within versus between countries is rejected for both the EU-15 (according to the *F*-test of $b - d = 0$ in Table 1) and all countries together (according to the *F*-test of $(a + b) - (c + d) = 0$ in Table 1).

We assess the robustness of the estimation results in several ways. First, we apply simultaneous quantiles regressions to check for the influence of potential outliers. As the results for the median, the lower, and the upper quartile regressions in Table 2 indicate, the parameters are very close to the OLS outcome and our results are not driven by a few influential observations. Second, we look at the longest available time span of data covering the period 1990 to 2000 (including the years of transitional recession and systemic transformation before 1993, also reported in Table 2). Even in this respect, the parameters prove to be relatively robust. Third, we use 1999 as an alternative base year to construct real wages, which obtains the same sign of all β-convergence coefficients as the baseline models in Table 1. (For the sake of brevity, we do not report these results. They are available from the authors.) Given these results, we can proceed with the analysis based on the estimates in Table 1.

Table 3 collects information on the speed of adjustment, expressed as the average annual closure of the gap between actual and steady-state real wage rates for the EU and the CEEC. To illustrate the role of intermediate goods trade, we report the estimated speed of adjustment as observed and a counterfactual situation with zero intermediate goods trade in the initial period. Since unconditional convergence is rejected at convenient levels of significance, we concentrate on the conditional convergence results (i.e., the lower block of results in the table). Intermediate goods trade significantly speeds up the convergence of real wage rates *within* the EU-15 countries. In fact, intermediate goods trade of these economies closed the intersectoral wage gap by 5.54% per annum when evaluated at variable means, whereas there was no such effect within the CEEC. Hence, in the EU-15 intermediate goods trade puts a significant pressure on industries with above-average real wage rates in the typical economy, while it leads to a faster increase of real wage rates in industries below the country average. Further, outsourcing significantly accelerates the speed of convergence *between countries* in both the EU (the difference between 1.79% and 1.45% is significant at 1%) and the CEEC (the difference between 1.82% and 1.45% is also

Table 1. Regression Results (β-convergence, 1993–2000)

Dependent variable: average log difference of real wages

Explanatory variables	Unconditional convergence		Conditional convergence	
	Coefficient	t	Coefficient	t
Within countries				
Initial level	0.026	1.93*	0.009	0.41
Initial level × initial outsourcing × CEEC dummy (a)	0.025	0.50	−0.023	−0.48
Initial level × initial outsourcing × EU-15 dummy (b)	−0.011	−2.13**	−0.024	−3.01***
Between countries				
Initial level	−0.016	−4.04***	−0.014	−3.72***
Initial level × initial outsourcing × CEEC dummy (c)	−0.002	−0.51	−0.008	−1.67*
Initial level × initial outsourcing × EU-15 dummy (d)	−0.001	−1.95*	−0.002	−3.40***
Constant	0.057	5.10***	0.037	2.87***
Number of observations	240		240	
R^2	0.18		0.33	
Root-mean-square error	0.03		0.03	
Residual d.f.	230		217	
	p-value		p-value	
Heteroskedasticity (Cook and Weisberg, 1983): $\chi^2(1)$	0.12		0.03**	
Ramsey RESET test: $F(3,$ residual d.f.$)$	0.01***		0.46	
F-tests:				
Industry effects: $F(13,220)$	—		0.00***	
Marginal initial value effects evaluated at means:				
$a - b = 0$; $F(1,$ residual d.f.$)$	0.11		0.04**	
$a - c = 0$; $F(1,$ residual d.f.$)$	0.59		0.75	
$c - d = 0$; $F(1,$ residual d.f.$)$	0.81		0.85	
$b - d = 0$; $F(1,$ residual d.f.$)$	0.04**		0.00***	
$(a + c) - (b + d) = 0$; $F(1,$ residual d.f.$)$	0.11		0.05**	
$(a + b) - (c + d) = 0$; $F(1,$ residual d.f.$)$	0.33		0.03**	

Notes: *** significant at 1%; ** significant at 5%; * significant at 10%. Reported *t*-statistics are heteroskedasticity corrected.

significant at 1%). Finally, the impact on the speed of adjustment of the CEEC is somewhat stronger (though only at $\alpha = 29\%$). Summing up, our results support Deardorff's (2001) notion that outsourcing facilitates factor price equalization across countries.

4. Conclusions

This paper proposes a new concept to distinguish the two dimensions of convergence—*between* and *within* countries. We analyze the impact of outsourcing on the adjustment

Table 2. *Conditional β-convergence Simultaneous Quantiles Regression Results and Longest Available Period Regression Result*

Dependent variable: average log difference of real wages

Explanatory variables	0.25 quartile (1993–2000) Coefficient	t	Median (1993–2000) Coefficient	t	0.75 quartile (1993–2000) Coefficient	t	Long period (1990–2000) Coefficient	t
Within countries								
Initial level	0.022	0.76	−0.015	−0.6	0.017	0.57	−0.013	−0.72
Initial level × initial outsourcing × CEEC dummy (a)	−0.092	−0.81	0.012	0.20	−0.004	−0.06	0.051	0.76
Initial level × initial outsourcing × EU-15 dummy (b)	−0.030	−2.62***	−0.019	−1.81*	−0.027	−2.03**	−0.017	−2.87***
Between countries								
Initial level	−0.016	−1.93*	−0.019	−3.45***	−0.017	−4.58***	−0.012	−3.25***
Initial level × initial outsourcing × CEEC dummy (c)	−0.019	−2.13**	−0.005	−0.77	0.003	0.6	−0.010	−1.91*
Initial level × initial outsourcing × EU-15 dummy (d)	−0.002	−2.78***	−0.001	−1.94*	−0.001	−1.87*	−0.001	−2.03**
Constant	0.033	1.13	0.055	2.95***	0.066	5.54***	0.037	2.89***
Pseudo-R^2/R^2	0.15		0.20		0.32		0.29	

Notes: *** significant at 1%; ** significant at 5%; * significant at 10%. Reported *t*-statistics are heteroskedasticity corrected.

Table 3. Estimated Speed of Convergence: Annual Closure of the Gap in Percent

	Within countries		Between countries	
	Overall	Without outsourcing	Overall	Without outsourcing
Unconditional convergence				
EU-15	−0.34	−2.41**	1.81***	1.66***
CEEC	−3.34**	−2.41**	1.76***	1.66***
Conditional convergence				
EU-15	5.54*	−0.92	1.79***	1.45***
CEEC	0.07	−0.92	1.82***	1.45***

Notes: ***significant at 1%; **significant at 5%; *significant at 10%.

of real wage rates in manufacturing of the EU-15 and 5-CEEC at the industry level. Specifically, we treat the impact of outsourcing transitorily and look at its effect on the speed of adjustment.

Based on β-convergence regressions, we significantly reject *unconditional convergence* within both the EU and the CEEC. Our estimation results furthermore suggest that intermediate goods trade of the CEEC has not fostered the pace of adjustment *within* these economies. By way of contrast, it has led to a closure of the gap between observed and steady-state wage rates *within* the EU countries.

Looking at the convergence *between* countries, cross-border outsourcing strongly fosters convergence *from below* for the CEEC and *from above* for most of the EU countries. Hence, our empirical estimates support the hypothesis derived from traditional models, namely that cross-border outsourcing increases the possibility of international factor price equalization (Deardorff, 2001).

References

Arellano, Manuel and Stephen Bond, "Some Tests of Specification for Panel Data: Monte Carlo Evidence and an Application to Employment Equations," *Review of Economic Studies* 58 (1991):277–97.

Arndt, Sven W., "Globalization and the Open Economy," *North American Journal of Economics and Finance* 8 (1997):71–9.

Baier, Scott and Jeffrey H. Bergstrand, "The Growth of World Trade: Tariffs, Transport Costs, and Income Similarity," *Journal of International Economics* 53 (2001):1–27.

Barro, Robert and Xavier Sala-i-Martin, *Economic Growth*, New York: McGraw-Hill (1995).

Carree, Martin and Luuk Klomp, "Testing the Convergence Hypothesis: a Comment," *Review of Economics and Statistics* 79 (1997):683–6.

Carree, Martin, Luuk Klomp, and A. Roy Thurik, "Productivity Convergence in OECD Manufacturing Industries," *Economics Letters* 66 (2000):337–45.

Cook, Dennis R. and Sanford Weisberg, "Diagnostics for Heteroscedasticity in Regression," *Biometrika* 70 (1983):1–10.

Deardorff, Alan V., "Outsourcing in Simple Trade Models," *North American Journal of Economics and Finance* 12 (2001):121–37.

Egger, Hartmut and Peter Egger, "Cross Border Sourcing and Outward Processing in EU Manufacturing," *North American Journal of Economics and Finance* 12 (2001):243–56.

Ethier, Wilfred J., "National and International Returns to Scale in the Modern Theory of International Trade," *American Economic Review* 72 (1982):950–9.

Feenstra, Robert C. and Gordon H. Hanson, "Foreign Investment Outsourcing and Relative Wages," in R. C. Feenstra, G. M. Grossman, and D. A. Irvin (eds.), *Political Economy of Trade Policy: Essays in Honor of Jagdish Bhagwati*, Cambridge, MA: MIT Press (1996):89–127.

———, "Foreign Direct Investment and Relative Wages: Evidence from Mexico's Maquiladoras," *Journal of International Economics* 42 (1997):371–93.

———, "The Impact of Outsourcing and High-technology Capital on Wages, 1979–1990," *Quarterly Journal of Economics* 114 (1999):907–40.

———, "Global Production Sharing and Rising Inequality: a Survey on Trade and Wages," in K. Choi and J. Harrigan (eds.), *Handbook of International Trade*, Oxford: Basil Blackwell (2001).

Fontagné, Lionel, Michael Freudenberg, and Deniz Ünal-Kesenci, *Statistical Analysis of EC Trade in Intermediate Products*, Paris: EUROSTAT (1996).

Greenaway, David, Robert C. Hine, and Peter Wright, "An Empirical Assessment of the Impact of Trade on Employment in the United Kingdom," *European Journal of Political Economy* 15 (1999):485–500.

Hummels, David, Jun Ishii, and Kei-Mu Yi, "The Nature and Growth of Vertical Specialization in World Trade," *Journal of International Economics*, 54 (2001):75–96.

Jones, Ronald W. and Henryk Kierzkowski, "A Framework for Fragmentation," in Sven W. Arndt and Henryk Kierzkowski (eds.), *Fragmentation: New Production Patterns in the World Economy*, Oxford: Oxford University Press (2001):17–34.

Kohler, Wilhelm K., "A Specific-factors View on Outsourcing," *North American Journal of Economics and Finance* 12 (2001):31–53.

———, "The Distributional Effects of International Fragmentation", *German Economic Review* 4 (2003):89–120.

Krueger, Alan B. and Lawrence Summers, "Efficiency Wages and the Inter-industry Wage Structure," *Econometrica* 56 (1988):269–93.

Krugman, Paul R., "Growing World Trade: Causes and Consequences," *Brookings Papers on Economic Activity* (1995):327–62.

Quah, Danny, "Galton's Fallacy and Tests of the Convergence Hypothesis," *Scandinavian Journal of Economics* 95 (1993):427–43.

Chapter 7

"Export Experience" under Borrowing Constraints

Saqib Jafarey and Sajal Lahiri

1. Introduction

One of the relationships frequently encountered in the literature on export-led growth is the so-called "export experience" effect.[1] Roughly speaking, this implies that a country's exports at one point of time have a positive relationship with its exports at future points of time. The most widespread theoretical reasoning behind this is that exporting firms, in particular those of developing countries, benefit from dynamic learning-by-doing that in turn arises from a variety of influences.[2]

Empirical tests have used data at various levels of aggregation to investigate this hypothesis. Using time-series data from Pakistan, for example, Akbar (2001) found that cumulative exports have a positive and significant effect on a measure of current export competitiveness. Using firm-level data from the electronics industry in Taiwan, Aw and Hwang (1995) found that, even after controlling for other important factors such as input use, exporting firms display higher levels of productivity than nonexporting firms.[3]

In opposition to the presumption of dynamic learning effects, Clerides et al. (1998) have argued—and provided evidence using data from Colombia, Mexico, and Morocco—that the greater efficiency of exporting firms could be due to reverse causation: more efficient firms tend to self-select into the exporting sectors. Over time, such self-selection could provide an alternative mechanism through which a positive serial correlation in export performance could arise. Furthermore, at a purely theoretical level, Dixit (1989) has shown that stochastic shocks combined with fixed entry and exit costs at the firm level can generate hysteresis, and therefore a pattern of serial correlation, in a country's trading behavior, again without any dynamic learning. In other words, it may be misleading to call observed serial correlation in exports an "experience" effect.

In this paper, we argue that—learning-by-doing, self-selection, and sunk costs aside—a separate explanation for the existence of what appears to be an export experience effect can arise for a country that borrows from abroad and does not face a perfectly elastic supply of credit. We model this conjecture using a two-period framework in which a small (with respect to commodity markets) and open economy produces two goods in each period, an importable and an exportable, using capital which is initially fixed but can be augmented through endogenous investment (which is in units of the importable) between the two periods. The amounts of investment and consumption are influenced by the presence of a constraint on overseas borrowing, which results in a wedge between its domestic interest rate and the world lending rate.[4]

Using this setup, we show that a temporary export subsidy (applied in the first period alone) can improve the country's current account in the first period. This reduces its demand for funds and lowers its domestic interest rate. The lower domestic interest rate stimulates greater investment and, on the assumption that greater investment leads to an increase in capital allocated to the export sector, the output of the exportable goes up in the second period. At the same time, the lower interest rate reduces the demand for consumption of the exportable in the second period. Through these two effects, the temporary export subsidy not only increases first-period exports but also contributes to a higher export volume in the second period. While our analysis also uncovers an offsetting effect on second-period exports, the important point is that, if the economy were small in credit markets and faced a perfectly elastic supply of credit, investment and interest rates would be unaffected by a temporary export subsidy and the mechanism which links export promotion to persistence in export performance would be missing.[5] In addition to identifying these mechanisms, we study how they vary with four different scenarios regarding how the amount that the country can borrow gets determined. The benchmark scenario looks at a case in which a borrowing constraint is exogenously imposed upon the country while the export subsidy is chosen optimally by its government. In all the other cases, we assume that the lenders are from a single foreign country and its government optimally sets the total amount of loan that they can provide. In other words, there is a game in which the lender-country government chooses how much can be lent while the borrowing country chooses its first-period export subsidy. These alternatives are: (i) a Nash game in which both countries act simultaneously, (ii) a Stackelberg game in which the borrowing country acts first and chooses the subsidy before the lending country chooses its lending level, and (iii) a Stackelberg game with the order of moves reversed.

In each scenario, we find that, starting from the equilibrium level of the temporary export subsidy that is appropriate for the game under consideration, a small increase in this subsidy contributes to creating an export experience effect through the mechanisms discussed above, but the effectiveness of the subsidy is greater in the case of exogenous borrowing (or when the lender is a leader) than in the other two cases. The reason for this is that, in the two other cases, the lender partially offsets the impact of the subsidy by tightening the borrowing constraint in response.

The benchmark model is outlined in section 2. Section 3 looks at the export experience effect under an exogenous borrowing constraint. Section 4 examines the three cases of an endogenous constraint. Section 5 concludes.

2. Benchmark Models

We consider an open economy which lasts two periods, labeled as $t = 1$ and $t = 2$, respectively. It produces two goods per period and is small in the world market for each good, so the international prices of the two goods are exogenous. Goods labeled 1 and 2 are produced during $t = 1$ while goods labeled 3 and 4 are produced during $t = 2$. Goods 1 and 3 are importables while goods 2 and 4 are exportables. P_i is the price of good i. Prices are normalized such that $P_1 = 1$.

The economy starts at $t = 1$ with K units of capital. At $t = 1$, it can add to this through investment, I, which becomes available at $t = 2$.[6] The economy faces a binding borrowing constraint on overseas credit, $\bar{b}$, which applies to both investment and consumption. All the markets are assumed to be competitive.

The government has one policy instrument which affects decisions made at $t = 1$ and this is a temporary specific export subsidy, denoted by s_1.[7]

The economy is described by the following equations:

$$E\left(1, P_2 + s_1, \frac{P_3}{1+r}, \frac{P_4}{1+r}, u\right) + I = R^1(1, P_2 + s_1, K) + \frac{R^2(P_3, P_4, K+I)}{1+r} - T, \qquad (1)$$

$$(1+r)\bar{b} = R^2 - P_3 E_3 - P_4 E_4, \qquad (2)$$

$$R_3^2 = 1 + r, \qquad (3)$$

$$T = s_1[R_2^1 - E_2]. \qquad (4)$$

Equation (1) represents the economy's intertemporal budget constraint. It states that the total discounted present value of consumption and investment expenditure is equal to the discounted present value of income minus a lump-sum tax. Equation (2) describes borrowing: total repayment (principal plus interest) in period 2 equals income minus expenditure in that period. The investment choice is described in (3), and is obtained by setting $(\partial u/\partial I) = 0$ from (1) at a given level of the interest rate r. The amount of lump-sum taxation, T, needed to pay the subsidy is defined by (4). Together the equations determine u, the indirect utility; r, the domestic interest rate; I, the level of investment; and T, the subsidy payment.

In the above equations, $E(\cdot)$ is the expenditure function, R^1 is the revenue function at $t = 1$, R^2 is revenue at $t = 2$, $R^2 - P_3 E_3 - P_4 E_4$ is the current account surplus at $t = 2$, and $R_2^1 - E_2$ is the level of exports of good 2 at $t = 1$.[8]

We assume that all goods are substitutes, both intra- and intertemporally, and that all the goods are normal. Formally:

$$E_{ij} > 0, \quad i \neq j = 1,2,3,4, \quad \text{and} \quad E_{i5} > 0, \quad i = 1,2,3,4.$$

This completes the description of our benchmark model. We now turn to its analysis.

3. Export Experience

In this section, we examine how a temporary subsidy for exports, s_1, in period 1 affects the level of exports in period 2. Before turning to this question, we analyze how s_1 affects a number of other variables. Differentiating (1)–(4), we get

$$\alpha du = -\frac{H}{(1+r)^2} dr - \beta ds_1, \qquad (5)$$

$$\Delta dr = -(1+r)d\bar{b} - \left[P_3 E_{32} + P_4 E_{42} - \frac{\beta\gamma}{\alpha}\right]ds_1, \qquad (6)$$

$$R_{33}^2 dI = dr, \qquad (7)$$

where

$$\alpha = E_5 - s_1 E_{25} > 0,$$

$$\beta = s_1 [R_{22}^1 - E_{22}],$$

$$G = s_1 (P_3 E_{23} + P_4 E_{24}),$$

$$H = (1+r)\bar{b} + G,$$

$$\Delta = \bar{b} - \frac{P_3 E_{33} + 2P_4 E_{34} + P_4 E_{44}}{1+r} - \frac{(1+r)}{R_{33}^2} - \frac{\gamma H}{\alpha(1+r)^2} > 0,$$

$$\gamma = P_3 E_{35} + P_4 E_{45} > 0.$$

$\alpha > 0$ is known as the Hatta normality condition. It can be shown that if good 1 is normal, then α is indeed positive. Walrasian stability in the credit market ensures that $\Delta > 0$.

Equation (5) shows that an increase in r lowers welfare. This is for two reasons. First, since the country is a borrower, it suffers from an intertemporal terms-of-trade loss. The second effect is via changes in subsidy payments. An increase in r makes period 2 consumption relatively cheaper and this reduces period 1 consumption and therefore increases period 1 exports as well as the tax revenue needed to finance the export subsidy (at given s_1).

An increase in s_1 (at given r) increases subsidy payments, both directly, at given level of exports, and indirectly, by increasing the domestic price of the exportable in period 1 and therefore the overall level of exports. This is welfare-reducing. Note that welfare is not directly affected by changes in I as it is optimally chosen (the envelope property). An increase in $\bar{b}$ increases the supply of loan and thus reduces the interest rate as can be seen from (6). An increase in s_1 has two opposing effects on the demand for loans and thus on r. First, it makes period 2 goods relatively cheaper, reducing the excess of income over consumption in period 2 and thus the demand for loans. This tends to reduce the interest rate. But an increase in s_1 also increases subsidy payments, for reasons mentioned above, and thus reduces period 1 disposable income. This increases the demand for loans and thus the interest rate. These two effects are reflected by the coefficient of ds_1 in (6). Equation (7) states that an increase in r reduces investment by reducing the present value of its returns.[9]

Having explained the basic equations, we now turn to the issue of export experience. Denoting by X the level of exports in period 2, where $X = R_2^2 - E_4$, a positive value of dX/ds_1 would imply that a temporary export subsidy can encourage exports into the future, reflecting an "export experience" effect.

Differentiating X we get

$$dX = R_{23}^2 dI + \left[\frac{P_4 E_{44} + P_3 E_{43}}{(1+r)^2} \right] dr - E_{45} du - E_{42} ds_1. \tag{8}$$

We shall now consider four scenarios. In the first, we assume that s_1 is optimally set by the borrower country, but $\bar{b}$ is exogenously given. In the second scenario, we consider a Nash equilibrium in which a single lending country optimally decides $\bar{b}$, while the borrowing country optimally sets s_1, each country taking the value at which the other country's instrument is set as given. In the third scenario, the borrowing country is assumed to move first in setting s_1, with the lending country setting $\bar{b}$ in response; in the fourth scenario, the order of play is reversed. The last three scenarios will be taken up in section 4.

Exogenous Credit Constraint

The first-order condition for s_1 is

$$\beta\Delta = \frac{H}{(1+r)^2}\left[P_3E_{23} + P_4E_{24} - \frac{\beta\gamma}{\alpha}\right]. \tag{9}$$

We denote the optimal value of s_1 by s_1^o.

When $\bar{b}$ is exogenously given and the initial value of s_1 is optimally set, from (8) we get

$$\frac{dX}{ds_1} = R_{23}^2\frac{dI}{ds_1} + \left[\frac{P_4E_{44} + P_3E_{43}}{(1+r)^2}\right]\frac{dr}{ds_1} - E_{42}. \tag{10}$$

The terms dr/ds_1 and dI/ds_1 can be eliminated by using the comparative static results derived earlier.

However, instead of deriving the complete reduced-form effect, it is more illuminating to consider each term in the above expression separately, since they correspond to various channels through which future exports are affected by a current subsidy. Substituting (9) into (6), we get

$$\left.\frac{\partial r}{\partial s_1}\right|_{s_1=s_1^o} = -\left[P_3E_{32} + P_4E_{42} - \frac{\beta\gamma}{\alpha}\right] = -\frac{(1+r^*)^2\beta\Delta}{H} < 0, \tag{11}$$

and therefore from (7) it follows that dI/ds_1 is positive. This means that an export subsidy leads to greater investment and a higher level of imports of the capital good. A positive value of R_{23}^2 means that a larger capital stock in period 2—coming about by investments in period 1—will lead to a higher output of the export good at $t = 2$. This will contribute a positive effect to exports at $t = 2$.[10]

We also know that dr/ds_1 is negative. Since the coefficient associated with it is negative, the second term also contributes a positive effect on exports at $t = 2$. Unlike the first term, however, this is a consumption-based effect. By lowering the domestic interest rate, the subsidy increases the relative price of consumption at $t = 2$ with respect to the current period. This tends to lower consumption of the exportable at $t = 2$, which in turn stimulates exports.

The third term captures the substitution effect between good 2 and good 4. Since the subsidy raises the cost to domestic consumers of the exportable at $t = 1$, it may induce substitution toward other goods; in particular to the export good at $t = 2$. This tends to raise consumption of the exportable at $t = 2$ and to discourage exports, offsetting the effects coming from the first term.

To summarize, an export experience effect can arise (i) if extra investment leads to greater production in the exports sector, and/or (ii) if the interest-rate effect on domestic consumption of the export good at $t = 2$ dominates the direct substitution effects. Note that if the country could borrow freely at an exogenous interest rate with no distortions, an export subsidy would neither change the interest rate nor induce additional investment in capital goods. It is in this context that the borrowing constraint plays a role in creating channels through which temporary export promotion generates future export growth.

4. Endogenous Borrowing Constraints

In the preceding section, we assumed that the amount that can be borrowed was determined exogenously. In this section, we introduce a foreign country which determines the amount of borrowing, $\bar{b}$, on the basis of its own optimization problem. In other words, we assume that, while the two countries are small open economies in the goods market in the sense that their actions do not alter commodity prices, they are large in the credit market.[11] In this framework, each country has one instrument at its disposal: an export subsidy, s_1, for the home country and an optimal level of lending, $\bar{b}$, for the foreign country.

The model describing the foreign country is

$$E^*\left(1, P_2, \frac{P_3}{1+r^*}, \frac{P_4}{1+r^*}, u^*\right) + I^* = R^{1*}(1, P_2, K^*) + \frac{R^{2*}(P_3, P_4, K^*+I^*)}{1+r^*} + \frac{(r-r^*)\bar{b}}{1+r^*}, \qquad (12)$$

$$(1+r)\bar{b} = P_3 E_3^* - P_4 E_4^* - R^{2*}, \qquad (13)$$

$$R_3^{2*} = (1+r^*). \qquad (14)$$

The above equations are analogous to (1)–(3) for the home country. We need to explain only the last term on the right-hand side of (12). As just mentioned, we assume that the foreign country imposes a quota on the amount of loan that can be given to the home country. This leads to an excess demand for loans in the home country and drives a wedge between the interest rates in the two countries. Following the treatment of quotas in the international trade theory literature, we assume that the foreign-country government applies competitive loan licensing and thereby collects a quota fee (or rent) amounting to $(r - r^*)\bar{b}$. The reader will immediately realize that our treatment of borrowing constraint is akin to the treatment of voluntary export restraints (VERs) in the international trade theory literature. There is an important difference, however, between the standard treatment of VERs in the literature and the way we deal with the borrowing constraint here, and this arises because of the dynamic nature of borrowing. In particular, one needs to make some assumption about the time period when the quota rent is collected by the government. Since the possible rent from lending arises only in period 2 when the loan is repaid, we assume that the foreign government collects the license fee also in period 2, and this quota rent is returned to foreign-country households in a lump-sum fashion.

Differentiating (12)–(14), we obtain

$$E_5^* du^* = (r - r^*)d\bar{b} + \frac{\bar{b}}{1+r^*} dr, \qquad (15)$$

where dr is as in (6). The second term on the right-hand side of (15) gives the terms-of-trade effect. Since the foreign country is the lender it benefits when the interest rate rises. The first term gives the change in the quota rent for given levels of interest rates.

We shall now consider three scenarios. In the first scenario, we assume that the two countries play a Nash game; i.e., the home country maximizes its welfare by optimally choosing s_1 taking the level of $\bar{b}$ as given, and at the same time the foreign country maximizes its own welfare by optimally choosing $\bar{b}$ taking s_1 as given. In the second scenario, we shall assume that the borrower country has a first-mover advantage. In particular, we consider a two-stage game. In order to obtain a subgame-perfect equilibrium, the game is solved via backward induction. In stage 2 of the game, the lender country decides on an optimal value of $\bar{b}$ contingent upon a given value for s_1. In stage

1, the borrower country decides on the level of s_1 by maximizing its welfare taking into account the reaction function from the second stage of the game. In the final scenario, the order of the game is reversed in the sense that the lender country is a follower and the borrower country is the leader. The three scenarios are considered in turn in the following three subsections.

In each scenario, we examine how, starting from each equilibrium, a unilateral increase in s_1 by the government of the borrowing country affects second-period exports, X. We also compare the magnitude of this effect in the different equilibria.

The Nash Game

In this subsection, we consider a Nash game in s_1 and $\bar{b}$. From (5), (6), and (15), by setting $\partial u/\partial s_1 = 0$ and $\partial u*/\partial \bar{b} = 0$, we obtain the following two first-order conditions, which are solved simultaneously to derive the Nash equilibrium values $(s_1^N, \bar{b}^N)$:

$$s_1 : \beta\Delta = \frac{H}{(1+r)^2} \cdot \left[P_3 E_{23} + P_4 E_{24} - \frac{\beta\gamma}{\alpha} \right],$$

(16)

$$\bar{b} : \varepsilon = \frac{r - r^*}{1+r},$$

(17)

where

$$\varepsilon = -\frac{d(1+r)}{d\bar{b}} \frac{\bar{b}}{1+r} (>0)$$

describes the elasticity of the borrowing country's interest factor with respect to the amount borrowed.

It is to be noted that both countries are large in the credit market and therefore have market power in this market. Thus, the intervention-free equilibrium is distorted from the point of view of each country, and equations (16) and (17) give the second-best non-cooperative values for the two instruments. Each country attempts to move the international terms of trade, r, in its favor by use of the instrument at its disposal.

From the f.o.c. for $\bar{b}$ (equation (17)) we get[12]

$$(\varepsilon + \varepsilon^*) \frac{d\bar{b}}{ds_1} = \frac{\partial r}{\partial s_1} \frac{\bar{b}}{1+r},$$

(18)

where

$$\varepsilon^* = \frac{d(1+r^*)}{d\bar{b}} \frac{\bar{b}}{1+r^*} > 0.$$

From (11) and (18) we get

$$\left. \frac{d\bar{b}}{ds_1} \right|_{s_1 = s_1^N} < 0;$$

(19)

i.e., starting from a Nash equilibrium, the lender country's government reacts to a small increase in the export subsidy by tightening the constraint on loans to the borrowing country. The intuition is straightforward. At the Nash equilibrium, the lender country earns positive quota rents, but a small increase in the export subsidy reduces these rents by reducing the interest rate in the borrowing country—the lender country fights this by tightening its supply of credit.

Using (5), (6), (18), (11), and (10), we get

$$\frac{dX}{ds_1}\bigg|_{\bar{b}=\bar{b}^N} = \frac{dX}{ds_1}\bigg|_{\bar{b}=\text{const.}} - \left[\frac{E_{23}}{R_{33}^2} + \frac{P_4 E_{44} + P_3 E_{43}}{(1+r)^2}\right]\frac{1+r}{\Delta}\frac{d\bar{b}}{ds_1} - \frac{E_{45}H}{(1+r)\alpha\Delta}\frac{d\bar{b}}{ds_1}. \tag{20}$$

Since $d\bar{b}/ds_1 < 0$ from (19), it follows from (20) that[13,14]

$$\frac{dX}{ds_1}\bigg|_{\bar{b}=\bar{b}^N} < \frac{dX}{ds_1}\bigg|_{\bar{b}=\text{const.}} \quad \text{if } E_{45} \simeq 0.$$

The above results can be explained intuitively as follows. Compared to the case where $\bar{b}$ is exogenous, under the Nash game, two additional terms arise because the Nash equilibrium value of $\bar{b}$ adjusts as s_1 is changed. We know from (19) that $d\bar{b}^N/ds_1 < 0$ and from (5) that $dr/d\bar{b} < 0$. Therefore, the additional term involves an increase in r. This in turn has two effects. First, the direct effect of an increase in r is that it reduces exports in period 2 as explained before. Second, it reduces income and therefore reduces consumption and increases exports in period 2. If the income effect does not fall on the consumption of good 2 in period 2, then this effect is insignificant and the direct effect dominates.

The Borrower Country has a First-mover Advantage

In this subsection we consider a two-stage game in which the borrower country acts as the leader. In this case, the first-order condition for s_1 is

$$\frac{\partial u}{\partial s_1} + \frac{\partial u}{\partial \bar{b}}\frac{d\bar{b}}{ds_1} = 0.$$

The first-order condition for $\bar{b}$ remains (17). The equilibrium here is denoted by $(\hat{s}_1, \hat{b})$.

Here, using (5), (6), (10), (11), and (18), we get

$$\frac{dX}{ds_1}\bigg|_{\bar{b}=\hat{b}} = \frac{dX}{ds_1}\bigg|_{\bar{b}=\text{const.}} - \left[\frac{E_{23}^2}{R_{33}^2} + \frac{P_4 E_{44} + P_3 E_{43}}{(1+r)^2}\right]\frac{1+r}{\Delta}\frac{d\bar{b}}{ds_1}. \tag{21}$$

We have proved elsewhere that $s_1^N > \hat{s}_1$.[15] From (6), it can be shown that r is a U-shaped function of s_1. Furthermore, from (11) it follows that at $s_1 = s_1^N$, r is a decreasing function of s_1. Since the optimal value of $\hat{s}_1 < s_1^N$, it follows that $dr/ds_1 < 0$ at $s_1 = \hat{s}_1$. From (21) it then follows that, without any restrictions on income effects, we have[16]

$$\frac{dX}{ds_1}\bigg|_{\bar{b}=\hat{b}} < \frac{dX}{ds_1}\bigg|_{\bar{b}=\text{const.}}.$$

The intuition is similar to that given for the previous case except that the income effect on exports is absent in this case as the effect of changes in welfare via induced changes in $\bar{b}$ is taken into account in determining the optimal value of s_1.

The Lender Country has a First-mover Advantage

In this subsection we consider a two-stage game in which the lender country is the leader. In the second stage of the game, the borrower decides on the level of s_1 by maximizing its welfare for a given value of $\bar{b}$. That is, the reaction function of the borrower is obtained from (16). The lender then maximizes its welfare subject to this reaction function. The first-order condition for the lender's objective function is

$$\frac{du^*}{d\bar{b}} = \frac{\partial du^*}{\partial \bar{b}} + \frac{\partial u^*}{\partial s_1}\frac{ds_1}{d\bar{b}} = 0. \tag{22}$$

We denote the equilibrium levels of the instruments by $(\tilde{s}_1, \tilde{\bar{b}})$. We now consider the effect of an increase in s_1 on the level of period 2 exports, X. Interestingly, in this case a change in s_1 will leave the level of $\tilde{\bar{b}}$ unchanged, and therefore qualitatively the effect of a change in s_1 on X in this case is exactly the same as it was in the case where $\bar{b}$ was exogenous. In fact, if the exogenous level of $\bar{b}$ is the same as $\tilde{\bar{b}}$, the magnitude of the effect will also be the same.

5. Conclusion

Export promotion is an extremely widespread phenomenon; most countries in the world have been trying to increase their share of the world market. There are many reasons why they do so. One of the arguments is that a current increase in exports is likely to have a permanent effect on exports, making export promotion activities very efficient. This is the so-called "export experience" effect. In the literature, people have put forward many theoretical reasons why there may be a persistence effect in exports, and many others have attempted to test whether there indeed is a learning-from-exporting effect.

In this paper we have identified a possible new channel via which a temporary promotion of exports can have long-lasting effects. In particular, we have shown that the presence of credit market imperfections can be a source for such persistence. We have also shown that the nature of the initial equilibrium determines the size of the export-experience effect.

To be more specific, we developed a two-period two-country multigood model with endogenous investment. The two countries are related only by the credit market, and the borrower home country is allowed to borrow only a specified amount by the lender country. In this framework we examined the effect of a period 1 export subsidy in the home country on the level of its exports in period 2. We considered a number of equilibria depending on how the initial level of export subsidy and the amount of credit are determined. We find that a temporary export subsidy, by affecting the interest rates and therefore the level of investment, consumption and production in period 2, can affect the level of exports in period 2.

References

Akbar, Mohammad, "Pakistan's Export Performance: 1972–1998," PhD dissertation, University of Essex (2001).

Aw, B.-Y. and A. R. Hwang, "Productivity and the Export Market: a Firm Level Analysis," *Journal of Development Economics* 47 (1995):313–32.

Balassa, Bella, "Exports and Economic Growth: Further Evidence," *Journal of Development Economics* 5 (1978):181–9.

Bhagwati, Jagdish N., "Export Promoting Trade Strategy: Issues and Evidence," *World Bank Research Observer* 3 (1988):27–57.

Chen, Tain-jy and De-piao Tang, "Comparing Technical Efficiency Between Import-substituting and Export-oriented Firms in a Developing Country," *Journal of Development Economics* 26 (1987):277–89.

Clerides, Sofronis K., Saul Lach, and James R. Tybout, "Is Learning by Exporting Important? Microdynamic Evidence from Colombia, Mexico, and Morocco," *Quarterly Journal of Economics* 113 (1998):903–47.

Dixit, Avinash, "Hysteresis, Import Penetration, and Exchange Rate Passthrough," *Quarterly Journal of Economics* 104 (1989):205–28.

Dixit, Avinash and Victor Norman, *Theory of International Trade*, Cambridge: Cambridge University Press (1980).

Djajic, Slobodan, "Temporary Import Quota and the Current Account," *Journal of International Economics* 22 (1987):349–62.

Edwards, Sebastian, "Openness, Trade Liberalization, and Growth in Developing Countries," *Journal of Economic Literature* 31 (1993):1358–93.

Edwards, Sebastian and Sweder van Wijnbergen, "The Welfare Effects of Trade and Capital Market Liberalization," *International Economic Review* 27 (1986):141–8.

Feder, Gershon, "On Exports and Economic Growth," *Journal of Development Economics* 12 (1986):59–73.

Grossman, Gene and Elhanan Helpman, *Innovation and Growth in the World Economy*, Cambridge, MA: MIT Press (1986).

Haddad, M., "How Trade Liberalization Affected Productivity in Morocco," World Bank policy research working paper 1096 (1993).

Jafarey, Saqib and Sajal Lahiri, "Trade Intervention and Capital Controls: Strategic Interactions and Commitments," Department of Economics, University of Essex (2002).

Jung, Woo S. and Peyton J. Marshall, "Exports, Growth and Causality in Developing Countries," *Journal of Development Economics* 18 (1985):1–12.

Lopez, Ramon and Arvind Panagariya, "Temporary Import and Export Quotas and the Current Account," *Journal of International Economics* 31 (1991):371–81.

Osang, Thomas and Stephen J. Turnovsky, "Differential Tariffs, Growth, and Welfare in a Small Open Economy," *Journal of Development Economics* 62 (2000):315–42.

Tybout, James R. and M. Daniel Westbrook, "Trade Liberalization and Dimensions of Efficiency Change in Mexican Manufacturing Industries," *Journal of International Economics* 31 (1995):53–78.

World Bank, *The East Asian Miracle*, New York: Oxford University Press (1993).

———, *World Development Report: The State in a Changing World*, New York: Oxford University Press (1997).

Notes

1. On the general topic of export-led growth, see, for example, Balassa (1978), Bhagwati (1988), Edwards (1993), Feder (1983), and Jung and Marshall (1985).

2. The World Bank (1997) identifies contact with "international best practise" as one source of such learning. Several authors have cited various forms of knowledge spillovers from foreign buyers to local exporters as another source (see Grossman and Helpman, 1991; World Bank, 1993).

3. Other empirical papers on this topic include Chen and Tang (1987), Haddad (1993), and Tybout and Westbrook (1995).

4. Formally, our analysis also goes through if, instead of a borrowing "constraint," the country is large in credit markets and faces an upward-sloping supply curve of loans. The only difference would be that, in the latter case, there would be no wedge between domestic and foreign interest rates, but the borrowing country's government would be able to manipulate both. But it is both convenient and more realistic to think of the borrowing country as facing a distorted interest rate.

5. As in Dixit (1989), the term "export experience" can be somewhat misleading here as there is no learning-by-doing involved and that is why it is under quotation marks. Positive serial correlation in this paper occurs due to policy-induced consumption smoothing and investments. In contrast, in Dixit (1989) shocks create the positive serial correlation. Since the purpose of this paper is to show that temporary export-promotion policy can generate an export "experience" effect even in the absence of learning-by-doing, we do not consider any stochastic shock in this paper.

6. Investment is in units of the *numéraire*, good 1.

7. It is to be noted that this benchmark model is similar in many ways to the one in Edwards and Wijnbergen (1986). The main difference in terms of the model structure is that, whereas they assume the borrowing constraint to fall entirely on investment expenditure, we assume that it applies to both investment and consumption. Three other papers which also have similar model structure are Djajic (1987), Lopez and Panagariya (1991), and Osang and Turnovsky (2000). The objectives of our paper are quite different from these four papers.

8. The expenditure function represents the minimum level of expenditure that can possibly attain a given level of utility. A revenue function is the maximum value of total output that can be achieved for given commodity prices, technology, and endowments. The partial derivative of an expenditure (revenue) function with respect to the price of a good gives the Hicksian demand (supply) for that good. E_i (R_i^j) is the partial derivative of the expenditure function (period-j revenue function) with respect to the ith argument. Moreover, the matrix of second-order partial derivatives with respect to the prices of an expenditure (revenue) function is negative (positive) semidefinite. For this and other properties of expenditure and revenue function see, for example, Dixit and Norman (1980). Since the endowments of factors other than capital do not vary in our analysis, they are omitted from the arguments of the revenue functions.

9. It should be noted that implicitly we are ruling out the Heckscher–Ohlin (HO) framework by assuming that $R_{33}^2 < 0$ since in an HO model endowments, provided they are in the cone of diversification, do not affect factor prices; i.e., $R_{33}^2 = 0$.

10. As mentioned in note 9, our model is a specific-factor model, and R_{23}^2 will indeed be positive if capital is specific to the export sector. Implicitly in the model, there are many other inelastically supplied endowments some of which are specific to a sector and some are mobile. Capital stock in this paper is interpreted as a factor that is specifically used in the export sector and investment in which is endogenous, without necessarily implying that the export sector is more capital-intensive. An observational corollary to this interpretation is that the mechanism through which export persistence arises will be weaker in an economy in which capital is not specific to the export sector.

11. The assumption of exogenous commodity prices is made for a number of reasons. First, it allows us to focus on the credit channel by not introducing complication from the commodity markets. Second, in a relative sense, a developing country has a greater potential market for its commodity imports and exports than it does for credit. That is, while goods can be bought and sold from a variety of countries, credit is available only from a handful of rich countries. Moreover, lending by the rich countries in turn tends to be dominated by large banks.

12. In order to avoid third-order derivatives, we assume that ε is constant.

13. A sufficient condition for $E_{45} \simeq 0$ is that income effects fall entirely on consumption in period 1 and on consumption of good 1 in period 2.

14. Implicitly, we assume that the exogenous level of $\bar{b}$ is the same as $\bar{b}^N$.

15. See Jafarey and Lahiri (2002).

16. We implicitly assume that the exogenous level of $\bar{b}$ is the same as $\hat{\bar{b}}$.

Chapter 8

Does Exporting Increase Productivity?
A Microeconometric Analysis of Matched Firms

Sourafel Girma, David Greenaway, and Richard Kneller

1. Introduction

As a key driver of the globalization process, exports figure prominently in the minds of policymakers. This is partly evidence-based: at an aggregate level, exports and economic growth are positively correlated.[1] But it also reflects the fact that the instincts of many policymakers are fundamentally mercantilist: exports are seen as key to wealth creation, imports are not. This preoccupation has resulted in extensive export promotion activity of one form or another, ranging from trade promotion activities, through to export subsidies, to state trading monopolies. There is probably not a government worldwide that does not engage in export promotion of one form or another. That is quite remarkable. What is equally remarkable, however, is the limited extent to which intervention has been informed by micro-level evidence linking exporting and firm performance.

Until recently, little was known about the characteristics of firms that export. Yet, as Bernard and Jensen (1999) point out, that is central to the design of effective policy. For instance, should support be targeted at encouraging firms to enter export markets or at firms already in those markets? Or should firms be encouraged to set up subsidiaries overseas and become multinationals rather than engage in arm's-length trade? It is not possible to make informed policy choices without robust information on the links between exporting and productivity.

Bernard and Jensen (1995) have pioneered a new literature on the microeconometrics of firm characteristics, exporting, and productivity, and there is now evidence on the relationship for a number (but still a small number) of countries using a range of investigative methods. This paper adds to that literature in two respects. First, it offers one of the first analyses of exports and productivity completed for a large panel of UK firms.[2] Since the UK is the fifth largest exporter of merchandise globally, it is clearly a nontrivial case to investigate. Second, it applies matching analysis, allowing a more targeted evaluation of causality than has been completed thus far, both to exporting and export intensity. Matching is a technique used widely in the labor economics literature. To our knowledge, this is the first study to apply matching and difference-in-differences to investigate the characteristics of exporting and nonexporting firms.[3]

In section 2, we set out the reasons why some firms export and some do not, as well as explaining why once firms begin exporting they *could* become more productive. This section also briefly reviews the evidence adduced thus far and summarizes the key results on the relative productivity of exporters and nonexporters and on causality between exporting and productivity. In section 3, we sharpen the focus to exporting and firm performance using our matching analysis and find evidence that firms become more productive even after they have commenced exporting. Section 4 concludes.

2. Exporting, Self-selection, and Learning

It is widely accepted that the starting point for explaining why some firms export and others do not is sunk costs. Entry costs associated with, for example, market research, product modification, compliance, and so on mean that profit-maximizing firms will enter export markets only if the present value of their profits exceeds the fixed costs of entry. Building on the work of Roberts and Tybout (1997), both Clerides et al. (1998) and Bernard and Jensen (2001a,b) have developed simple but elegant dynamic optimizing models to analyze entry and exit decisions of exporting firms. The essentials can be gleaned from Figure 1, based on Clerides et al. (1998).

Clerides and colleagues assume a monopolistic setting which generates downward-sloping demand curves and ensures that strategic interaction is not an issue. They further assume that marginal costs (c) are invariant to both output and market. Trade frictions, in the form of transportation costs and/or man-made barriers, consume some of the revenue generated by exporting. Thus the firm's foreign demand and marginal revenue schedules lie everywhere below its domestic equivalents, as shown in Figure 1. Gross profits (π) from exporting are therefore the shaded area. But net profits will be less, because of the fixed start-up costs of becoming an exporter, F. Clearly, entry will take place only when

$$\pi f(c, z^f) > F, \tag{1}$$

where c is marginal costs and z represents demand shifters.

Clearly, if F is positive, as the figure neatly shows, firms with marginal costs below some threshold will self-select into export markets. This then underpins the proposition that firms that export will be more productive than firms that do not. The model also has something to say about exit. Firms that become less productive will tend to leave export markets, though not necessarily in the period in which productivity dips. In other words, in any given period, it may still be optimal to continue to export if expression (1) is not satisfied, to avoid re-entry costs and/or in anticipation of cost reductions. This generates a further testable proposition: firms that leave export markets will be less productive, but a fall in productivity may appear only with a lag.

The sunk costs/entry models also offer a framework for gaining insight into a third dimension of firm behavior, namely learning. There are plausible reasons for thinking that, having entered export markets, firms become more productive. The central idea behind this is that a combination of learning from buyers, competition with other firms, and generally gaining greater exposure to best practice results in reductions in c. As a consequence, exporters that were more efficient to start with become even more efficient by virtue of their presence in export markets. This then generates a third testable proposition, that exporting boosts productivity.[4]

Melitz (2003) has constructed a dynamic model with heterogeneous firms to show how, given the opportunity to engage in international trade, more productive firms export, less productive firms produce only for the domestic market, and the least productive firms exit production entirely. This work has now been extended by Helpman

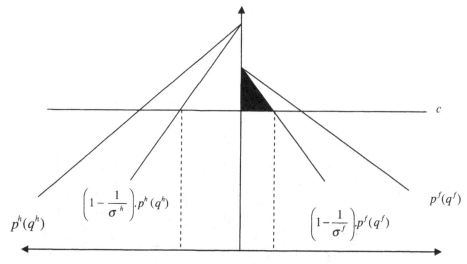

Figure 1. Gross Operating Profits from Exporting

et al. (2004) to encompass the wider menu of options which globalization might bring, namely direct affiliate production overseas as an alternative to exporting. In this paper, we do not investigate that particular option but focus only on exporting/non-exporting.

The propositions that more productive firms self-select into export markets, and might become more productive by virtue of being there, have been exposed to micro-level investigation in a number of recent studies. Table 1 summarizes details of ten papers on ten countries: Aw and Hwang (1995) on Taiwan; Bernard and Jensen (1995, 1999) on the US; Clerides et al. (1998) on Colombia, Mexico, and Morocco; Bernard and Wagner (1997) and Wagner (2002) on Germany; Kraay (1999) on China; Castellani (2002) on Italy; Delgado et al. (2002) on Spain; and Alvarez (2002) on Chile. The studies cover a range of time periods and use a variety of methodologies. Aw and Hwang (1995) and Castellani (2002) are cross-section analyses of firm-level data, for one year in the former and four years in the latter. Delgado et al. (2002) is a novel application of nonparametric analysis of productivity distributions for a five-year period, again using firm-level data. All of the other studies work on panels at the firm or plant level and apply best-practice panel-data estimation.

With regard to outputs, every single study finds that exporters have higher productivity than nonexporters. They also typically find that exporting firms are bigger, more capital-intensive, and pay higher wages. This in itself is quite striking since it is unusual to find such unanimity across the totality of a literature in any area of applied economics (even one as small as this). The literature is also at one on the self-selection hypothesis: exporters are typically more productive *before* they enter export markets. Some, like Bernard and Jensen (1999), Bernard and Wagner (1997), and Clerides et al. (1998), also investigate the characteristics of quitters and find that firms are less productive after they leave export markets. The learning hypothesis receives somewhat less support, however. Castellani (2002) reports some evidence suggesting that the productivity of exporting firms may increase with increases in export *intensity*. For Chinese firms, Kraay (1999) reports evidence of learning-by-exporting. But that is it. The evi-

Table 1. Summary of the Key Features of Studies of Exports and Productivity

Study	Country	Sample	Methodology	Results
Bernard and Jensen (1999)	US	50–60,000 plants 1984–92	Linear probability with fixed effects	Self-selection of exporters Absence of learning from exporting Higher productivity of exporters
Delgado et al. (2002)	Spain	1,766 firms 1991–96	Nonparametric analysis of productivity distributions	Higher productivity of exporters Self-selection of exporting firms Inconclusive evidence on learning
Aw and Hwang (1995)	Taiwan	2,832 firms 1986	Translog production function Cross-section	Higher productivity of exporters Self-selection Absence of learning from exporting
Castellani (2002)	Italy	2,898 firms 1989–94	Cross-section	Higher productivity of exporters Learning associated with export intensity
Kraay (1999)	China	2,105 firms 1988–92	Dynamic panel	Higher productivity of exporters Learning from exporting
Clerides et al. (1998)	Colombia Mexico Morocco	All plants 2,800 firms All firms 1981–91 1986–90 1984–91	FIML of cost functions Panel data	Exporting firms more efficient than nonexporting firms Quitters less productive No learning from exporting in Colombia and Mexico Some learning from exporting in Morocco Spillovers from exporters to nonexporters
Bernard and Wagner (1997)	Germany	7,624 firms 1978–92	Panel data	Higher productivity of exporting firms Self-selection of exporters
Wagner (2002)	Germany	353 firms 1978–89	Panel data; matching	Higher productivity of exporting firms Absence of learning from exporting
Alvarez (2002)	Chile	5,000 plants 1990–96	Ordered probit; pooled data	Higher productivity of exporting firms Self-selection of exporters

dence in Delgado et al. (2002) is inconclusive; and Bernard and Jensen (1995, 1999), Bernard and Wagner (1997), Clerides et al. (1998), and Aw and Hwang (1995) explicitly test for, but fail to find, any evidence to support the learning-by-exporting hypothesis.

In sum, the literature thus far consistently finds evidence to support the proposition that firms that export are generally more productive than those that do not, and that they become more productive in order to export. However, the majority of studies fail to find any convincing evidence of further productivity benefits from exporting after entry has occurred.

3. Does Exporting Lead to Better Performance?

The Microeconometric Evaluation Problem

Our aim is to evaluate the causal effect of exporting on some performance indicator (Δy). In our analysis, Δy represents the growth rate of employment, output, labor productivity, or total factor productivity. Δy is sometimes referred to as the "outcome" in the evaluation literature.[5] Let $EXP_{it} \in \{0, 1\}$ be an indicator (dummy variable) of whether firm i entered the export markets for the first time at period t, and Δy_{it+s}^1 the outcome at time $t + s, s \geq 0$, following entry. Also denote by Δy_{it+s}^0 the outcome of firm i *had it not started exporting*. The causal effect of exporting for firm i at time period $t + s$ is defined as

$$\Delta y_{it+s}^1 - \Delta y_{it+s}^0. \tag{2}$$

The fundamental problem of causal inference is that the quantity Δy_{it+s}^0 is unobservable. Thus the analysis can be viewed as confronting a missing-data problem. In common with most of the microeconometric evaluation literature (cf. Heckman et al., 1997), we define the *average* effect of exporting on export market entrants as

$$E\{\Delta y_{t+s}^1 - \Delta y_{t+s}^0 \mid EXP_{it} = 1\} = E\{\Delta y_{t+s}^1 \mid EXP_{it} = 1\} - E\{\Delta y_{t+s}^0 \mid EXP_{it} = 1\}. \tag{3}$$

Our causal inference relies on the construction of the counterfactual for the last term in equation (3), which is the outcome entrants would have experienced, on average, had they not participated in export markets. The counterfactual is estimated by the corresponding average value of firms that remain nonexporters: $E\{\Delta y_{it+s}^0 \mid EXP = 0\}$.

An important feature in the construction of the counterfactual is the selection of a valid control group. We assume that all the difference in Δy (except that caused by exporting) between exporters and the appropriately selected control group is captured by a vector of observables X and the pre-entry *level* of the outcome variable y_{it-1}. The basic idea of matching is to select from the reservoir of nonexporters those firms in which the distribution of the variables affecting the outcome variable is as similar as possible to the distribution of the exporting firm. To do so, we adopt the "propensity score matching" method of Rosenbaum and Rubin (1983). Thus we first identify the probability of exporting (or "propensity score") for all firms using the following probit model:

$$P(EXP_{it} = 1) = F(TFP_{it-1}, size_{it-1}, ownership_{it-1}, wages_{it-1}). \tag{4}$$

Here *F is* the normal cumulative distribution function, and the full set of regional sectoral and time dummies is also included.[6] Let P_{it} denote the predicted probability of exporting at t for firm i, which is an actual (eventual) exporter. A nonexporting firm j, which is "closest" in terms of its "propensity score" to an exporting firm, is then selected as a match for the former, using the "nearest-neighbor" matching method.[7] More formally, at each point in time and for each new exporter i, a nonexporting firm j is selected such that[8]

$$|P_{it} - P_{jt}| = \min_{k \in \{EXP_{kt}=0\}} \{P_{it} - P_{jt}\}. \tag{5}$$

This type of matching procedure is preferable to randomly or indiscriminately choosing the comparison group because it is less likely to suffer from selection bias by picking firms with markedly different characteristics.

Database Construction and Sample Characteristics

Our sample of firms was drawn from the *OneSource* database.[9] This has a number of attractions: it is one of a very small number of datasets to contain recent firm-level export data; information on employment, physical capital, output, and wages is provided in a consistent way across firms; and it has a time-series element, allowing investigation of the dynamics of exporting/productivity links.

Our dataset contained information on 8,992 companies over the period 1988 to 1999, yielding a maximum of 54,130 observations.[10] To allow intertemporal comparisons, we converted current to constant price values using highly disaggregated price deflators.[11] For each of 101 three-digit sectors, we generated firm-level measures of total factor productivity (TFP) as residuals from a Cobb–Douglas production function with time-specific effects. TFP for each firm is therefore expressed relative to the industry average. Of the 8,992 firms in our initial sample, 4,031 have exported in at least one year. As a result of switching in and out of export markets, the percentage exporting in any given year is lower than this, however.[12] We found that behavior is highly persistent. Around 96% of firms who export in one period do so again in the next period, whereas 94% of firms who did not export continue not to do so in the next period also. The probability of a firm starting or stopping exporting across two years is correspondingly quite low. Only 6% of nonexporters become exporters in the next period, while only 4% of exporters stop exporting.[13] Like other authors, we interpret this as prima facie evidence of sunk costs.

Nearest-neighbor matching means that we can use data only from a subset of the sample, specifically 781 nonexporting firms as a match for the 1,387 new export-market entrants. Having selected the comparison group, we adopt the difference-in-differences methodology[14] to isolate the role of exporting in the performance dynamics of firms. As Blundell and Costa Dias (2000, p. 438) argue, a combination of matching and difference-in-differences will generally improve the quality of nonexperimental evaluation studies. The difference-in-differences approach is a two-step procedure. First, the difference between the average growth rates before and after entry in the export market is calculated for the exporting firms, conditional on past performance, size, age, industry, and regional and time characteristics. However, this difference cannot exclusively be attributed to exporting since the post-entry period growth rate might be affected by factors that are contemporaneous with entry. To adjust for this, the difference obtained at the first stage is further differenced with respect to the before and after difference for the control group of nonexporters. The difference-in-differences estimator therefore removes effects of common shocks, and provides a more accurate description of the impact of exporting.

The importance of appropriate matching cannot be overemphasized. In the labor economics literature that evaluates the impact of a job training program on earnings, it is frequently observed that enrollment into a program is more likely if a temporary loss in earnings occurs just before the start of the program, the so-called "Ashenfelter's dip." Since faster earnings growth is expected to follow such a dip (irrespective of whether the individual in question participates in the program or not), difference-in-differences based on randomly matched individuals is likely to overestimate the earnings impact of training. The converse of this phenomenon might be present here, if exporting firms experience a surge of productivity just before entry,[15] in which case they might be expected to grow less slowly in subsequent periods.

Econometric Results

Our difference-in-differences equation based on the sample of matched firms can be written as

$$\Delta y_{it} = \alpha y_{it-1} + \beta X_{it-1} + \sum_{s=-1}^{2} \gamma_s EXP_{it-s} + D_{jrt} + \varepsilon_{it}, \tag{6}$$

where i, t, r, and j index firms, time periods, industries, and regions respectively, and D represents the full set of four-digit industry, region, and time dummies. As before, Δy denotes the change in the outcome variable (employment, output, wages, labor productivity, or TFP). X is a vector of firm-specific control variables, and EXP_{it} is a dummy which is set to 1 if firm i switches to exporting at time t. Thus we study the contemporaneous and lagged (up to two years after entry) effects of exporting to consider whether changes to the growth of the various business performance indicators, if any, take time to occur. We also use an indicator which predates exporting (E_{it+1}) with a view to further controlling for any performance-exporting relationship in the pre-exporting period that is not captured by the matching procedure.

Our key findings are summarized in Table 2. In general we have found that older and bigger firms grow more slowly. A high initial performance *level* is also found to be associated with relatively modest growth rates, suggesting a β-convergence among the firms. Like Bernard and Jensen (1995), we found some evidence to suggest that the decision to begin exporting raises the growth of employment and output. The growth rate of output (employment) is raised by 3.6 (2.8) and 2 (1.3) percentage points in the first and second periods of exporting. It fact growth of output outstrips that of employment, suggesting post-entry productivity improvement. Evidence also exists that the faster rate of growth of employment and output predate the decision to export. Where our results differ from those of Bernard and Jensen in an important way is in the uncovering of a causal relationship from exporting to TFP growth. On entry year, exporting firms experience a TFP growth rate which is higher by about 1.6 percentage points than would be the case had they remained nonexporters. Moreover, TFP continues to grow by an extra percentage point in the following year. By contrast, TFP growth prior to entry is found to be no faster than that of the nonexporting one. This suggests that our matching strategy has succeeded in selecting control firms in a manner that adjusts for potentially confounding effects of the pre-exporting period

Table 2. Does Entry into the Exports Market Improve Performance?

	Employment growth	Output growth	Labor productivity growth	TFP growth
Wage growth	−0.167			
	(10.65)**			
Capital growth	0.107			
	(7.13)**			
Initial value	−0.021	−0.026	−0.085	−0.103
	(14.25)**	(12.47)**	(9.53)**	(19.64)**
Age	−0.001	−0.001	−0.012	−0.001
	(5.58)**	(4.40)**	(1.67)	(2.38)*
Pre-entry period	0.008	0.019	0.003	0.002
	(1.31)	(1.95)	(0.43)	(0.23)
Entry year	0.028	0.036	−0.122	0.016
	(3.46)**	(2.92)**	(0.12)	(1.64)
One year later	0.013	0.020	1.518	0.011
	(2.26)*	(2.43)*	(2.23)*	(1.60)
Two years later	−0.002	−0.003	0.404	0.001
	(0.41)	(0.36)	(0.57)	(0.09)

Notes: Robust t-statistics are in parentheses. Initial values are the lagged values of the relevant variables. For example, in the TFP growth equation, lagged value is the level of TFP in the previous period. The point estimates give change in the growth rate of the relevant variable that is caused by exporting. * Significant at 10%; ** significant at 5%; *** significant at 1%. The full set of four-digit industry, region, and time dummies is included. Initial value refers to the lagged value of the relevant variable in levels.

productivity characteristics. (The results for labor productivity follow the same pattern as for TFP.)

As we saw earlier, past export experience is a very powerful predictor of current export behavior. This has led some, like Castellani (2002), to investigate whether export intensity has a role to play. In our sample, firms that are more export-intensive (in the sense of having a relatively high share of exports in total sales) are more likely to continue to export, but this effect decreases as the share of exports in sales increases. In other words, increasing the amount of experience a firm has in exports markets matters more when the share of exports to total sales is low than when it is high.

Does the productivity effect depend upon the growth rate of export intensity? To explore this, we augment our baseline specification as

$$\Delta y_{it} = \alpha y_{it-1} + \beta X_{it-1} + \gamma_{-1} EXP_{t+1} + \gamma_0 EXP_{it} + \sum_{s=1}^{2} \gamma_s \Delta expint^* EX_{it-s} + D_{jrt} + \varepsilon_{it}. \quad (7)$$

That is, we interact the two lagged export entry dummies by the (contemporaneous) export intensity growth rate. Our findings are reported in Table 3 and they provide some interesting insights. In the period following entry, the rate of growth of output increases with the share of exports in total output. A 10-percentage-points increase in export intensity causes output growth to accelerate by about 2.5 percentage points. However, the export-intensity parameters are insignificant in the employment

Table 3. Export Market Entry, Export Intensity, and Performance

	Employment growth	Output growth	Labor productivity growth	TFP growth
Pre-entry period	0.008	0.019	0.007	0.002
	(1.31)	(1.97)**	(0.83)	(0.24)
Entry year	0.028	0.036	0.009	0.016
	(3.46)***	(2.92)***	(0.87)	(1.64)*
One year later	0.012	0.017	0.007	0.009
	(2.13)**	(2.15)**	(1.09)	(1.31)
Interaction term	0.074	0.246	0.175	0.207
	(1.05)	(2.03)**	(1.67)	(2.03)**
Two years later	−0.002	−0.004	0.003	0.0
	(0.35)	(0.47)	(0.48)	(0.05)
Interaction term	−0.035	0.078	0.103	0.035
	(0.48)	(0.60)	(0.89)	(0.33)

Notes: Robust *t*-statistics are in parentheses. * Significant at 10%; ** significant at 5%; *** significant at 1%. The interaction term is the product of the relevant post-entry dummy with the corresponding export intensity growth rate.

equation, implying that any output growth must have resulted from a more efficient utilization of factors of production (including labor). This point is reinforced by inspection of the productivity results. An increase in the share of exports raises the rate at which TFP grows in the period after entry. The estimate, which is statistically significant, suggests that a firm increasing its share of exporting by 10 percentage points enjoys an additional 2.1-percentage-points TFP growth, whereas firms that did not increase export intensity do not benefit from this additional productivity boost.[16] In the sample, only 25% of the newly exporting firms have significantly increased their export intensity, so that the benefit of exporting at the post-entry period is not universal.

To summarize, our difference-in-differences estimates suggest that exporting has helped improve performance. Most of the effects of exporting are confined to the first two years following entry, and the rate of growth of export intensity plays an economically important role. The reliability of the difference-in-differences methodology is, of course, dependent on the assumption that exporting and nonexporting firms are similarly affected by macro factors that are contemporaneous with entry. During most of our study period (1988–99), British manufacturing firms have had to operate under exchange rate uncertainty. It is possible that exporting firms respond to exchange rate uncertainties in a different way from nonexporting firms. If so, and if this had a deleterious impact on their performance, our estimation method will *underestimate* the true degree of the performance-enhancing effect of exporting. This conjecture appears to have found some justification from difference-in-differences estimates based on all firms (i.e., the unmatched sample) which are reported in Table 4. Compared to the results in Table 2, it seems that there is a more pronounced and significant productivity boost a year after entry. These findings are only suggestive, however, as the two sets of results are not strictly comparable. Results based on the matched sample are the only ones that can allow us to make a causal inference from exporting to performance dynamics.

Table 4. Export Market Entry and Performance: Difference-in-Difference Estimates from the Unmatched Sample

	Employment growth	Output growth	Labor productivity growth	TFP growth
Pre-entry year	0.0110	0.0275	0.0129	0.0112
	(2.00)**	(3.34)***	(1.85)	(1.59)
Entry year	0.0258	0.0338	0.0096	0.0170
	(3.89)***	(3.24)***	(1.09)	(2.02)**
One year later	0.0112	0.0231	0.0131	0.0158
	(2.37)**	(3.21)***	(2.17)**	(2.69)***
Two years later	−0.0003	0.0002	0.0052	0.0030
	(0.06)	(0.02)	(0.84)	(0.47)

Notes: The baseline specification described in equation (2) is used.
Robust *t*-statistics are in parentheses.
**Significant at 5%; ***significant at 1%.
Estimated coefficients or the control variables in equation (8) are available from the authors.

4. Conclusions

Promoting exports is a high priority for most governments, on the assumption that it is good for productivity and growth. Until recently, however, there was little robust evidence linking exporting and performance at the firm level. Following the seminal work of Bernard and Jensen, a number of microeconometric studies have now been completed on a range of developed and developing countries.

In this paper we apply a novel methodology to investigate exporting and firm performance for a large panel of UK firms. In applying matching analysis we ensure that the characteristics of exporters and nonexporters are as close as they can be, allowing us to drive out effects that can be reliably attributed to exporting. We find that exporters are typically larger and more productive than nonexporters; and, like all other analysts, we find that they self-select, in that they were more productive before they entered. Some of our other key findings are in contrast to other work, however. The major contrast with most other work is that exporting may boost productivity. This may be a consequence of the methodology we have used, or it may be due to underlying structural differences between the UK and US. For example, since the US is a larger and more competitive market, with more firms closer to the technological frontier, potential learning benefits from exporting are likely to be less than for UK firms. This is an issue worthy of further investigation.

References

Alvarez, A., "Determinants of Firm Export Performance in a Less Developed Country," mimeo, University of California at Los Angeles (2002).

Aw, B. Y. and A. R. Hwang, "Productivity in the Export Market: a Firm Level Analysis," *Journal of Development Economics* 47 (1995):313–32.

Bernard, A. and J. B. Jensen, "Exporters, Jobs and Wages in US Manufacturing: 1976–1987," *Brookings Papers on Economic Activity, Microeconomics* (1995):67–119.

———, "Exceptional Exporters' Performance: Cause, Effect or Both?" *Journal of International Economics* 47 (1999):1–25.

——, "Exporting and Productivity: the Importance of Reallocation," mimeo, Dartmonth College (2001a).

——, "Why Some Firms Export," NBER working paper 8349 (2001b).

Bernard, A. and J. Wagner, "Exports and Success in German Manufacturing," *Weltwirtschaftliches Archiv* 133 (1997):134–57.

Bleaney, M. and K. Wakelin, "Efficiency, Innovation and Exports," *Oxford Bulletin of Economics and Statistics* 64 (2002):3–15.

Blundell, R. and M. Costa Dias, "Evaluation Methods for Non-experimental Data," *Fiscal Studies* 21 (2000):427–68.

Castellani, D., "Export Behaviour and Productivity Growth: Evidence from Italian Manufacturing Firms," *Weltwirtschaftliches Archiv* 138 (2002):605–28.

Clerides, S., S. Lach, and J. Tybout, "Is Learning by Exporting Important? Microdynamic Evidence from Columbia, Mexico, and Morocco," *Quarterly Journal of Economics* 113 (1998):903–48.

Delgado, M., J. Farinas, and S. Ruano, "Firm Productivity and Export Markets: a Nonparametric Approach," *Journal of International Economics* 57 (2002):397–422.

Edwards, S., "Openness, Trade Liberalisation and Growth in Developing Countries," *Journal of Economic Literature* 31 (1993):1358–93.

——, "Openness, Productivity and Growth: What Do We Really Know?" *Economic Journal* 108 (1998):383–98.

Girma, S., D. Greenaway, and R. Kneller, "Export Market Exit and Performance Dynamics," *Economics Letters* 80 (2003):181–8.

Heckman, J., H. Ichimura, J. Smith, and P. Todd, "Matching as an Econometric Evaluation Estimator: Evidence from Evaluating a Job Training Programme," *Review of Economic Studies* 64 (1997):605–54.

Helpman, E., M. Melitz, and S. Yeaple, "Export versus FDI," *American Economic Review* 94 (2004):300–16.

Kraay, A., "Exports and Economic Performance: Evidence from a Panel of Chinese Enterprises," mimeo, World Bank (1999).

Melitz, M., "The Impact of Trade on Intra-industry Reallocations and Aggregate Industry Production," *Econometrica* 71 (2003):1695–725.

Meyer, B., "Natural and Quasi-experiments in Economics," NBER technical working paper 170 (1994).

Roberts, M. and J. Tybout, "The Decision to Export in Colombia," *American Economic Review* 87 (1997):545–65.

Rosenbaum, P. and D. B. Rubin, "The Central Role of the Propensity Score in Observational Studies for Causal Effects," *Biometrika* 70 (1983):41–55.

Sianesi, Barbara, "Implementing Propensity Score Matching Estimators with Stata," available at http://fmwww.bc.edu/RePEc/usug2001/psmatch.pdf (2001).

Wagner, J., "The Causal Effects of Exports on Firm Size and Labour Productivity: First Evidence from a Matching Approach," *Economics Letters* 77 (2002):287–92.

Notes

1. See, for example, Edwards (1993, 1998).

2. Bleaney and Wakelin (2002) investigate the links between exporting and productivity for a sample of innovating and noninnovating firms in the UK.

3. Independently, Wagner (2002) has used plant-level German data to evaluate causal effects of exporting on plant performance. In a companion paper, Girma et al. (2003) use matching to investigate the performance of firms that exit export markets.

4. Clerides et al. (1998) solve their model numerically and generate transitions consistent with these outcomes.

5. For a comprehensive review on the microeconometric evaluation literature see Blundell and Costa Dias (2000).

6. It goes without saying that the success of the matching method depends on correctly identifying the variables that determine export participation.

7. The matching is performed in Stata version 7 as described in Sianesi (2001).

8. A nonexporting firm can be matched to more than one exporting firm.

9. For our analysis we used the OneSource CD-ROM entitled "UK Companies, Vol. 1" for October 2000. These data are derived from the accounts that companies are legally required to deposit at Companies House.

10. To ensure that we flush out any "exporting" effects, we excluded a range of observations. First, foreign companies are omitted, since they arguably have different export motives (e.g., intrafirm trade) to domestically owned companies. Second, parent companies were omitted, since if they had consolidated accounts this would have led to double-counting. Third, only companies whose main activity is manufacturing were chosen. Fourth, the top and bottom one-percentile firms in terms of employment, labor productivity, and wages, and firms with annual employment or wages growth exceeding 100%, were omitted, to mitigate the impact of outliers.

11. Although the use of firm-level prices is the ideal way of constructing real values, such data are not available and five-digit price indices help to ameliorate problems associated with more aggregate price deflators.

12. Taking 1995 as a representative year in the middle of the sample period, we find that 35% of firms exported and 65% did not. These results are robust to the use of 1993 as an alternative year.

13. These results are robust across time. There is no obvious trend in the decision not to export.

14. See Meyer (1994) for a review of this approach.

15. Recall that we have already established that good performance predates export market entry.

16. In other words, the entry effect on TFP for those firms is confined to the 1.6-percentage-point growth at entry year.

Chapter 9

Outsourcing under Imperfect Protection of Intellectual Property

Amy Jocelyn Glass

1. Introduction

Globalization means many things to many people. Economies are becoming more integrated. National borders matter less for the exchange of goods and services. Many more countries are opening up to trade and exporting their products to increasingly global markets. One way these changes may be manifested is through growth in international outsourcing. US firms (and firms from other developed countries) have increasingly been outsourcing production to countries where production costs are lower.

Outsourcing can appear in the data through both imports and exports. When firms shift production of some components abroad and assemble the components into final goods at home, the components are imported. When firms produce some components at home and assemble the components into final goods abroad, the components are exported. Feenstra (1998) provides an excellent summary of data representing the increasing extent of international outsourcing. He suggests merchandise trade relative to value-added, and shifts in the composition of trade by end use, as measures.

Merchandise trade relative to value-added has been growing steadily for the major developed countries since at least 1960. As Table 1 shows, values for the United States have tripled from 9.6% to 35.8% over the 30-year period from 1960 to 1990. Other countries, such as the United Kingdom and Canada, have seen their values double, starting from higher initial levels (33.8% to 62.8%, and 37.6% to 69.8%, respectively).

Trade in capital goods provides a rough measure of trade in intermediate goods. Capital goods contain items such as machinery, electrical parts, and other components. Shares of capital goods in both imports and exports have been rising for the United States since at least 1925. As Table 2 shows, the US import share of capital goods rose from 0.4% to 33.6% from 1950 to 1995, and the export share rose from 8.7% to 42.4%.

Why has outsourcing been expanding and what are its consequences? This paper examines whether the effects of outsourcing depend on the reasons behind the expansion in outsourcing. Glass and Saggi (2001) constructed a North–South product-cycle model to help identify forces leading to increased outsourcing and a lower Northern relative wage. That work countered the claim that international outsourcing of production must be detrimental to the welfare of workers in industrialized countries by arguing that faster innovation could create gains sufficient to offset the decline in Northern wages. The Glass–Saggi model (hereafter, GS) assumed no Southern imitation for simplicity.

Table 1. *Merchandise Trade Relative to Value-added (percentages)*

	United States	United Kingdom	Canada	Germany
1960	9.6	33.8	37.6	24.6
1970	13.7	40.7	50.5	31.3
1980	30.9	52.6	65.6	48.5
1990	35.8	62.8	69.8	57.8

Table 2. *Shares of Capital Goods in US Trade (percentages)*

	Imports	Exports
1925	0.4	8.7
1950	1.3	22.4
1965	7.1	31.4
1980	19.0	35.0
1995	33.6	42.4

This paper adds imitation to address whether changes in exposure to imitation could be behind the expansion in outsourcing and whether, if so, the increased outsourcing occurs together with increased innovation. I find that an increase in the intensity of imitation decreases the rate of innovation and the extent of outsourcing, while increasing the Northern wage relative to the Southern wage. Thus an expansion in outsourcing, together with a decline in the Northern relative wage and faster innovation, could stem from a decline in imitation. Southern imitation may be declining due to efforts to strengthen protection of intellectual property in the South. The results suggest that as the TRIPs agreement becomes fully implemented, outsourcing may rise further.

In addition to examining the effects of imitation, the model is useful for determining how the effects of other parameters are altered by imitation. In the GS model, labor supplies did not affect the relative wage across countries. Thus, increased labor supplies (alone) could not account for the increase in outsourcing because the Northern relative wage would not fall in response, according to the original model. This feature was unfortunate because greater availability of labor in the South seems intuitively to be a plausible explanation.

Along with increases in outsourcing, Southern (effective) labor supplies have been increasing. Young (1995) found evidence of factor accumulation due to rising participation rates (primarily for women), shifts in labor from agriculture to manufactures, improved education, and increased investment for the East Asian newly industrialized countries (Hong Kong, Singapore, Korea, and Taiwan). The fraction of the workforce with at least a secondary education has essentially tripled (or more) in these countries over the past three decades. Also, the opening of China and other countries may act like an increase in the Southern labor supply available for outsourcing.

Adding imitation to the model allows increased Southern labor supplies to possibly explain increased outsourcing occurring with a reduction in the relative wage across countries. Once imitation is added, labor supplies do affect the relative wage across countries, indirectly through their effect on the rate of innovation. The relative wage across countries adjusts to keep the value of a firm (the present discounted value of profits) the same whether or not the firm outsources. Whether outsourcing or not, firms are always exposed to the chance that a rival will invent an even better generation of their product; however, when outsourcing, there is the additional risk of imitation. The rate of innovation alters the degree of discounting when outsourcing relative to when not: if innovation occurs frequently, the additional risk of imitation will be relatively less important.

Either increased labor supplies or decreased imitation could be raising the incentives for international outsourcing. What is the impact of these changes? Do both countries benefit or is there conflict between the interests of the North and the South? Does the impact of outsourcing depend on whether reduced imitation or increased labor supplies are the driving force?

Three separate welfare effects operate in this model: effects on expenditure, average price level, and average quality consumed. Decreased imitation and increased labor supplies increase the rate of innovation and thus the average quality of products consumed. On the other hand, they decrease expenditure and might increase the average price level. However, the growth effect (innovation) will dominate the level effects (expenditure and average price level) for each country provided the discount rate is sufficiently low (must be patient enough). Therefore, the South need not be hurt by reducing imitation through tighter protection of intellectual property. Furthermore, outsourcing need not hurt the North. Decreased imitation and increased labor supplies join the list in GS of forces that could increase outsourcing and yield welfare benefits for the North, despite declines in the Northern relative wage.

There is evidence that increased outsourcing reduces the gap in wages across countries. Egger and Pfaffermayr (2004, this issue) find that outsourcing generates convergence in average real wage rates across countries. Scheve and Slaughter (2002) examine a different type of concern of Northern workers: uncertainty in employment and wages due to outsourcing. Such concerns should act like level effects and thus benefits from faster innovation could more than compensate. Girma and Görg (2004, this issue) find that high wages are positively related to outsourcing decisions (including both domestic and international outsourcing), so the cost motive does seem important.

An innovator may shift production to the South by licensing a Southern firm or by forming a subsidiary for that purpose—foreign direct investment (FDI). Lai (1998) has argued that an increase in the intensity of imitation of multinationals' products causes a reduction in FDI and innovation. Here I consider the more general case where some, but not necessarily all, stages of production are shifted to the South and find a similar result. Additionally, in the Lai (1998) model, innovations are new varieties, whereas here they are quality improvements.

2. International Outsourcing Model

Each country is composed of a representative consumer and many firms. Consumers are willing to pay a premium for quality because they derive more utility from higher quality levels of products. This premium gives Northern firms an incentive to develop quality improvements. Once successful in inventing a higher quality level of a product, a Northern firm can then outsource some stages of production to the low-cost South.

However, by outsourcing, the Northern firm exposes itself to imitation. The degree that shifting production to the South lowers costs is determined endogenously through the relative wage across countries.

Consumers

Consumer preferences are as described in the quality ladders product cycle model of Grossman and Helpman (1991). Identical consumers live in one of two countries, North and South, $i \in \{N, S\}$. Consumers choose from a continuum of products indexed by $j \in [0, 1]$, where products are available in a discrete number of quality levels indexed by m. A consumer has additively separable intertemporal preferences given by lifetime utility

$$U = \int_0^\infty e^{-\rho t} \log u(t) dt, \tag{1}$$

where ρ is the common subjective discount rate, instantaneous utility is

$$\log u(t) = \int_0^1 \log \left[\sum_m \lambda^m x_m(j, t) \right] dj, \tag{2}$$

λ^m is the assessment of quality level m, and $x_m(j, t)$ is consumption of quality level m of product j at time t. Each quality level m is λ-times better than quality level $m - 1$, where λ denotes the size of the quality increment. By the definition of quality, higher quality levels are valued more: $\lambda > 1$.

Since preferences are homothetic, aggregate demand can be found by maximizing lifetime utility (1) subject to the aggregate intertemporal budget constraint

$$\int_0^\infty e^{-R(t)} E(t) dt \leq A(0) + \int_0^\infty e^{-R(t)} Y(t) dt, \tag{3}$$

where $R(t) = \int_0^t r(s) ds$ is the cumulative interest rate up to time t and $A(0)$ is the aggregate value of initial asset holdings. Aggregate income is

$$Y(t) = \sum_i L_i w_i(t), \tag{4}$$

where $w_i(t)$ is the wage in country i at time t and L_i is the labor supply in country i, so $L_i w_i(t)$ is the total labor income in country i at time t. Labor and wages are measured in efficiency units. Aggregate spending is

$$E(t) = \int_0^1 \left[\sum_m p_m(j, t) x_m(j, t) \right] dj, \tag{5}$$

where $p_m(j, t)$ is the price of quality level m of product j at time t.

The consumer's maximization problem can be broken into three stages: the allocation of lifetime wealth across time, the allocation of expenditure at each instant across products, and the allocation of expenditure at each instant for each product across available quality levels. In the first stage, each consumer evenly spreads lifetime spending for each product across time; in the second stage, each consumer evenly spreads spending at each instant across products; see Grossman and Helpman (1991) for details. In the final stage, each consumer allocates spending for each product at each instant to the quality level with the lowest quality adjusted price, p_m/λ^m. Thus, consumers are willing to pay a premium of λ for a one-quality-level improvement in a product.

Producers

To produce a given quality level of a product, a firm must first design it. However, due to assumed differences in technological knowledge across countries, only Northern firms innovate: innovation by Southern firms is assumed to be sufficiently difficult that it does not occur. The innovation process is the same as in Grossman and Helpman (1991). Assume innovation races occur simultaneously for all products, with all Northern firms able to target the quality level above the current highest quality level for each product. Normalize the Southern wage to one, $w_S = 1$, so $w \equiv w_N/w_S = w_N$ is the Northern wage relative to the Southern wage. Assume undertaking innovation intensity ι for a time interval dt requires $a\iota dt$ units of labor at a cost of $wa\iota dt$ and leads to success with probability ιdt.

In Grossman and Helpman's model, Northern firms must produce only in the North. Similar to Glass and Saggi (2001), in my model Northern firms can purchase some stages of production from Southern firms. Normalize the unit labor requirement in production to one. Of the one unit of labor needed to produce one unit of the final product, the fraction β can be outsourced and the remaining $(1 - \beta)$ cannot. The output of any stage is a tradable intermediate good so different stages of production can be located in different countries. Production of components could occur in the South and assembly in the North, or the reverse, or other more complicated divisions of the production process between countries.

To outsource production, a firm must first adapt its production process for the South. For simplicity, assume this adaptation process is costless (but uncertain). Undertaking outsourcing intensity ϕ for a time interval dt leads to success with probability ϕdt. If successful at its efforts, a firm outsources the fixed fraction β of production. The uncertain process involved with outsourcing could involve a search for appropriate licensing partners.

A firm's problem can be broken down into two stages. First, when undertaking innovation, the firm chooses its intensity of innovation to maximize its expected value, given the innovation intensities of other firms. Once successful in innovation, the firm then chooses the price of its product and intensity of adaptation to maximize its value, given the prices and innovation intensities of other firms. Current producers do not undertake any innovation due to the familiar profit destruction argument (Grossman and Helpman, 1991).

To generate a finite intensity of innovation, expected gains must not exceed cost, with equality when innovation occurs with positive intensity

$$v_N \leq wa, \quad \iota > 0 \Leftrightarrow v_N = wa, \tag{6}$$

where v_N is the value a firm gains from successful innovation. Costs exceeding benefits would choke off innovation, whereas benefits exceeding costs would lead to innovation at an infinite intensity (and could not persist given free entry into innovation races). Similarly, expected gains from international outsourcing must not exceed the cost of zero, with equality when outsourcing occurs with positive intensity

$$v_O - v_N \leq 0, \quad \phi > 0 \Leftrightarrow v_O - v_N = 0, \tag{7}$$

where $v_O - v_N$ is the capital gain from outsourcing production.

Why doesn't outsourcing provide any excess returns? If the value from outsourcing were to exceed the value from keeping all production located in the North, then the intensity of outsourcing would be infinite, and so all successful innovators would outsource immediately. We are interested in cases where some but not all Northern firms outsource production (to see how changes in imitation risk affect outsourcing decisions), so we assume that firms earn the same value of their present discounted profits regardless of whether they choose to outsource. For equilibria with both innovation and outsourcing, both of these conditions must hold with equality and thus $v_N = v_O = wa$.

The reward to innovation is the discounted stream of profits from production. A Northern firm that successfully innovates earns the reward

$$
v_N = \frac{\pi_N + \phi v_O}{\rho + \phi + \iota},
$$
$$
(\rho + \phi + \iota)v_N = \pi_N + \phi v_O,
$$
$$
(\rho + \iota)v_N = \pi_N + \phi(v_O - v_N), \tag{8}
$$
$$
v_N = \frac{\pi_N + \phi(v_O - v_N)}{\rho + \iota} = \frac{\pi_N}{\rho + \iota},
$$

where I have used $v_N = v_O$ to simplify the expression. Because outsourcing yields no excess returns, the reward to innovation v_N is not directly affected by the opportunity to outsource. Upon successfully adapting its technology for Southern production, the firm's value becomes

$$
v_O = \frac{\pi_O}{\rho + \iota + M} \tag{9}
$$

until rival innovation or imitation terminates its value, where M is the intensity of Southern imitation. As in Helpman (1993) and Lai (1998), the intensity of imitation can be interpreted as reflecting the degree of intellectual property protection in the South (with stronger protection leading to lower values of M).

Note that the value of a firm being the same regardless of whether outsourcing $v_N = v_O$ implies that profits when outsourcing must be larger relative to profits when not outsourcing in proportion to the intensity of imitation:

$$
\frac{\pi_O}{\pi_N} = \frac{\rho + \iota + M}{\rho + \iota} = 1 + \frac{M}{\rho + \iota} > 1. \tag{10}
$$

In general, imitation might also target goods even when they are produced entirely in the North, in which case the relevant ratio would be $(\rho + \iota + M)/(\rho + \iota + \underline{M})$, where $\underline{M}$ is the imitation intensity targeting Northern production and the risk of imitation rises with outsourcing $M > \underline{M}$. The model should be robust to allowing imitation of Northern production; increases in M would then be thought of as occurring relative to $\underline{M}$.

Under Bertrand competition, the most recent innovator for each product engages in limit pricing behavior by choosing a price that just keeps its closest rival from earning a positive profit from production. Each most recent innovator has a one-quality-level lead over the closest rival and so chooses a price equal to λ times the rival's marginal cost.

Assume all old technologies have full international outsourcing potential. Old technologies are designs that have already been improved. Once technologies no longer yield profits in equilibrium, these old technologies become fully available to Southern firms. This assumption provides a common marginal cost of production of one for all technologies that are no longer produced in equilibrium.

Thus each producing Northern firm charges price $p = \lambda$ and makes sales $x = E/\lambda$ (as aggregate expenditure is price times sales $E = px$) regardless of whether the firm outsources production. International outsourcing does affect production costs, and thus profits (price minus costs times sales). Let $\delta \equiv 1/\lambda$. Firms that do not outsource production have marginal cost w, yielding instantaneous profits

$$\pi_N = (\lambda - w)\frac{E}{\lambda} = E(1 - w\delta). \tag{11}$$

Firms that outsource production have marginal cost $c \equiv \beta + (1 - \beta)w$, a weighted average of costs in the North and the South, where $0 < \beta < 1$ represents the labor share in outsourced production, yielding instantaneous profits

$$\pi_O = E(1 - c\delta) = E[1 - w\delta + \beta\delta(w - 1)]. \tag{12}$$

I assume that there are sufficiently many potential suppliers in the South that Northern firms are able to purchase items at cost. Even though outsourcing lowers costs, Northern firms do not lower their prices because they price at a markup relative to the cost of Southern firms.

Comparing the profit expressions, profits rise with outsourcing in proportion to the size of the cost savings, the fraction of production outsourced, and the volume of sales: $\pi_O - \pi_N = E\delta\beta(w - 1)$. Or in terms of ratios:

$$\frac{\pi_O}{\pi_N} = \frac{E[1 - w\delta + \beta\delta(w - 1)]}{E(1 - w\delta)} = 1 + \frac{\beta\delta(w - 1)}{1 - w\delta} > 1. \tag{13}$$

The cost savings of outsourcing increase profits, which provides an incentive for firms to outsource, despite the increased risk of imitation. Combining (10) and (13) yields

$$1 + \frac{M}{\rho + \iota} = 1 + \frac{\beta\delta(w - 1)}{1 - w\delta} \rightarrow \frac{M}{\beta} = \frac{\delta(w - 1)(\rho + \iota)}{1 - w\delta}. \tag{14}$$

Inserting profits (11, 12) into the producing firm valuations (8, 9) and inserting those values into the innovation and adaptation conditions (6, 7), under equality, yields the valuation conditions

$$E(1 - w\delta) = wa(\rho + \iota), \tag{15}$$

$$E[1 - w\delta + \beta\delta(w - 1)] = wa(\rho + \iota + M), \tag{16}$$

which must hold for an equilibrium with both innovation and outsourcing.

The assumption that all production never occurs in the South is supported by more fundamental assumptions. Suppose that, while the unit labor requirement in basic production in the South is one (by normalization), the unit labor requirement in advanced production in the South is $\zeta > 1$. Provided the unit labor requirement in advanced production in the South is greater than the Northern wage in equilibrium $\zeta > w$, producing the basic stage will be cheaper in the South while producing the advanced stage will be cheaper in the North.

Additionally, outsourcing all production could expose the firm to imitation at an intensity substantially higher than M, say $\overline{M} \gg M$ (with $\overline{M} > M/\beta$), so that the additional cost savings do not justify the much larger imitation risk

$$\frac{\overline{M}}{\rho+\iota} \gg \frac{\delta(w-1)}{1-w\delta}. \tag{17}$$

Or equivalently the valuation condition for full outsourcing is an inequality:

$$E(1-\delta) < wa(\rho+\iota+\overline{M}). \tag{18}$$

The structure of the model suggests that if firms are free to split the production process across borders to any degree and face an imitation risk M increasing in the fraction outsourced β, firms will pick β to minimize M/β. The condition (14) needed for both valuation conditions to hold simultaneously fixes the ratio of M/β. If a firm were to choose a β that led to a higher M/β, its outsourcing would lead to a lower rate of return than the outsourcing of other firms. While it would reap additional cost savings, the additional exposure to imitation would be excessive.

Market Measures and Resources

A quality level of a product is produced entirely in the North following innovation, partially in the North, and partially in the South once outsourced, and entirely in the South following imitation. Let n_N denote the fraction of products produced entirely in the North, n_O denote the fraction of products outsourced, and n_S denote the fraction of products produced entirely in the South. In a steady state, the flows into must equal flows out of outsourcing, so that the fraction of products outsourced n_O remains constant. The flows into outsourcing are ϕn_N while the flows out are $(\iota + M)n_O$; therefore

$$\phi n_N = (\iota + M)n_O. \tag{19}$$

Similarly, the flows into and out of pure Southern production must be the same. The flows into pure Southern production are $M n_O$ while the flows out are ιn_S; therefore

$$M n_O = \iota n_S. \tag{20}$$

These product measures must sum to one:

$$n_N = 1 - n_O - n_S. \tag{21}$$

These last two equations can be rewritten and combined as $n_S = M n_O/\iota$ and $n_N = 1 - n_O(1 + M/\iota)$.

The labor constraints for each country will complete the model. The fixed supply of labor is allocated between innovation and production in the North. All products are targeted for innovation and hence the labor demand for innovation is $a\iota$. Sales by Northern firms are $x_N = x_O = E\delta$ regardless of whether a product is outsourced. The fraction n_N of products are produced entirely in the North and the fraction n_O have only some stages produced in the North, so labor demand for production in the North is $n_N E\delta + (1 - \beta)n_O E\delta$. The North has a fixed labor supply of L_N and so the Northern labor constraint is

$$a\iota + [n_N + (1-\beta)n_O]E\delta = L_N. \tag{22}$$

Labor is used only for production in the South since Southern firms are assumed to not innovate and imitation is assumed to be costless. The South produces only some stages in markets with outsourcing and all stages for products that have been imitated. Labor demand for production of outsourced products is $\beta n_o E \delta$. I assume that following imitation, all Southern firms become able to produce the entire product and thus set price equal to the cost of production of one (need one unit of labor to produce one unit of output by normalization, and the Southern wage is one by normalization). Thus, sales of imitated products are $x_S = E$ and labor demand for pure Southern production is $n_S E$. The South has a fixed labor supply of L_S and so the Southern labor constraint is

$$(\beta n_o \delta + n_S)E = L_S. \tag{23}$$

Studying the two labor constraints reveals that an increase in the fraction of products that are outsourced, n_o, or in the fraction of labor demand for outsourced production, β, leads to a shift in labor demand from the North to the South.

Define the extent of international outsourcing as the fraction of all production outsourced to the South, $\chi \equiv \beta n_o$, the fraction of products outsourced times the fraction of production outsourced for each product. Since $n_o = \chi/\beta$, the steady-state constant measure conditions $n_S = M n_o/\iota$ and $n_N = 1 - n_o(1 + M/\iota)$ can be rewritten in terms of the extent of outsourcing as $n_S = M\chi/(\beta\iota)$ and $n_N = 1 - (\chi/\beta)(1 + M/\iota)$. The market measures can then be eliminated from the resource constraints, leaving the Northern labor constraint

$$a\iota + \left[1 - \chi\left(1 + \frac{M}{\beta\iota}\right)\right]E\delta = L_N \tag{24}$$

as $n_N + (1 - \beta)n_o = 1 - \chi[1 + M/(\beta\iota)]$, and the Southern resource constraint

$$\chi E\left(\delta + \frac{M}{\beta\iota}\right) = L_S \tag{25}$$

as $\beta n_o \delta + n_S = \chi\delta + M\chi/(\beta\iota) = \chi[\delta + M/(\beta\iota)]$. An increase in the extent of outsourcing, χ, not only shifts labor demand for production from the North to the South, it also increases the overall demand for labor since imitated products have lower prices and thus larger sales.

These two resource constraints, (24) and (25), combined with the two valuation conditions, (15) and (16), comprise the system. The four equations determine aggregate spending E, the Northern relative wage w, the rate of innovation ι, and the extent of international outsourcing χ.

3. Steady-state Equilibrium with Outsourcing and Imitation

The primary goal of this paper is to determine the effect of the intensity of imitation M on the rate of innovation ι and the extent of outsourcing χ, as well as on aggregate expenditure E and the Northern relative wage w. To determine these effects, solve the four equations for the four endogenous variables in turn. Start by solving the innovation valuation condition (15) and the outsourcing valuation condition (16) for aggregate expenditure

$$E = \frac{a\left[\dfrac{M}{\beta} + \delta(\iota + \rho)\right]}{\delta(1 - \delta)} > 0 \tag{26}$$

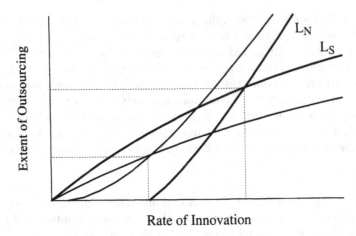

Figure 1. Effect of Imitation on Outsourcing and Innovation

and the relative wage

$$w = \frac{\dfrac{M}{\beta} + \delta(\iota + \rho)}{\dfrac{M}{\beta}\delta + \delta(\iota + \rho)} > 1 \tag{27}$$

(noting $\delta \equiv 1/\lambda < 1$ as $\lambda > 1$) consistent with innovation and outsourcing occurring in equilibrium. A higher aggregate expenditure increases the incentives for both innovation and outsourcing through larger sales. A higher relative wage reduces the incentives for innovation (due to lower profits in the product market) and expands the incentives for international outsourcing of production (due to larger cost savings).

For various extents of international outsourcing $\chi \in (0, \beta)$, Figure 1 traces the rate of innovation ι that equates labor demand and labor supply in each country. The Northern resource constraint is represented by

$$L_N = a\iota + \left[1 - \chi\left(1 + \frac{M}{\beta\iota}\right)\right]\left[\frac{a\left[\dfrac{M}{\beta} + \delta(\iota + \rho)\right]}{\delta(1 - \delta)}\right]\delta \tag{28}$$

and the Southern resource constraint by

$$L_S = \chi\left[\frac{a\left[\dfrac{M}{\beta} + \delta(\iota + \rho)\right]}{\delta(1 - \delta)}\right]\left(\delta + \frac{M}{\beta\iota}\right). \tag{29}$$

The intersection of the two resource constraints indicates the equilibrium extent of outsourcing and rate of innovation.

Imitation Intensity

An increase in the intensity of imitation M clearly shifts the Southern resource constraint down: for any given rate of innovation ι, the extent of outsourcing χ must fall.

More imitation raises the measure of Southern production $n_S = \chi M/(\beta \iota)$, holding ι and χ fixed, so more labor is needed for Southern production. In addition, aggregate expenditure (26) rises with M, and the larger volume of sales raises demand for labor both in Southern production and in outsourcing of production in the South.

The shift in the Northern resource constraint due to an increase in M is less clear. More imitation reduces the measure of Northern production $n_N = 1 - \chi(1 + M/\beta \iota)$ but increases aggregate expenditure. However, the production shifting effect dominates, so the Northern resource constraint shifts up with a larger extent of outsourcing for any given rate of innovation. Consequently, the new intersection occurs at a lower extent of outsourcing and a slower rate of innovation.

To demonstrate the effects on χ and ι more formally, solve the Southern resource constraint (25) for the extent of outsourcing

$$\chi = \frac{L_S \delta \iota (1 - \delta)}{a\left(\delta \iota + \dfrac{M}{\beta}\right)\left[\dfrac{M}{\beta} + \delta(\iota + \rho)\right]} > 0 \tag{30}$$

consistent with the labor demand for production equaling the labor supply in the South. A higher extent of outsourcing increases the demand for labor in the South and decreases the demand for labor in the North by shifting production to the South. Finally, differentiate the Northern resource constraint with respect to the rate of innovation and the intensity of imitation (the Northern labor constraint involves squared terms of ι and so solving for ι is not convenient) to find

$$\frac{d\iota}{dM} = -\frac{a(\beta \delta \iota + M)^2 + L_S \beta^2 \delta \iota (1 - \delta)^2}{\beta\left[a(\beta \delta \iota + M)^2 - L_S \beta \delta M (1 - \delta)^2\right]} < 0 \quad \text{if } \rho < \bar{\rho}, \tag{31}$$

where $\bar{\rho} \equiv (L_S/a)(1 - \delta)(\iota + M\delta)/(M + \iota \beta \delta)$, which should be true since the discount rate should be quite small (virtually zero)—see the Appendix for details. So indeed an increase in the intensity of imitation decreases the rate of innovation.

The effects on the other endogenous variables can then be determined using the chain rule. The extent of outsourcing increases with the rate of innovation

$$\frac{\partial \chi}{\partial \iota} = \frac{L_S \beta^2 \delta (1 - \delta)[M(M + \beta \delta \rho) - \beta^2 \delta^2 \iota^2]}{a(\beta \delta \iota + M)^2 [M + \beta \delta(\iota + \rho)]^2} \tag{32}$$

if $M(M + \beta \delta \rho) > \beta^2 \delta^2 \iota^2$, and decreases with the intensity of imitation

$$\frac{\partial \chi}{\partial M} = -\frac{L_S \beta^2 \delta \iota (1 - \delta)[2M + \beta \delta(2\iota + \rho)]}{a(\beta \delta \iota + M)^2 [M + \beta \delta(\iota + \rho)]^2} < 0. \tag{33}$$

An increase in the intensity of imitation therefore alters the extent of outsourcing according to

$$\frac{\partial \chi}{\partial M} = \underbrace{\frac{\partial \chi}{\partial M}}_{-} + \underbrace{\frac{\partial \chi}{\partial \iota}}_{?} \underbrace{\frac{d\iota}{\partial M}}_{-}. \tag{34}$$

Using the expressions for the partials establishes that an increase in the intensity of imitation must decrease the extent of outsourcing $d\chi/dM < 0$—see the Appendix.

The relative wage decreases with the rate of innovation

$$\frac{\partial w}{\partial \iota} = -\frac{\beta M(1-\delta)}{\delta(M+\beta(\iota+\rho))^2} < 0, \tag{35}$$

and it increases with the intensity of imitation

$$\frac{\partial w}{\partial M} = \frac{\beta(1-\delta)(\iota+\rho)}{\delta(M+\beta(\iota+\rho))^2} > 0; \tag{36}$$

but it does not depend directly on the extent of outsourcing. An increase in the intensity of imitation therefore increases the relative wage.

$$\frac{dw}{dM} = \underbrace{\frac{\partial w}{\partial M}}_{+} + \underbrace{\frac{\partial w}{\partial \iota}\frac{d\iota}{dM}}_{-\quad -} > 0. \tag{37}$$

Aggregate expenditure increases with the rate of innovation

$$\frac{\partial E}{\partial \iota} = \frac{a}{1-\delta} > 0, \tag{38}$$

and it increases with the intensity of imitation

$$\frac{\partial E}{\partial M} = \frac{a}{\beta\delta(1-\delta)} > 0; \tag{39}$$

but it does not depend directly on the extent of outsourcing. An increase in the intensity of imitation therefore increases aggregate expenditure if the direct effect dominates:

$$\frac{dE}{dM} = \underbrace{\frac{\partial E}{\partial M}}_{+} + \underbrace{\frac{\partial E}{\partial \iota}\frac{d\iota}{dM}}_{+\quad -}. \tag{40}$$

Using the expressions for the partial establishes that aggregate expenditure does indeed increase with the imitation intensity $dE/dM > 0$—see the Appendix.

PROPOSITION 1. *An increase in the intensity of imitation reduces the rate of innovation, reduces the extent of international outsourcing, increases the relative wage, and increases aggregate expenditure.*

Note that in the partial solutions for aggregate expenditure (26) and for the relative wage (27)—which can take the place of the two valuation conditions—and in the Northern and Southern labor constraints (28) and (29), the intensity of imitation M enters only relative to the fraction of production that is basic enough to be outsourced, β. Similarly, β enters those four equations only in relation to M.

Suppose Northern firms can choose β, but face a tradeoff between a larger share of production outsourced β and a larger intensity M. An increase in both M and β would act like an increase in M for a given β (at least in terms of the direction of effects) if M/β rises. So if firms choose to outsource a larger fraction of the production of their products (a larger β), and as a result face a larger intensity of imitation M, and if M/β rises, the rate of innovation will fall. If β rises but M/β falls, the rate of innovation would rise.

Glass and Saggi (2001) found, in the absence of imitation, that an increase in β (which was called α) always increased innovation. So the addition of imitation risk would seem to have introduced the possibility of reversing the prior result that more outsourcing (due to expanding the share of each product that is outsourced) leads to faster innovation. But the discussion of the condition (14) implied by the two valuation conditions holding implied that firms would pick β to minimize M/β as so doing would maximize the rate of return generated by outsourcing. Thus firms would never in equilibrium pick a β that increased M/β. So the GS result regarding an increase in β is robust to the addition of imitation risk when outsourcing.

Labor Supplies

However, the effect of the labor supplies turns out to be somewhat different with imitation than in Glass and Saggi (2001). One might think that one reason international outsourcing has been on the rise is an increase in the Southern labor supply since outsourcing is a way of shifting labor demand from the North to the South.

In the original model, the labor supplies had no effect on the relative wage. The point of the original model was to argue that faster innovation could offset lower relative wages and thus cause Northern workers to benefit from forces that increased outsourcing. Since increasing the Southern labor supply did not lower Northern wages (relative to the South), it did not fit the scenario being considered. Why was there no effect of labor supplies on the relative wage? Without imitation, the relative wage was determined exclusively by the two valuation conditions. Without imitation, the profit streams before and after outsourcing were discounted to the same degree (by $\rho + \iota$). Thus, the relative wage was all that was left to ensure that both valuation conditions held.

But with imitation, outsourcing profits are discounted by more than they were prior to outsourcing due to the increased risk that the profit stream will be terminated by imitation. Imitation adds a term involving the relative effective discount rates $(\rho + \iota + M)/(\rho + \iota) = 1 + M/(\rho + \iota)$. So now the partial solution for the relative wage (27) is a function of the rate of innovation. There is still no direct effect of labor supplies on the relative wage, but there is now an indirect effect that operates through the effect of the labor supplies on innovation.

An increase in the rate of innovation makes the risk of imitation less important. If there is almost no innovation, the expected duration of profits will be substantially shortened when outsourcing because imitation would almost surely occur prior to the next innovation. Therefore, the relative wage would need to be high to generate sufficient cost savings from outsourcing to justify the imitation risk. But if innovation is especially quick, the next innovation will almost always occur prior to imitation, so the expected duration of the profit stream will be essentially unchanged by outsourcing. In that case, the relative wage would fall to almost one as little cost savings are needed from outsourcing.

Since an increase in either labor supply increases the rate of innovation, it follows that the relative wage falls regardless of which labor supply increased. With imitation, it is now possible that an increase in the Southern labor supply can lead to an increase in the extent of outsourcing together with a reduction in the Northern relative wage and an increase in the rate of innovation.

PROPOSITION 2. *An increase in the Northern or Southern labor supply leads to a faster rate of innovation, a larger extent of outsourcing (if imitation is sufficiently large), a larger aggregate expenditure, and a lower relative wage.*

The rate of innovation rises as

$$\frac{d\iota}{dL_N} = \frac{a(\beta\delta\iota + M)^2 - L_S\beta\delta M(1-\delta)^2}{(1-\delta)(\beta\delta\iota + M)^2} > 0 \quad \text{if } \rho < \bar{\rho}, \tag{41}$$

$$\frac{d\iota}{dL_S} = \frac{a(\beta\delta\iota + M)^2 - L_S\beta\delta M(1-\delta)^2}{\delta(1-\delta)(\beta\delta\iota + M)(\beta\iota + M)} > 0 \quad \text{if } \rho < \bar{\rho}, \tag{42}$$

where the numerator in each is the same as the large term in the denominator of $d\iota/dM$ that was shown to be positive if the discount rate is small enough. Expanding labor supplies increase innovation, so this economy exhibits scale effects. The expressions for the derivatives of the rate of innovation with respect to the labor supplies, however, suggests that the magnitude of the scale effect shrinks as the Southern labor supply expands. Segerstrom and Dinopoulos (2003) have recently constructed a North–South quality-ladders model without scale effects but no outsourcing.

Aggregate expenditure rises as there is no direct effect and it rises with the rate of innovation. Similarly, the relative wage falls as there is no direct effect and it falls with the rate of innovation. Recall that the extent of outsourcing increases with the rate of innovation $\partial\chi/\partial\iota > 0$ if $M(M + \beta\delta\rho) > \beta^2\delta^2\iota^2$. The Southern labor supply has a direct effect of increasing the extent of outsourcing

$$\frac{\partial\chi}{\partial L_S} = \frac{\beta^2\delta\iota(1-\delta)}{a(\beta\delta\iota + M)^2[M + \beta\delta(\iota + \rho)]^2} > 0. \tag{43}$$

Applying the chain rule, an increase in the Southern labor supply should increase the extent of outsourcing if the intensity of imitation is sufficiently high:

$$\frac{d\chi}{dL_S} = \underbrace{\frac{\partial\chi}{\partial L_S}}_{+} + \underbrace{\frac{\partial\chi}{\partial\iota}}_{?}\underbrace{\frac{d\iota}{dL_S}}_{+}. \tag{44}$$

There is no direct effect of the Northern labor supply, so if outsourcing increases with innovation, then an increase in the Northern labor supply should increase the extent of outsourcing:

$$\frac{d\chi}{dL_N} = \underbrace{\frac{\partial\chi}{\partial\iota}}_{?}\underbrace{\frac{d\iota}{dL_N}}_{+}. \tag{45}$$

Because there is a direct positive effect for the Southern labor supply, if imitation is low so that outsourcing falls with innovation, outsourcing could rise with the Southern labor supply and fall with the Northern labor supply.

Table 3 summarizes the analytical results for the effects of increases in the imitation intensity, the Southern labor supply, and the Northern labor supply on the Northern relative wage, aggregate expenditure, the rate of innovation, and the extent of outsourcing.

Welfare Effects and Numerical Examples

Is the North hurt by outsourcing due to the reduction in its relative wage reducing income and thus consumption? Do the effects of outsourcing on Northern (or Southern) welfare depend on why outsourcing expanded? Is the South hurt if it adopts

Table 3. *Signs of Effects of Imitation and Labor Supplies*

	M	L_S	L_N
w	$+$	$-$	$-$
E	$+$	$+$	$+$
l	$-$	$+$	$+$
χ	$-$	$\pm$	$\pm$

policies such as stronger protection of intellectual property that decrease imitation? Or if Northern or Southern labor supplies expand?

To address these questions, return to the expressions for utility and examine them for a steady-state equilibrium. By the law of large numbers, the expected number of innovations arriving in time period t is $\overline{m} = ut$. The average price paid by consumers is

$$\overline{p} = (1 - n_S)\lambda + n_S = \lambda - n_S(\lambda - 1) \tag{46}$$

since they pay price λ for all but imitated products, which have a price of one. Instantaneous utility (2) is

$$\log u(t) = \log E - \log \overline{p} + \overline{m} \log \lambda. \tag{47}$$

Lifetime utility (1) is

$$U = \frac{\log E + \left(\dfrac{l}{\rho} - 1\right)\log \lambda - \log[\lambda - n_S(\lambda - 1)]}{\rho}. \tag{48}$$

The first term indicates that utility rises with expenditure, the second term that utility rises with innovation due to higher average quality of products consumed, and the third term that utility declines with the average price level. The average price level declines if the measure of pure Southern production rises so that a larger fraction of products have had their highest available quality level imitated.

A larger extent of outsourcing can be caused by a reduction in imitation or an expansion in labor supplies. Whichever the source, innovation will rise and generate a positive growth effect on welfare due to the higher average quality of products. However, the Northern relative wage always falls, so the amount of expenditure by Northern consumers will fall, a negative level effect on their welfare. So the North can benefit if it is patient enough. A series of numerical examples will help illustrate the conflict between growth and level effects for both countries.

The numerical examples will also check that the condition for the imitation intensity to be large enough, $M(M + \beta\delta\rho) > \beta^2\delta^2 l^2$, can be true in equilibrium, so increases in labor supplies can expand outsourcing. And the examples will illustrate possible ways in which the average price level might adjust. Set the quality increment to $\lambda = 3$ (so $\delta = 1/3$), the share of each unit of production that can be outsourced to $\beta = 1/2$, the unit labor requirement in innovation to $a = 1$, and the discount rate to $\rho = 1/12$. The base case parameters will be imitation intensity $M = 1/2$, Southern labor supply $L_S = 1$, and Northern labor supply $L_N = 2$. Then consider increasing the imitation intensity $M' = 2/3$, Southern labor supply $L_S' = 3/2$, and Northern labor supply $L_N' = 3$, each in turn. The outcomes are presented in Table 4.

Table 4. Numerical Examples

	Base	$M' = 2/3$	$L'_S = 3/2$	$L'_N = 3$
w	2.19	2.63	2.08	1.82
E	5.53	6.45	5.79	6.62
ι	0.602	0.217	0.776	1.33
χ	0.091	0.024	0.160	0.139
n_O	18.1%	4.8%	31.9%	27.8%
n_N	66.8%	80.5%	47.5%	62.0%
n_S	15.1%	14.7%	20.6%	10.2%

Table 5. Welfare Effects for Numerical Examples

	M'	L'_S	L'_N
$\Delta \log E$	+0.19, +0.001	−0.06, −0.004	−0.19, −0.002
$\left(\frac{\Delta \iota}{\rho} - 1\right)\log \lambda$	−5.07	+2.29	+9.61
$\Delta \log \bar{p}$	+0.003	−0.04	+0.03
Total effect	−4.89, −5.07	+2.19, +2.24	+9.46, +9.64

Increases in either the Northern or the Southern labor supply do increase the extent of outsourcing in this numerical example. The measure of pure Southern production increases with the Southern labor supply but decreases with increases in imitation or the Northern labor supply. Therefore, increases in the Southern labor supply or decreases in imitation may reduce the average price level, but increases in the Northern labor supply may increase the average price level.

These numerical examples can then illustrate possible welfare effects. Table 5 calculates the three components of the overall welfare effect for each of the three parameter changes. In the row for $\Delta \log E$, the first number is for the North and the second is for the South.

Reducing imitation would mean reversing the signs on the column for M': negative level effects though expenditures net of the price level effect and positive growth effect through imitation. Increases in the labor supplies have similar consequences, although increases in the Northern labor supply elevate the price level slightly. The total effect is $\log E + (\iota/\rho - 1)\log \lambda - \log \bar{p}$ (subtract the third row from the sum of the first two rows) and change in lifetime utility ΔU is this total effect divided by the discount rate. For these numerical examples, the discount rate is sufficiently slight that both countries gain from increased outsourcing, regardless of its cause.

4. Conclusion

This paper has developed a quality ladders model with both outsourcing and imitation. Glass and Saggi (2001) is extended to capture the possibility that outsourcing stages of production to the South, while lowering costs, may expose the firm to a greater risk of imitation. This extension is useful for discovering what the effects of imitation

risk are on the rate of innovation, the extent of outsourcing, the North-to-South relative wage, and aggregate expenditure. The new model is also useful for examining
whether the effects of increases in the Northern or Southern labor supplies on these
endogenous variables are altered by the addition of imitation risk.

The first result is that an increase in the intensity of imitation reduces the rate of
innovation and the extent of outsourcing, and increases the relative wage and aggregate expenditure. The main point of GS, that the decline in the relative wage due to
outsourcing can be offset by faster innovation, is shown to be robust, even if the
increased outsourcing stemmed from reduced imitation risk.

The second result is that increases in either labor supply lead to a decline in the
relative wage, along with a faster rate of innovation. There was no effect of labor
supplies on the relative wage in the original model without imitation. However, the
addition of imitation generates an indirect effect of labor supplies on relative wages
that occurs through the rate of innovation. Increases in innovation make the imitation
risk less important, and so the relative wage falls as cost savings from outsourcing
do not need to be as large to compensate for the shorter expected duration of profits.
Provided imitation is large enough, increased labor supplies increase the extent of
outsourcing. So increased Northern or Southern labor supplies can be added to the list
of forces that could be behind the trend toward greater outsourcing.

Appendix

Signing $d\iota/dM < 0$

The expression for the extent of outsourcing (30) is inserted into the Northern labor
constraint (28), which is then solved for the Northern labor supply. That value for
L_N is then used to simplify the derivative of the rate of innovation with respect
to the imitation intensity (31) since starting from an equilibrium. The condition
on the discount rate ρ is found by inserting the partial solution for χ (30) into
$n_N = 1 - (\chi/\beta)(1 + M/\iota) > 0$. The discount rate being small enough, $\rho < \bar{\rho}$, together
with some products being produced entirely in the North, $n_N > 0$, ensures that the denominator of $d\iota/dM$ is positive. The value of the Southern labor supply needed for
the denominator to be negative, $a(\beta\delta\iota + M)^2/[\beta\delta M(1 - \delta)^2]$, exceeds the maximum
L_S allowed for $n_N > 0$.

Signing $d\chi/dM < 0$

Plug the corresponding expressions for the partials to find

$$L_S < \tilde{L}_S \equiv \frac{\bar{L}_S + a\left(\dfrac{2M}{\beta\delta} + 2\iota + \rho\right)}{1 - \delta} \rightarrow \frac{d\chi}{dM} < 0, \tag{49}$$

where

$$\bar{L}_S \equiv \frac{a\left(\dfrac{M}{\beta} + \delta(\iota + \rho)\right)}{\delta(1 - \delta)}\left(\delta + \frac{M}{\beta\iota}\right) \tag{50}$$

is an upper bound on the supply of Southern labor such that $L_S < \bar{L}_S$ is required
for the extent of outsourcing to remain complete, $\chi < \beta$ (that is $n_O < 1$). Since $\tilde{L}_S > \bar{L}_S$

as $a[2M/(\beta\delta) + 2\iota + \rho] > 0$ and $1/(1 - \delta) > 1$ due to $\delta < 1$, the upper bound $L_S < \overline{L}_S$ implies that the condition $L_S < \tilde{L}_S$ is satisfied.

Signing dE/dM > 0

The level of Southern labor supply required to make the derivative negative exceeds the maximum allowed for the measure of Northern production to be positive.

References

Egger, Peter and Michael Pfaffermayr, "Two Dimensions of Convergence: National and International Wage Adjustment Effects of Cross-border Outsourcing in Europe," this issue.

Feenstra, Robert C., "Integration of Trade and Disintegration of Production in the Global Economy," *Journal of Economic Perspectives* 12 (1998):31–50.

Girma, Sourafel and Holger Görg, "Outsourcing, Foreign Ownership, and Productivity: Evidence from UK Establishment-level Data," this issue.

Glass, Amy J. and Kamal Saggi, "Innovation and Wage Effects of International Outsourcing," *European Economic Review* 45 (2001):67–86.

Grossman, Gene M. and Elhanan Helpman, "Quality Ladders and Product Cycles," *Quarterly Journal of Economics* 106 (1991):557–86.

Lai, Edwin L.-C., "International Intellectual Property Rights Protection and the Rate of Product Innovation," *Journal of Development Economics* 55 (1998):133–53.

Scheve, Kenneth and Mathew J. Slaughter, "Economic Insecurity and the Globalization of Production," NBER working paper 9339 (2002). Forthcoming in *American Journal of Political Science*.

Segerstrom, Paul S. and Elias Dinopoulos, "A Theory of North–South Trade and Globalization," mimeo (2003). Available at http://bear.cba.ufl.edu/dinopoulos/PDF/Northsouth.pdf.

Young, Alwin, "The Tyranny of Numbers: Confronting the Statistical Realities of the East Asian Growth Experience," *Quarterly Journal of Economics* 110 (1995):641–80.

Index